JUDAS

D1617166

JUDAS

BETRAYER
OR FRIEND
OF JESUS?

WILLIAM KLASSEN

FORTRESS PRESS
MINNEAPOLIS

JUDAS
Betrayer or Friend of Jesus?

Lyrics from *Jesus Christ Superstar* copyright © MCA Music Ltd. Used by permission.

All translations from the Greek New Testament and from other foreign language sources are by the author except where otherwise indicated.

Cover and text designed by Joe Bonyata.

Cover art: *The Taking of Christ,* Valentin (called Valentin de Boulogne), French (worked in Rome), 1591–1632, oil on canvas, 58 × 77 in., Juliana Cheney Edwards Collection. Courtesy, Museum of Fine Arts, Boston. Used by permission.

Library of Congress Cataloging-in-Publication Data

Klassen, William.
    Judas : betrayer or friend of Jesus? / William Klassen.
      p. cm.
    Includes bibliographical references.
    ISBN 0-8006-2968-X (alk. paper)
    1. Judas Iscariot.   2. Bible.   N.T. Gospels—Biography.
  I. Title.
  BS2460.J8K52   1996
  226'.092—dc20
                                                  96-6390
                                                     CIP

Manufactured in the U.S.A.   AF-2968

00   99   98   97   96   1   2   3   4   5   6   7   8   9   10

CONTENTS

To David Flusser

In celebration of that Jew who prayed that his enemies might receive
forgiveness

οὐ γὰρ οἴδασιν τί ποιοῦσιν

PREFACE

As a teacher of early Christian literature in a university setting, I have had the privilege of introducing a generation of students to the historical Jesus. In that connection particular attention was paid to Judas. For some reason students from certain faith backgrounds in particular kept insisting that questions about Judas be addressed.

As one attempt to address those questions I played the role of Judas, first to my classes and then increasingly to congregations that requested it. The format was simple. I appeared dressed in first-century garb as Judas at the point in time when he had just learned that Jesus had been delivered to Pilate by the high priest. The whole hour revolved around questions that the audience asked me and that I sought to answer. The questions had to come out of what they had read in the New Testament about Judas. In this way I sought to deal with the complexity of the New Testament sources: what they say about Judas, his role, and his destiny.

One of the most astonishing results of this bit of drama was the anger that so many people displayed toward me in the role of Judas. It seems as though people are not able to reassess the person of Judas and the role he played in the life and death of Jesus. Many, of course, are open to doing so, and it is those people for whom I write this book.

I am grateful to David Noel Freedman for assigning me the article on Judas for the *ABD* (1992), 3:1091–1096. That article, written some six years ago, represents the first results of my quest for the historical Judas. This book is a much different and, I hope, more mature work. I owe that in part to the Catholic Biblical Association of America for nominating me to be its visiting research scholar in Jerusalem in the fall of 1991. To them and to members of the community at the École Biblique who graciously invited Dona and me, hosted us and assisted us in far more ways than we can ever record, our warmest thanks. It was a memorable experience to work again in their magnificent library and to participate in their spiritually and intellectually invigorating common life. Terry Prendergast, S.J., now auxiliary bishop of Toronto, read the complete manuscript while he was Visiting Research Professor at the École in 1995 and gave many helpful criticisms.

Many people have listened patiently to my emerging research conclusions about Judas, none more patiently than my wife, Dona Harvey, who also edited and reedited the whole manuscript at a time when she had other urgent assignments. It has become a joint effort between us. We spent a memorable wedding anniversary walking through the Valley of Gehinnom, to explore the place called Akeldama, where, according to tradition, Judas came to his end. Many hours have been spent trying to make available to reflective readers the fruits of scholarly research. Her work as a journalist has enriched me personally and helped me to rededicate my efforts at making first-century stories make sense to us today.

Two scholarly contributions have been particularly valuable to me, those of Hans-Josef Klauck and Werner Vogler. Both have been supportive of my work; in turn I have tried to record my indebtedness to them in the usual way. Where my conclusions coincide with theirs, it does not necessarily mean that I derived them from their work, although I owe them more than I can record here. I have pushed the borders of research beyond theirs. At the same time, encouragement to do so came from their work. In the revision stages of my work I benefited greatly from the work of Raymond Brown and Elaine Pagels. With both I disagree on major issues. But it is an argument based on respect for their work.

It is a pleasure also to record my scholarly debt to two university communities where I have worked while writing this book. They are the University of Toronto, where Peter Richardson especially was a strong support to me, not least because of his ability to pursue critical questions in a supportive way. I respect him as a scholar and cherish him as a friend. There is also the University of Waterloo, quite different from the respectable old University of Toronto, but supportive through its grant programs both for the beginnings and for the conclusions of the writing of this book. My colleagues at St. Paul's United College bore patiently my dedication to trying to get people to understand that perhaps Judas also belonged in the roster of Christian disciples. I am also grateful to Peter Frick for putting at my disposal his expertise both in Greek and in computer technology. The Social Sciences and Humanities Research fund at the University of Waterloo was of critical assistance to me providing partial support for editorial work and computer assistance, the latter performed flawlessly by Arlene Sleno at various stages of the work.

No work of this nature can ever be published without the courageous support of editors and publishing houses. Here my thanks go in the first instance to the staff of Fortress Press, who demonstrated again that what regular commercial houses will not touch for economic reasons and univer-

sity presses cannot touch because their system precludes such political incor-
rectness, a press based in the church can and will. Special thanks go to Dr.
Cynthia Thompson for her interest, encouragement, and support and to
Marian Noecker for careful copyediting.

I dedicate this book to David Flusser, whose friendship I have cherished
for over twenty years. My intellectual and spiritual life has been enormously
enriched by the hours spent in his home in Jerusalem. I wish him and Han-
nah and their family much strength and continuing joy for their life in the
city in which both Jesus and Judas offered up their final days.

—WILLIAM KLASSEN

ABBREVIATIONS

AB	Anchor Bible
ABC	Anchor Bible Commentary
ABD	*Anchor Bible Dictionary*
AJT	*Anglican Journal of Theology*
ANRW	*Aufstieg und Niedergang der römischen Welt*
ASTI	*Annual of the Swedish Theological Institute*
ATANT	Abhandlungen zur Theologie des Alten und Neuen Testaments
ATRS	*Anglican Theological Review.* Supplement Series
B. Qam	*Baba Qamma*
B.C.E.	Before Common Era
Bauer, *Lexicon*	*A Greek-English Lexicon of the New Testament,* by Walter Bauer
BETL	Bibliotheca ephemeridum theologicarum lovaniensium
BEvTh	Beiträge zur evangelischen Theologie
BR	*Biblical Review*
BVC	*Bible et Vie Chrétienne*
BWANT	Beiträge zur Wissenschaft vom Alten und Neuen Testament
BZ	*Biblische Zeitschrift*
CBQ	*Catholic Biblical Quarterly*
CD	Damascus Document
C.E.	Common Era
ChH	*Church History*
CJ	*Concordia Journal*
CToday	*Christianity Today*
DACL	*Dictionnaire d'Archéologie Chrétienne et de Liturgie*
Did	*Didache*
DJG	*Dictionary of Jesus and the Gospels*
DRev	*Downside Review*
DtPfrBl	*Deutsches Pfarrerblatt*

EB	Echter Bibel
EnJ	*Encyclopaedia Judaica*
ET	*Expository Times*
EthEn	*Ethiopic Enoch*
ETL	*Ephemerides Theologicae Lovanienses*
ETR	*Etudes Théologiques et Religieuses*
EvQ	*Evangelical Quarterly*
EvTh	*Evangelische Theologie*
EWNT	*Evangelisches Wörterbuch zum Neuen Testament*
Exp	*Expositor*
FBBS	Facet Books, Biblical Series
FRLANT	Forschungen zur Religion und Literatur des Alten und Neuen Testaments
FS	Festschrift
FTS	Freiburger Theologische Studien
HDB	Hastings, *Dictionary of the Bible*
Hochl	*Hochland* (Kempten and Munich)
HTR	*Harvard Theological Review*
HWDA	*Handwörterbuch des deutschen Aberglaubens,* ed H. Bächtold-Stäubli, 1927–1942.
IB	Intepreters Bible
ICC	International Critical Commentary
IDB	*Interpreter's Dictionary of the Bible*
J. Ter	Jerusalem Targum, *Terumot*
JAAR	*Journal of the American Academy of Religion*
JB	*Jerusalem Bible*
JBL	*Journal of Biblical Literature*
JE	*Jewish Encyclopedia*
JEGP	*Journal of English and Germanic Philology*
JJS	*Journal of Jewish Studies*
JL	*Jüdisches Lexicon*
JQ	*Jewish Quarterly*
JQR	*Jewish Quarterly Review*
JR	*Journal of Religion*
JSNT	*Journal for the Study of the New Testament*
JSNTSup	Journal for the Study of the New Testament, Supplement Series
JThS	*Journal of Theological Studies*
JThSA	*Journal of Theology for South Africa*
JW	Josephus, *Wars of the Jews*
KTWBNT	Kittel, *Theologisches Wörterbuch zum Neuen Testament*
LavTP	*Laval Théologique et Philosophique* (Quebec)

LCL	Loeb Classical Library
LD	*Lectio Divina*
LM	*Lutherisches Monatsheft*
LSJM	Liddell, Scott-Jones & McKenzie, *Greek-English Lexicon*
LThK	*Lexicon für Theologie und Kirche*
LXX	Septuagint
MGWJ	*Monatsschrift für Geschichte und Wissenschaft des Judentums*
MLR	*Modern Language Review*
MTZ	*Münchener theologische Zeitschrift*
NEB	New English Bible
NIDNTT	*New International Dictionary of New Testament Theology*
NIV	New International Version
NJB	New Jerusalem Bible
NJBC	New Jerusalem Bible Commentary
NRSV	New Revised Standard Version
NT	*Novum Testamentum*
NTAbh	Neutestamentliche Abhandlungen
NT, Sup	Novum Testamentum, Supplement
NTOA	Novum Testamentum et Orbis Antiquus
NTS	*New Testament Studies*
NYTBR	*New York Times Book Review*
OBO	Orbis biblicus et orientalis
OCP	Orientalia Christiana Periodica (Rome)
PG	Migne, *Patrologia Graeca*
PL	Migne, *Patrologia Latina*
PMLA	*Proceedings of the Modern Language Association*
1QH	Qumran, Hodayoth Scroll
1QS	Qumran, Serek Scroll
RB	*Revue Biblique*
RevQ	*Revue de Qumran*
RevScRel	*Revue des Sciences Religieuses*
RE	*Realencyklopädie für protestantische Theologie und Kirche.* 3rd ed., ed. A. Hauck. Leipzig 1896–1913.
RGG	*Die Religion in Geschichte und Gegenwart*
RHPR	*Revue d'Histoire et de Philosophie Religieuses*
RHR	*Revue de l'Histoire des Religions*
SAC	*Studien zur Antike und Christentum*
Sanh	*Sanhedrin*
SANT	Studien zum Alten und Neuen Testament
SEÅ	*Svensk Exegetisk Årsbok*
sh	shekel, shekelim
SLJT	*St. Luke's Journal of Theology*

SNTSMS	Society for New Testament Studies, Monograph Series
SST	Studies in Sacred Theology
STBibEChrist	Studia Biblica et Christianis
StMed	*Studia Medievalis*
StNT	Studium Novum Testamentum
T. Gad	*Testament of Gad*
ThA	Theologische Arbeiten
THKNT	*Theologischer Handkommentar zum Neuen Testament*
ThLZ	*Theologische Literaturzeitung*
ThPQ	*Theologische-Praktische Quartalschrift*
TPI	Trinity Press International
TJ	*Toledoth Jeshua*
TPC	Torch Preacher's Commentary
TRE	*Theologische Realenzyklopädie*
WUNT	Wissenschaftliche Untersuchungen zum Neuen Testament
WUS	Washington University Studies
WZ	*Wissenschaftliche Zeitschrift*
ZNW	*Zeitschrift für die neutestamentliche Wissenschaft*

INTRODUCTION

Judas has not been a marginal figure in Christendom. He presents us with a central human and Christian problem: how to deal with the enemy, the foreigner, and our understanding of evil.

—Bernhard Dieckmann[1]

One of the most noteworthy aspects of the life of Jesus of Nazareth was the way in which he gathered a community of undistinguished people around him. These followers, known as his disciples, became responsible for keeping his memory alive by retelling his story and putting it in written form. Among the followers were twelve men who represented continuity with the twelve tribes of Israel. Of these twelve, Peter and Judas Iscariot receive the most attention as the Gospel writers tell the story of Jesus. It is generally agreed that the Passion narratives, the story of Jesus' last days and his death on the cross, form the heart of the first Gospels. In those accounts, Judas is a dominant figure. In subsequent times, he has been almost universally condemned for his role in the arrest of Jesus.

The Synoptic Gospels (Matthew, Mark, and Luke) first introduce Judas to the reader as a disciple but always list him last among the Twelve.[2] It is nevertheless significant that he was among those of the disciples whom Jesus selected to be named an "apostle."[3] Together with the other eleven, Judas was called "to be with Jesus," sent forth to preach, empowered to cast out demons and to heal all kinds of sickness.[4]

In the Gospel of John we hear nothing about Judas until, in chapter 6:59-71, an incident is recorded as taking place at Capernaum early in Jesus' ministry after Jesus preached in the synagogue. Upon hearing his words, specifically that "unless you eat the flesh of the Son of Man and drink his blood, you can have no life in you" (6:53, NEB), many of Jesus' disciples turn against him, exclaiming: "This is more than we can stomach! Why listen to such talk?" (6:60, NEB). In this small village on the northern shores of the Sea of Galilee where Peter, and perhaps even Jesus, made his home

(Mark 2:1, 15), many of his disciples scornfully reject Jesus and leave him. In John 6:64, Jesus dismisses these people as those "who have no faith."

Then John provides an editorial comment: "Jesus knew all along who were without faith and who was to deliver him over" (6:64). Thus John brings together the faithless who left Jesus in Capernaum and Judas, tainting him with the brush of defection. Soon thereafter John has Jesus saying: "Have I not chosen you, all Twelve? Yet one of you is a devil." John explains: "He meant Judas, son of Simon Iscariot. He it was who would hand him over, and he was one of the Twelve." No other Gospel writer has so openly exposed Judas as a devil; none even attributes demonic influence to him, so early in Jesus' life.

Scholars have been skeptical about the historical authenticity of this account. While John uses it to solve one problem (how could Jesus not know about Judas?), he in fact creates another. How could a "devil" be tolerated among the disciples over such a long period of time? Was not one of the hallmarks of Jesus and his disciples their ability to cast out demons?

All the Gospels join in bringing Judas to the fore during the last week of Jesus' life. Here Judas is shown complaining about the waste of money to prepare Jesus' body for burial (although this occurs only in John 12:4-8), as taking part in the Last Supper, and as going to the high priest to arrange for handing Jesus over to the religious authorities.

At the Last Supper, Jesus indicates to the disciples that someone will hand him over. With some vagueness he seems to suggest the deed will be performed by Judas. Jesus expresses alarm at the fate of this person but ultimately gives the signal for Judas to carry out his mission: to go to the high priest and bring a small group of officials to meet Jesus in Gethsemane to hand him over. Judas goes to the religious authorities to tell them of Jesus' whereabouts, an act for which he accepts payment of thirty pieces of silver. In the garden, Judas kisses Jesus so that the arresting party will know who he is, and instructs them to arrest Jesus, bind him tight, and take him away.

Judas apparently continues to observe what happens to Jesus. When he learns that Jesus has been handed over by the high priest to Pontius Pilate, the Roman official in charge, he returns to the Temple and, in anguish born of remorse, proclaims that he has made a mistake. When the high priests refuse to take back the thirty pieces of silver, he throws them back into the Temple and then either hangs himself (Matt 27:1-10) or, according to Luke (Acts 2:15-22), falls forward on the ground and his body bursts open, pouring out his entrails in an ignominious death.

This is the story of Judas that has laid a considerable hold on our imaginations over the centuries. The following issues have made it impossible for us to let the story lie dormant:

1. How could Jesus choose a traitor to be one of his disciples? This choice in some way reflects upon Jesus, with respect either to his lack of insight into the person of Judas or to his inability to reform Judas once he became a follower, to exorcise the demons that allegedly possessed him.

2. How could Judas do what he did? What motive might he have had? If his deed of "handing Jesus over" was evil, how could he have been so impervious to the good influences of Jesus?

3. What lesson is there to be learned from Judas, his deed, and his end? Must we not take heed that if Judas, who lived so close to Jesus, could turn defector or even traitor, does not a similar possibility exist for each one of his followers?

4. What symbol or image lies behind the figure of Judas? Is it the patriarch Judah who handed Joseph over? The eternal Jew? The devoted servant wishing to risk everything for the sake of loyalty to his master? Or, on a more mundane level, merely the treasurer, the one charged with overseeing the money?

5. To what extent has Judas served as a "scapegoat" for many church people? The annual Jewish atonement service in ancient times chose a goat on whom the lot fell and on whom the sins of the people were loaded by the priest after he had heard their confessions. The goat was then sent out to a desert cliff to die, carrying the sins of the people into oblivion. Have members of Western society chosen Judas as "scapegoat" and unloaded on him their anger and insecurity, harassing and killing Jews in place of Judas to free themselves of their collective guilt? This may well be the most difficult question raised by our reading and misreading of the Judas story. This question makes it imperative that we seek to discover anew the Judas story and find its meanings for today.

Kirk Hughes has addressed the Judas question imaginatively in an essay that uses the analogy of framing a picture.[5] He notes that "Judas frames Jesus." Judas stands central to the Christian passion story. The figure of Judas looms at the periphery of Jesus' Last Supper and his story "forms a narrative frame around the Gospel account of the Last Supper." Through a superb selection of writings about Jesus by ancient church authors, medieval scholars, and contemporary literary figures and commentators, Hughes draws a complex picture of what Judas seen as "traitor" means for the present. But he also sharpens our ability to view Judas in the perspective of the whole. In a very real sense, then, Jesus also frames Judas. And each of the Gospel writers does so as well.

History of the Debate

The Person of Judas in Recent Times

Of the twelve apostles, Judas Iscariot is the disciple who, over many centuries, including our own, has attracted the most sustained attention on the
part of the church as well as historians of folklore[6] and culture. Whether in
art,[7] literature,[8] or music about the life of Jesus, it is the disciple Judas who
has captured and held the most interest. Even the color of his hair (red,
some authors maintain) has been subjected to study.[9] These portraits of Judas
have developed along a variety of lines, each one offering a distinct typology
or portrait.

Judas as Evil Man: The Traitor

For the most part, the name Judas is equivalent to the demonic. At times
Judas is portrayed as the epitome of evil in the form of hypocrisy, greed,
unfaithfulness, ingratitude, and, above all, betrayal.[10] His name is equivalent
to "traitor." In many writings about him, authors spare themselves the effort
of using Judas's name and refer to him mainly as "the traitor," implying
thereby that his act of betrayal of Jesus is what made him stand out among
the twelve apostles. His deed, they judge, stands unique in perversity in the
annals of human history.[11] "The most notorious criminal in Christian history," a recent writer calls him.[12] "The man who in the Christian conscious-
ness personifies the most odious of traitors and the blackest of treachery,"
another writes.[13]

Beyond the action associated with the arrest of Jesus, the name of Judas
has achieved a widespread value as a symbol. Even a book of the Bible, the
Revelation to John, is described as "sub-christian, the Judas of the New
Testament"[14] because it does not meet the standards of a given author. There
are even at least three gravestones that bear the "curse of Judas," one from
Argos, two are Attic inscriptions from the third or fourth centuries.[15]

Søren Kierkegaard, that insightful gadfly of the nineteenth century, auda-
ciously suggested that the modern incarnations of Judas do not take their
thirty pieces of silver at once. Rather, they take form as professors of theology, say, guaranteeing themselves a certain sum of money for life.[16] Moreover, he describes as "almost laughable so that on internal grounds one is
nearly tempted to doubt if it is historically true, that a Jew—and that is
what Judas was after all—that a Jew had so little understanding of money
that for thirty pieces of silver he was ready (if one would put it so) to dispose
of such a prodigious money value as Jesus Christ represented, the greatest
source of revenue ever encountered in the world, on which a million qua-
drillions have been realized, to dispose of it for thirty pieces of silver!"[17]

The degree to which Judas represents evil can be seen in the German law that forbids parents to give a child the name Judas (along with Satan) for the good of the child.[18] It must be a difficult dilemma for Jewish parents in Germany who wish to name their son Yehudah, a historically well loved name among Jews down through the centuries, even before the time of Jesus.

Interest in Judas has also been sustained by the fact that throughout the history of the church, there have been those who have been obsessed by his evil nature, almost gloating over it.[19]

Taking into consideration how very little is said about Judas in the New Testament, it is a marvel that theologians have produced volumes about him as a model of evil. One such case is Carl Daub, who, next to Friedrich Schleiermacher, is considered by some "probably the most original systematic theologian of the early nineteenth century Germany." For Daub, the disciple Judas represents "the embodiment of the metaphysical opposition to the good that is, in turn, overcome by God."[20]

In his first chapter, Daub seeks to show the fundamental difference between Judas and Jesus, the latter embodying perfect goodness and the former unparalleled evil. No one can ever be as evil as Judas was. There are many common forms of evil, but Judas represents an apotheosis of evil. Among the descendants of Adam, "Judas remains the only one in whom sin reached its highest peak. He provides a view of sin at its most repulsive and abhorrent manifestation. Faithless, loveless, ungrateful himself, he betrayed with the kiss, the sign of faithfulness, love and gratitude."[21]

Never in the history of the human race has evil been manifested so brazenly in the presence of God's goodness, God's own son. In the face of that act, anything the other disciples did, especially Peter, or any sins described in Holy Writ, pale in significance because Judas betrayed the Son of God. Even his repentance ended in despair.[22] Daub concludes that Judas Iscariot is the only one to whom the verdict of condemnation applies; it has to be expressed because he rejected the wholly innocent one. The assurance of condemnation is based on several things that Judas knew: Judas knew the complete innocence of Jesus; he sinned not by doing evil but by committing an evil act against one who is fully good. Thus there was no excuse for Judas and repentance was impossible. He was unable to accept the divine grace.[23]

Daub wants to prevent any plea on Judas's behalf that he did not know what he was doing. In fact, an important part of his book is to deal once and for all with those who defend Judas. Daub devotes the second part of his treatise to the various defenses that have been launched on behalf of Judas.[24] He ably states the case in defense of Judas and has a particular interest in those who as moral psychologists and exegetes come forward with a more humane Judas. He does not name his partners in dialogue but there is

every reason to think that he was aiming, in part at least, at the new approach to Judas that was led by Friedrich Gottlieb Klopstock and supported
by poets such as J. W. von Goethe.[25]

Judas as Instrument of Salvation

To be sure, other voices have been raised against demonizing Judas in the
history of the church. Origen (a third-century church father), for example,
tried to insert some integrity into the discussion and took seriously the
differences among the four Gospels.[26]

The study of Judas has also been motivated by the conviction that, whatever Judas may have done specifically, as one Polish Catholic scholar recently
noted in a learned journal, "the theme of Judas is the one theme that is
essential to the divine economy of salvation."[27] Harald Wagner, who receives special attention later in this book, tries to sort out the divine and
human elements in the actions of Jesus, concluding that Judas is a "determining" influence in the saving history of God. Thus, his deed is part of
saving history, for out of the deed of Judas grows an event upon which the
salvation of humankind depends.[28]

Judas the Archetypal Jew

Finally, there is that pernicious connection between Judas and anti-
Semitism, a subject so vast that we can only touch on it here but one that
deserves some sustained attention if for no other reason than to help explain
how a selfless act of love, such as Jesus dying on a cross for others, can have
such diabolic side effects. No doubt the link between Judas and anti-
Semitism accounts at least in part for the keen interest displayed by Jewish
scholars in this disciple (see chapter 11, below).

Judas a Follower of Jesus

From the beginning there have also been those who have presented the
other side of Judas—that of trusted disciple. They underscore that he was
called by Jesus to be a disciple, that he was chosen to be one of the Twelve,
and, if the tradition can be trusted, that he was a treasurer of the disciple
group and as such must have enjoyed the sustained trust, if not the respect
and affection, of his fellow members of the community.

Novelist Dorothy Sayers concludes: "One thing is certain: he cannot
have been the creeping, crawling, patently worthless villain that some sim-
ple-minded people would like to make out; that would be to cast too grave
a slur upon the brains and character of Jesus."[29]

From the time of the second century, when a Gospel according to Judas
was composed, to our own time, voices have been raised in defense of Judas.

Within the Catholic church, Vinzenz Ferrer (1350–1419), an influential Dominican preacher, said in a sermon in 1391:

> Judas who betrayed and sold the Master after the crucifixion was overwhelmed by a genuine and saving sense of remorse and tried with all his might to draw close to Christ in order to apologise for his betrayal and sale. But since Jesus was accompanied by such a large crowd of people on the way to the mount of Calvary, it was impossible for Judas to come to him and so he said to himself: Since I cannot get to the feet of the master, I will approach him in my spirit at least and humbly ask him for forgiveness. He actually did that and as he took the rope and hanged himself his soul rushed to Christ on Calvary's mount, asked for forgiveness and received it fully from Christ, went up to heaven with him and so his soul enjoys salvation along with all elect.[30]

It is a remarkable retelling of the Judas story that stands almost alone and was considered heretical by the leadership of the church but warmly received by the common people.[31]

In recent times the popular rock opera *Jesus Christ Superstar* offers this explicit statement of Judas while he was among the Temple dignitaries:

> Jesus wouldn't mind that I was here with you
> I have no thought at all about my own reward
> I really didn't come here of my own accord.

The anguish of Judas comes to expression in his dramatic dialogues with Jesus and his plaintive admission: "I don't know how to love him," and the haunting question: "Does he love me too? Does he care for me?" Authors Tim Rice and Andrew Lloyd Webber have picked up the motif of the Fourth Gospel that Jesus did love his own, including Judas, until the very end (John 13:1) and even washed his feet to demonstrate that love in the form of menial service.[32]

One-seventh of the libretto of *Jesus Christ Superstar* is devoted to Judas. In the movie of the same title, Judas is the one who is resurrected; Jesus is not. Indeed, the whole movie begins and ends with Judas. An apocryphal account, denied by Tim Rice, has it that the first name given to this production was "The Gospel According to Judas," but the title fell victim to marketing advice which assumed that it is easier to identify with Jesus as Superstar than with Judas, the consummate "loser" in Christian history.[33] Whatever the truth, the opera's marketing strategy paid off handsomely.

At the conclusion of *Jesus Christ Superstar*, the character Judas comes to believe that he was the victim of an act of betrayal rather than its perpetrator.

> My God I'm sick, I've been used
> And you knew all the time
> God! I'll never know why you chose me for this crime
> You have murdered me! You have murdered me!

Such a presentation is, of course, a display of pure poetic license arising from the imagination of the artist. Presentations at the other end of the spectrum stating with dogmatic certainty that Judas betrayed Jesus, why he did so, and why this sin is unforgivable arise out of exactly the same source: their artistic imagination. Theologians are not above using their imaginations, nor above offering dogma as fact. For example, E. W. Hengstenberg is quoted as saying, "Judas is the only man of whom we know for certain that he is damned for eternity."[34] R. L. Barry says "Christian tradition has held that [Judas] is the only person certainly excluded from the kingdom because he did not repent of his suicide," citing John 6:71 and 13:27.[35]

How else can we account for the assertions made by Daub that "among all people, Judas is the only one about whom one can and must pronounce the verdict of damnation" or that Judas's guilt is "the only one which has to be considered unerasable"?[36] Even in modern times Judas is held responsible for the death of Jesus and his suicide is cited as God's punishment for his act.[37]

Others seek a way out of the dilemma by suggesting that during the Temple action Judas was captured by the officials of the high priest and forced to help them locate Jesus and arrest him.[38] It is, of course, sheer speculation but is a way out of a very difficult historical problem.

Why is the human mind so fascinated with one "evil" person to the exclusion of the eleven "good" people? In the end, that question—although appealing to some theologians—must be left to psychologists. What does engage us is the topic upon which scripture scholars have been working so responsibly and diligently: What can we say with relative certainty about the historical figure, Judas Iscariot?

The purpose of this book is to introduce the reader to the results of recent research on Judas and to draw some conclusions about what we should not say about Judas because it so clearly goes beyond the sources available to us. We can then make some tentative historical judgments and affirmations about Judas.

Notes

1. Dieckmann, *Judas als Sündenbock,* 141.
2. Mark 3:19//Matt 10:4//Luke 6:16.
3. Luke 6:13.
4. Luke 6:13//Matt 10:1-2//Mark 3:14.
5. Hughes, "Framing Judas," 223–237.
6. On the theological side, K. Lüthi, *Judas Iskarioth,* published a fine history of the treatment of Judas since the Reformation. Klassen, "Judas," gives a brief summary of Judas in the early church as do Haugg, *Judas,* 19–61; Vogler, *Judas,* 119–134; and Klauck, *Judas,* 125–135. For a broader treatment, see W. D. Hand, "A Dictionary of Words and Idioms Associated with Judas Iscariot."

7. The magnificent and monumental work of Walter Puchner, *Studien*, provides rich documentation of the impact of Judas on Eastern church art.

8. Jeffrey, ed., *A Dictionary of Biblical Tradition*, 418–420, does not begin to do justice to the materials on Judas.

9. Mellinkoff, "Judas's Red Hair," *Journal of Jewish Art*, 31–46.

10. H.-J. Klauck suggests seven interpretive types of Judas and considers the "incarnation of evil" as dominant, *Judas*, 17.

11. E.g., Schille, *Die urchristliche Kollegialmission*. In the index under "Judas," the reader is referred to the entry under "Traitor: Verräter"!

12. Gillooly, *New York Times Book Review*, 18, in a review of Mario Brelich, *The Work of Betrayal*.

13. Guardini, *The Lord*, 348.

14. Fiorenza, *The Book of Revelation*, "Critics of Rev have pointed out that the book preaches vengeance and revenge but not the love of the Sermon on the Mount [Collins, 1980, 204]." The designation "Judas" is Fiorenza's, not A. Y. Collins's.

15. "And if anyone should dare to open this tomb, . . . he will share the lot of Judas / all things will become darkness to him, / and God will destroy him on that day." B. McLean, "A Christian Epitaph: The Curse of Judas," and P. W. van der Horst, "A Note on the Judas Curse." John Henry Kent even supplies the name Judas on an inscription dated between 267 and 268 C.E. found in Corinth, although there is no evidence of his name, (*Corinth*), 200.

16. *Journals* under the heading "Holding Out," 1852–1854, 230–231.

17. Lowrie, trans., Kierkegaard, *Attack upon Christendom*, 36.

18. Dieckmann, *Judas*, 15.

19. Daub, *Judas Ischariot oder das Böse im Verhältnis zum Guten*.

20. Jack C. Verheyden in Schleiermacher, *The Life of Jesus*, 413, note. Daub's work itself was consulted in the University of Chicago Library.

21. Daub, *Judas*, 2–3.

22. Daub, *Judas*, 8–10.

23. Daub, *Judas*, 20–21.

24. Daub, *Judas*, 22–51: "Judas und seine Vertheidiger" (Judas and His Defenders).

25. Goethe's *Faust* is quoted in the preface. Although his major partners are philosophers and theologians, it is evident that he is trying to bring the humanists into the discussion and seeks to bridge the chasm between those who argued that Judas was totally determined to do evil and those who argued that he had an opportunity to exercise his own will. See Daub, *Judas*, 44–45. For Goethe's role in the Judas story, see Dieckmann, *Judas*, 149–157.

26. S. Laeuchli, "Origen's Interpretation of Judas."

27. Bartnik, "Judas l'Iscariote," 62.

28. Wagner, *Judas Iskariot*, 11.

29. Sayers, *The Man Born to Be King*, 30.

30. Dieckmann, *Judas*, 139–140.

31. Dieckmann found only one other case in which compassion is shown to Judas, *Judas*, 141.

32. [Lines from this musical are cited by permission from both Tim Rice and Leeds Musical, now MCA Music Ltd.] On *Jesus Christ Superstar*, see Ellis Nassour and Richard Broderick, *Rock Opera: The Creation of Jesus Christ Superstar. Jesus Christ*

Superstar is cited not as a faithful guide to the meaning of the NT text but rather as an example of playwrights who ask questions of the text that deserve answers.

33. To be sure, Charlie Brown in the cartoon strip "Peanuts" demonstrates the perennial appeal of the "loser." An earlier musical, *For Heaven's Sake,* had a haunting song about Jesus entitled "He Was a Flop at Thirty-Three." It caught one important dimension of the Jesus story.

34. Lüthi in *Geschichte,* 109. He cites *Evangelische Kirchenzeitung* [1883], 370. The latter was inaccessible to me.

35. Barry, "Suicide."

36. The oft-quoted verdict of Carl Daub, cited by Klauck, 147, from Daub's work, cited above, 1:16, 20. Daub is also quoted by Karl Barth, "The Election," 502. The University of Chicago copy of Daub came from Hengstenberg's library and it can be assumed that the latter's sharp words of despair in connection with Judas's ultimate fate come from Daub. It offers an interesting case, perhaps, of a biblical scholar taking direction not from the text itself but from a systematic theologian!

37. R. Brown: "Peter was not responsible for Jesus' death and Judas was. . . . Judas had done something so heinous that no ordinary repentance affects it" (*Death,* 641). "God's punishment for that guilt was evidenced in Judas' suicide" (*Death,* 836).

38. John Crossan accepts as historical the treachery of Judas and guesses "that Judas may have been captured from among Jesus' companions during the Temple action" (*Who Killed Jesus?* 81). A similar suggestion is also made by M. Myllykoski, *Die letzten Tage Jesu,* 146.

CHAPTER
ONE

THE NATURE OF OUR
SOURCES

Recognizing the differences between the Gospels and ancient biographies, as
well as the diversity in the different types of biography of the ancient Greco-
Roman and Semitic worlds, a growing number of scholars maintain that biography is the only generic text type with which the gospel genre can be
compared. . . . Although the Gospels fall short in literary style and language
usage, they are nothing less than biographies.

—W. Vorster[1]

No purely objective life history of Judas exists, although
attempts can be made to arrive at some facts. The pursuit is difficult, in part
because of the biased nature of our sources. No one will deny that the quest
for a historical person of the ancient world, be that Socrates, Cleopatra,
Josephus, Herodias, Musonius Rufus, or Xanthippe, is fraught with peril,
because most writers tried to present more or less than verifiable facts. At
the same time the quest is of a very different nature in the case of the first-
century Jewish historian Josephus, who wrote extensively about himself,
and that of Socrates, who as far as we know wrote nothing about himself.
With respect to Jesus, we have only writings by people who loved him and
sought to honor him by keeping his memory and teaching alive.

In the case of Judas, we will show that there is a progressively degenerat-
ing trend in which he is portrayed in increasingly more negative terms. One
reason, I suggest, is simply that he left the close fellowship of the followers
of Jesus and did not return. Generally speaking, small groups dedicated to a
cause cannot bear people who desert them. Even when they go in peace,
the motives of those who leave are often presented in a hostile light as others
seek to interpret the reasons for their departure.

Writers and those who hand on oral traditions also find it convenient
to have an "evil" person as a foil when they describe a "good" person.
For example, Xanthippe, the wife of Socrates, is quite bland in the earliest

portraits of her. But shortly after a Plato-led movement started to portray
Socrates as a just man, Xanthippe began to appear as a cantankerous shrew
who made life very difficult for Socrates. There is no historical evidence to
support this portrait of Xanthippe—but it served the cause well, for it made
Socrates look so much better of a man. Indeed, before too long Socrates is
portrayed as having two wives, both of them "distracting" him from his
quest to become an imperturbable man.[2]

We must, therefore, review some of the factors involved in retelling the
stories of people's lives in ancient times.

Ancient Biography

Two considerations direct our work. One is the nature of first-century biographical writings. In the Jewish world, apart from Josephus, who wrote his
autobiography, no one wrote biographies in the modern sense.[3] A modern
biography seeks to set the subject into his or her historical context and
usually to narrate the life of a person chronologically from birth to death.
The physical appearance of the subject is described, as is the psychological
and intellectual growth of the person. Modern biographers try to delineate
external influences that had a major impact on the subject's life and, in turn,
the important influence of the subject on people and events of his or her
time. Biographers try to restrict themselves to what is historically verifiable,
or at least plausible, to describe events and not just myths, beliefs, or traditions. Strictly speaking, a modern biography does not seek simply to praise
or defame; it seeks a degree of objectivity so that the reader can make up
his or her own mind.

By contrast, ancient biographers saw their role primarily as mythmaking,
to honor the community's heroes and to condemn its scoundrels for all
time. Biographers were meant to serve a moral purpose to shape the actions
of the community. The sources on Judas available to us, mainly the four
Gospels, share much more with their contemporaries than they do with our
notions of a biography. Among Jews and Gentiles there was a lively interest
in the life of a distinguished person and in reading what a writer (e.g.,
Plutarch in his famous *Lives*) might say about that person when seeking to
portray distinctive features. Lucian described the biographer's task as taking
from many things a very few that will suffice to give "readers a notion of
the sort of man he was" (*Demonax,* 67). There are clearly some connections
between ancient "lives" and what modern biographers try to do. So Talbert
concludes, "Given these rather obvious links between certain early Christian Gospels and the ancient biographical genre, a growing consensus re-
gards certain ancient 'lives' as the closest analogy to the canonical four and
perhaps a few other early Christian Gospels as well."[4]

The Sources

The second consideration is that we are dealing with four written sources, and they have some kind of relationship to each other. Four authors from the New Testament mention Judas. Each one wrote a Gospel, and behind each lies a community within which a creative writer functioned. None of them had any intention of writing about Judas as such, and all four did so almost exclusively in order to depict his role in the death of Jesus. In some respects, Judas appears as just a minor character in the drama of the Passion. Nevertheless, of the disciples only Peter gets more lines of coverage from the Gospel writers than does Judas, who receives about the following number of words: Mark, 169; Matthew, 309; Luke and Acts, 233; John, 489. After making allowances for relative length, we can see that the writer of the Fourth Gospel has considerably more interest in Judas than does any other author. With the increase in interest comes also an undisguised hostility toward Judas. Hard as it may be for us to admit it, it is possible for the writers of the earliest Gospels simply to have yielded to the sin of vilification. There is certainly a consensus that John "must have mortally loathed Judas," as Romano Guardini put it.[5] Vilification is a popular theme now among New Testament scholars, but little attention has been paid to John's vilification of Judas, which we explore at length in chapter 8. Although Peter is mentioned seven times as often as Judas (154 versus 22 times), Judas has absorbed the attention of writers in subsequent years.

Jesus and His Disciples

Jesus' relation to his disciples as a group appears to be of subsidiary interest to the editors who compiled the Gospels in the form we have them today. They apparently sought to explain how Jesus (whom, by the time they wrote, each of them acclaimed as Messiah) could have been taken captive, crucified, and raised from the dead. To be sure, the disciples play a role in the life of Jesus, but that role had little to do with the clarification or accomplishment of Jesus' own mission. The Gospels are unanimous in saying that in Gethsemane on the night that Jesus wrestled with the crucial decision he had to make, the disciples were quite soundly asleep, presumably feeling the effects of the Passover celebration.

They are depicted as singularly obtuse and unhelpful, even in supporting Jesus in what he was coming to believe was his mission. Rather, they sought to dissuade him from meeting his death in Jerusalem. Their main goal seems to have been to get a *real* kingdom established as soon as possible and to get for themselves the best positions in it. No doubts are ever recorded about Jesus being a King. Their questions were: when would the kingdom take shape, what would it be like, and what rank would each one have in it?

And where does Judas fit in? As one of the other ten disciples he presumably joined in rebuking the two sons of Zebedee for their raw ambition
reflected in their request of Jesus to have positions of power and position
when Jesus began his reign.[6] At the same time, the evidence of the four
Gospels suggests that the ten—and many other disciples, with the notable
exception of the women—agreed with the sons of Zebedee in their understanding of the kingdom. The resentment of the ten at the sons' request
may have come as much from knowing where it would leave the ten if the
two were granted their request as it does from any objection in principle.
Our sources do not suggest that the ten had a different view of the kingdom
than the two did or that they had listened more closely to what Jesus had
said about it. In any event, Judas takes his place among the ten.

In our search for the historical Judas, our sources are not only very limited, they are also tendentious—so much so that one of the most respected
New Testament scholars of our century, Johannes Weiss, concluded that the
"Judas problem is, in spite of all efforts, thus far insoluble. . . . A scientific
answer cannot be found; here fantasy has to do the task; consequently this
subject is the domain of the poet."[7] Two questions haunted Weiss: How
could Judas do what he did after such a long association with Jesus, and how
could Jesus have chosen such a person and kept him in his company?

Joseph Blinzler finds comfort in the fact that Judas came from Judea and
not Galilee. "This makes his difference in character appear a little more
comprehensible. Otherwise, this dark and sinister figure presents a psychological puzzle which even the poetic imagination cannot completely illuminate."[8] A similar point is made by Michael Grant, who claims that as a non-
Galilean "he lacked this particular regional basis of loyalty."[9]

We have some sympathy for Weiss's position. Nevertheless, we do not
give up our responsibilities as serious students of the biblical narratives. The
nature of the sources must be respected. First of all, they must be read in
the light of the goal and purpose of each Gospel writer. Each wrote, of
course, in the assurance that Judas's side of the story would never be told.
It has been left to the novelists, dramatists, and painters to depict that side.
But the Gospel writers, too, had their own agendas. They wrote with a
certain body of tradition, written and oral, at their disposal. They wrote as
custodians of a shared communal theology (a *Gemeindetheologie*), which they
sought to hand down to their followers but which they also hoped would
address certain critical problems faced by their communities. They were
creative shapers of their tradition. Each had access to certain sources unique
to them. Some of those sources may in fact have been written and/or been
committed to memory. Writing history today is not, it would seem, any
easier.

A Modern Parallel

In modern times, an earthshaking event such as the assassination of President John F. Kennedy is examined and reexamined using motion picture cameras, still-life photography, and eyewitness accounts. When author William Manchester worked for nearly three years "a hundred hours a week" to write *The Death of a President,* a history of that tragic event, he found that eyewitnesses changed their stories a year after they were interviewed.[10] As difficult as it was for him to write a definitive history of the assassination, no one doubted that the killing had transpired. But there was, and is, no unanimous agreement on who killed President Kennedy or why. People who believe in conspiracies point to the astounding fact that the Dallas police department apparently has no verbatim record of the critical interrogations they held with the prime suspect, Lee Harvey Oswald, before he was gunned down a few days later.[11] Those who reject the conspiracy theory draw from equally compelling evidence.

The Nature of the Tradition

In the case of Judas there are similar problems with the recounting of history. The four authors who mention him—Mark, Matthew, Luke, and John—had no intention of writing about Judas as such, and all four did so only as part of their efforts to depict the death of Jesus. This accounts for the fact that in Mark and Matthew—it could be argued in all four Gospels—Judas is quite peripheral to the action, which seems to be directed by God.

And what is Judas's role? It differs with each writer. Each of the Gospel writers has a distinct purpose in writing. They wrote in the first instance as missionaries intending to persuade others but also as those who were committed to keeping their own Christian community faithful to the risen and historical Jesus: "Not archivists but missionaries formulated the tradition from which the evangelists drew," says Martin Dibelius.[12]

It has been observed that the practice of "handing on" in which the Gospel writers engage is the same word always used for the act of Judas. It remains to be seen whether there are indications that in this process of "handing on" the writers of the Gospels were faithful to Judas and to Jesus himself. We must allow for the possibility that those who passed along the traditions about Judas were unfaithful to both Jesus and Judas. It may well be the case that the later tradition betrayed both of them by demonizing Judas and portraying Jesus as a dupe. To give them the benefit of the doubt we may conclude that in Mark's account we have the briefest treatment of Judas, for Mark confines himself to portraying Judas as a person. In John, however, Judas has become a character, not a central character, to be sure, but one who gives a certain element of color and brings dramatic tension to the narrative.

A Methodological Consideration

Nearly two hundred years ago Friedrich Schleiermacher insisted that individual writers of the biblical books were entitled to be read in their own right. Thus Luke could be read as Luke, his intentions analyzed, his evidence treated without asking how the Lukan text deviates from Mark or Matthew. That principle has only recently been applied to accounts involving Judas.[13] Although Origen had made some shrewd methodological observations, Gospel studies were generally done in a harmonistic way. The great commentators of the Reformation period—Bucer, Calvin, and Luther—tended to treat the four Gospels as one. This meant that John's highly dramatized, negative view of Judas overpowered Mark's more objective presentation. In the early years of the church, John's Gospel was the most popular.

Many scholars use data from the Fourth Gospel to malign Judas; some, such as Karl Barth, draw mainly from the Fourth Gospel. Although John provides surely the most biased and malicious portrait of Judas, he sets the norm. Other Gospel writers are accused of "softening" the true picture of Judas.

Fortunately, such an unhistorical treatment of sources is becoming less and less prevalent. It appears most frequently among commentators who are at a loss to explain the absence of information relating to Judas's act. The monographs on Judas have been able to avoid this trap with increasing success. One would wish it could also be said of commentators.

The first scholar to base his study of Judas on the four Gospel portraits of Judas, if I mistake not, was Donatus Haugg in 1930.[14] While Haugg distinguishes between the Gospels, he assumes that the Markan tradition rests on Peter, and he believes that this presentation of Judas "deserves full trustworthiness."[15] The Synoptics offer only the facts, not the interpretation thereof: "They [Synoptic writers] remain objective historians, which does not rule out a theological consideration of Judas." Moreover, Haugg accepts John's portrait as totally within the borders of that presented by the Synoptics; "consequently it cannot be a tendency towards vilification on John's part when he presents Judas as an avaricious thief."[16] John was not trying to accuse his fellow apostle of any evil; he simply calls attention to the evil influence of Satan, "seeking thereby to distribute the guilt."

He sees the theology of John as no hindrance to the historian. John is an eyewitness who "saw with greatest depth into the secrets of Judas' soul from the very beginning."[17] He concludes that both the older Synoptic-Petrine and the later Johannine presentation of the Judas narrative deserve "full historical trust" (*volles geschichtliches Vertrauen*). Unfortunately, he also treats as historically reliable the Capernaum incident as reported by John (6:59-71). When this is done, the figure of Judas becomes transformed because the investigator must conclude that Judas acted hypocritically for a number of years.[18]

Haugg's work was an important beginning even though the results have been reassessed. We cannot today speak as blithely about the historical reliability of the Gospels, and certainly we cannot treat John's vilification of Judas without asking some very direct questions about it.

The Human Need for Scapegoats

The most difficult problem in dealing with the Judas story is not, however, the biases of the Gospels but the intense aversion to—if not hatred for—Judas that has accumulated over the centuries, focusing primarily on Judas as scapegoat.

The word "scapegoat" came into the English language through Tindale's translation of Lev 16:8, 10, 26 when he rendered the Hebrew עֲזָאזֵל, Azazel, which literally means desert demon, as "the goote on which the lotte fell to scape." Most modern translations[19] avoid "scapegoat" and stay with the Hebrew original or a literal translation such as "Precipice" (NEB).[20] The phenomenon that it describes of blaming or punishing people for the sins of others is very old and cannot be ended by removing the word "scapegoat" from the Bible. Certainly Judas as scapegoat surfaces as a persistent folk and literary type.[21] One explicit reference to Judas as the "goat who fled" goes back at least to Cyril of Syria, about 279-303 C.E. (see below, p. 178).

In our time, René Girard has provided fresh impetus to an analysis of the scapegoat phenomenon. He specifically deals with the Bible's scapegoat texts and also with the violent sacrificial aspect of Jesus' death. Although, curiously, Judas does not figure in Girard's discussion to any extent, his impetus has affected Catholic thinkers differently from Protestant.[22] In his study of Girard, Raymund Schwager touches on Judas several times, blaming him for having been caught up in what he calls "the spirit of Jerusalem" that eventually killed Jesus, and condemns Judas for his act of betrayal as being the determining act that caught Jesus by surprise and began the death process. Most important, he thinks the Gospels saw the people who in one way or another were active in bringing about Jesus' death as representatives of whole peoples, and attributed to their deeds a fundamental character (*eine grundsätzliche Bedeutung*).[23]

Quite a different tack is taken by Robert Hamerton-Kelly, who studies Mark from the standpoint of Jesus becoming the scapegoat to replace the violence of the Temple hierarchy. The priests "buy through Judas" their new scapegoat; for Christians, Jesus should then mark the end of all scape-goating.[24]

Shortly after the First World War, Margaret Plath made an astute observation in her analysis of why the early church valued the Judas narrative. After discussing the value of the stories for self-examination and the element of warning in the Judas narratives, she lists another gap that the stories of Judas fill:

> Another practical religious need to be kept in mind by those who encounter the Judas story: the need to hate—for not a few the most preferred, indeed perhaps the only form they have of showing their love for their Lord; many can still muster honourable hatred against the traitors and enemies of Jesus even though they find it difficult to express in deeds their love for their Lord through following him in the attitudes he demands: meekness, purity of heart, and peacemaking.[25]

To her list of Jesus' demands, we could certainly add his exhortation to love one's enemies. Millions of Christians have been unable to follow this command to love one's enemies, enemies that for them include even Judas. As one such example, let us consider Abraham Santa Clara.

Abraham Santa Clara

Vividly I remember sitting in the library of the University of Tübingen in the summer of 1991, reading the sermons of Abraham Santa Clara, one of the most gifted preachers of the Austrian church of the late seventeenth century,[26] described by one historian as one of the "most effective writers and speakers of all time."[27] Friedrich Schiller described him as "a man of wonderful originality whom we must respect, and it would be an interesting though not at all an easy task to approach or surpass him in mad clever-ness."[28] His influence was most strongly felt in the German pulpit, in part because he brought "wit, gaiety, entertainment (to) dominate the Bavarian and Austrian pulpits in the next decades."[29] As Kann describes it: "Nobody in the intervening period between the early eighteenth and the late nine-teenth centuries in German-Austrian history handled the complex instru-ment of mass appeal with the mastery of Abraham. . . . Nobody . . . came even remotely as close . . . to the position of spokesman of the feelings of an urban lower middle class faithful to their religious and political traditions."[30]

For more than ten years Santa Clara was obsessed with Judas. Virtually every Sunday for an entire decade he preached about him, or, perhaps better said, *against* him. By way of warning to his faithful, Santa Clara proclaimed that Judas's mother had talked too much; listeners were urged not to let this happen to them lest they bring forth another Judas!

The concluding sermons in his interminable series consist of cursing all parts of Judas's anatomy, beginning with his red hair and ending with his toes. How could such a gifted preacher put his finest efforts into such an eloquent series of maledictions against a disciple whom Jesus apparently never scolded?[31] How could this gifted but misguided preacher stay in touch with the gentle gospel of Jesus when he devoted such passionate skill to pouring out venom toward one of Jesus' disciples? Did it not even once occur to him that Judas, too, could have been a servant of both God and the Messiah in handing Jesus over to the Jewish authorities?

What drew me to Abraham Santa Clara during those summer hours? An interest in Judas, to be sure. But it went beyond that to a recognition that both the monk, who served as court preacher, and I belong to the same community of disciples—a community of faith, hope, and love—as did Judas. We seek to find the meaning of discipleship; to serve the same teacher. From the outset it was obvious that I could not come out where Abraham Santa Clara did. But where was our common ground? And on what basis could I make an informed decision different from his? An exploration of these questions helped form the context for this book.

It is evident that Santa Clara stood in a very strong tradition regarding Judas. In fact, his position on Judas is part of the cultural heritage of Austria and Western Europe in general.

One of the reasons the denigrations of Judas have been so successful is that the writers have possessed excellent literary skills, beginning with the Fourth Gospel itself. We owe the pervasiveness of the negative tradition about Judas to at least two sources:

1. The gospel epic called *Carmen Paschale,* written by Sedulius at the beginning of the fifth century (before 431 C.E.). Meant to introduce Christians to beautiful Latin prose in Christian form so that they would not have to read pagan writers, this epic influenced the attitude of educated Christians for almost thirteen centuries.

It is highly likely that Sedulius, more than any other person, is responsible for the negative portrait of Judas so common among the educated, especially the theologians and clergy. "[The *Carmen Paschale*] was required reading in schools throughout the Middle Ages and a source of inspiration for Latin and the vernacular Biblical epics well into the 17th century. . . . It was a work which centuries of European readers found of enduring value," writes a modern student of the epic.

Sedulius shows no moderation in connection with Judas. His longest literary "intrusion" deals with Judas. His imprecation against Judas, for which there is no biblical precedent, sets the standard for later writers.

Although he was called the most Christian writer, it seems clear that the passion with which Sedulius condemns Judas and the particular indictments he offers against him far exceed any historical evidence.[32] His vituperation, therefore, has to be rejected not only on historical grounds but also on moral grounds, especially since epic writers claimed they were telling the truth.[33] That the connection between his work and the negative reputation of Judas apparently has never been noted before shows how effective the tradition has been. Few things fascinate people as much as stories about those whose actions they cannot comprehend. A time-honored way of dealing with these individuals is to consider them evil. Should we not also note that telling stories like this, without basis, constitutes slander?

2. The *Legenda Aurea,* a collection of apocryphal stories first gathered by the Dominican Jacob of Virragio (1230–1298), was widely circulated from the fourteenth and fifteenth centuries and beyond. What the *Carmen Paschale* did for the educated, this collection did for the uneducated. It "enveloped the whole intellectual life of the Middle Ages" and, according to one writer, remains the most popular book of edification of the West.[34]

Since the Enlightenment, there have been efforts to reverse the negative reputation that Judas has acquired in the church. Writing six decades after Santa Clara, Friedrich Gottlieb Klopstock[35] in his epic piece, *The Messiah* (1773), took Judas seriously as a person and saw Judas as trying to force Jesus' hand, "to move him to erect his long-awaited kingdom." Klopstock influenced Goethe, among many others, and made the way for a break with the traditional way of looking at Jesus and Judas.

A direct link exists also between the German writers and Thomas de Quincey, who was responsible for bringing their writings to the attention of British literary circles in the nineteenth century. In his writing on Judas, de Quincey makes explicit reference to a hypothesis that had been known in Germany for some time: "Not one thing, but all things, must rank as false which traditionally we accept about him [Judas]. That neither any motive of his, nor any ruling impulse, was tainted with the vulgar treachery imputed to him, appears probable from the strength of his remorse."[36] Rather, the grand scheme of Jesus was being neutralized by the character of Christ himself, whom de Quincey describes as "sublimely overgifted for purposes of speculation, but like Shakespeare's great creation, Prince Hamlet, not correspondingly endowed for the business of action and the clamorous emergencies of life."[37] Judas therefore believed that Jesus needed to be "precipitated into action by a force from without." His miscalculation was based on a total spiritual blindness which he fully shared with his fellow disciples. He outran them only in his presumption.

De Quincey viewed it as an important correction to see that Judas's act came not out of perfidy but from a belief in Jesus and in his kingdom. It must, he says, "always be important to recall within the fold of Christian forgiveness any one who has been long sequestered from human charity, and has tenanted a Pariah grave. In the greatest and most memorable human tragedies Judas is a prominent figure. . . . The crime, though great, of the Iscariot . . . was to promote the purposes of Christ . . . by means utterly at war with their central spirit. As far as can be judged, it was an attempt to forward the counsels of God by weapons borrowed from the armoury of darkness."[38]

It was not only educated and literate people who protested the traditional view of the "evil" Judas. In popular piety, a beautiful hymn dating to the sixteenth century offers a bit of pure gospel:

> Ah twas our great sins and serious transgressions
> Nailed Christ, the true son of God to the Cross
> For this, let us not sorely scold poor Judas
> Nor the company of Jews; the guilt is ours![39]

This book is not an effort to correct all that theologians have done with Judas. Its goal is more modest. Whatever theologians have said, the people in their own good sense, in strong touch with the gospel, have made a place for Judas. In addition to the hymn cited above, consider this line from an African-American slave song:

> When you get to heaven,
> rub poor lil' Judas' head.

What to make of this line needs more research and reflection than we can give it here. At the very least, it assumes that black slaves—at least the ones who created this line—expected to see Judas in heaven. It also refuses to cast Judas into the enemy role as the traitor who deserves only punishment; rather, it places him among the oppressed as someone to whom one is to bring relief. It speaks, above all, of compassion and thus goes to the central nerve of the gospel.[40]

Bernhard Dieckmann referred to Judas as a key figure for one's under-standing of Christianity and the church.[41] For him, the unbelief of the disci-ples was the decisive point in our understanding of Judas.[42] He recognized that since the traditional Judas picture appealed to a specific interpretation of the New Testament, any criticism of this traditional picture must relate to the New Testament and, indeed, be based on it. Not only does the New Testament permit a different interpretation of Judas, he suggested, but it even demands it.[43]

What is needed is a biblical-theological reworking of the Judas narrative. This is a very complex endeavor that must begin by considering each asser-tion about Judas in each of the Gospels, in the context of that Gospel's theology, before one can ask how it can be accepted today.[44] Basic work has been done in this area, mostly in German, to be sure; but a beginning has been made.[45] In this work, I seek to add to the quest of Dieckmann and others for the historical Judas. His significance in the history of Christian theology is of secondary importance. I have previously called attention to the lack of communication between persons writing commentaries and those who write monographs on Judas or related themes. Sometimes this lack of communication can, however, be overcome when the same person does both. One illustration of that is the work of Raymond Brown.

The treatment of Judas is complicated in the case of Brown. Already in his commentary on John he had dealt with the picture of Judas drawn by the Fourth Gospel (see below, chapter 8). In his recent monumental work, a detailed analysis of the Passion narratives,[46] he has abundant occasion to deal with Judas, for he is trying to depict the death of the Messiah in faithfulness to the Gospel writers. Therefore Judas is treated from the perspective of each Gospel writer but also in synoptic fashion in an overall treatment.

Brown now shows an appreciation for the complexity of the verb used to describe Judas's act. He has "insisted (211–213) that the verb *paradidonai,* applied to Judas, means "to give over," not "to betray" (1399). He notes that the classical word for "betray" appears only once in connection with Judas in the New Testament and wonders whether the Gospel writers preferred the word meaning "to hand over" because of their reading of Isaiah 53 (1399, note). He states that the handing over involved bringing the arresting party to find Jesus and identifying him for them, for he is described as the one "who gave Jesus over" (29). The evidence of the Gospels is that "the iniquity [sic] of Judas was to give over his teacher and friend to the *Jewish* authorities."[47] In his use of Popkes, Brown recognizes that *paradidōmi* means that "Jesus was given over (nay betrayed)" (211), thus introducing a critical contradiction. While praising the work of Popkes, Brown nevertheless refers to the act of Judas as "betrayal" (89, 120, 140, 144, 246, 251, 256, 263), and Judas himself as the "Traitor" (214) or the "betrayer" (242, 243, 244, 245, 246). He is one who "failed definitively" (49), while the others succeeded (141). He is described as a "mysterious, villainous figure" (242) whose presence is "otiose" in John's description of the arrest.[48] For Brown, the exchange of silver retains its traditional connotation of "a bribe" (60).

Nevertheless, in his thorough excursus "The Overall Treatment of Judas Iscariot," Brown explores the various issues in some detail. Using the latest literature, he presents evidence of the meaning of the word "to hand over" and rejects the notion that "a subject like Judas was created at a later level." He accepts the idea that Judas handed Jesus over to the authorities who arranged his death. He then adds: "In the tradition little more may have been known about Judas, except that he died a sudden, violent death" (1397).

In trying to answer the question, "What did Judas betray?" Brown insists that "the verb *paradidōmi*, applied to Judas, means to 'give over,' not to 'betray.'" He objects to all theories that Judas handed any information on to the authorities, seeing as their "fatal objection" that Judas did not appear as a witness against Jesus. But could it not be that he did not appear precisely because Jesus was handed over so quickly to the *Roman* authorities? Brown himself offers the possibility that Judas changed, "almost as if he did not know that this would be the outcome" (1401) when he saw Jesus was handed over to Pilate.

Evidence that Brown cannot rid himself of the long and persistent tradition of Judas as a sinner in this connection is indicated by his statement, "The *iniquity* [my italics] of Judas was to give over his teacher and friend to the *Jewish* authorities." He provides no evidence for his affirmation that "the Gospels agree that Judas had turned against Jesus by the time of the Last Supper" (1401). To his credit, although using some evidence from the *Golden Legend,* Brown concludes: "We cannot be certain the portrayal of Judas as avaricious is not a later denigration of his character on the principle that one who did such an evil act must have embodied all evil" (1401). The tentativeness of this statement is eloquent.

Brown has learned from recent writers such as Popkes and Klauck, and his portrait of Judas has changed from what it was in earlier writings. Not as frequent are the references to the maliciousness and evil of Judas (see below on John), and he is prepared to limit the amount of historicity attributed to the death accounts of Judas. Most significant is the way in which he recognizes that the fundamental meaning of the word used to describe Judas's act is not "betray" but to "hand over." Once that is recognized, possibilities emerge to remove the evil connotations of this word. He more frequently allows for the possibility that certain aspects of the Judas picture must be attributed to the evangelist and need not be historically valid.

Even more important, a connection is now made between the handing over that Judas carried out and God's. Brown has not yet been able to remove from his vocabulary the word "betray" in connection with what Judas did. But he is to be commended for consistently avoiding the word "betray" in his translation of the passion narrative (1583–1608). Even though he reminds us that it is a "painfully literal translation" (ix), he thereby makes significant progress toward helping us remove the stigma from Judas's deed by letting the text speak for itself. One can only hope that Brown will complete that journey and that all translators will follow suit.

The next step would be to relate the statements he made about Judas in

his work on First John to the portrait of Judas in the Fourth Gospel. For
the Johannine community, Judas was the "archetype of the secessionist
movement" and a son of perdition and evil.[49] The language of "going out"
is applied to Judas as well as to the secessionists.

The book *The Death of the Messiah,* in any case, already marks a major
breakthrough. For the key figure in the death of the Messiah is not Judas.
He plays a relatively minor role, which Brown recognizes. His work is a
fresh study of the passion of Jesus, a superb endeavor that courageously deals
also with the prickly question of the responsibility for Jesus' death. Although warned by some to avoid this question, Brown tackles it head-on a
number of times.[50] Not only does he treat the Gospels judiciously as historical sources, he also introduces the reader to a superb historical survey of the
state of the question and explains why certain positions held by the Gospels
are untenable today.

His distinction between guilt and responsibility is very servicable in this
context. Matthew, Brown holds, considers Judas and Pilate responsible for
Jesus' death. So Judas "could not escape guilt for having set in motion a
destructive process that could not be reversed. God's punishment for that
guilt was evidenced in Judas' suicide" (836). Is this Matthew speaking or
Brown? Either way surely it is impossible to make a leap from suicide to
guilt and even more problematic to see in the act of suicide evidence of
God's punishment. Does Matthew really say that?

It is part of the purpose of this book to address that question.

Summary

This book seeks to build on a foundation that has already been laid and
attempts to let the sources speak for themselves. Readers are invited to have
an open mind in approaching these texts. In the last analysis, you, the reader,
must make up your own mind and arrive at your own conclusion on the
basis of the same evidence available to all of us. As you do so, you may be
drawn to the conclusion that I have reached: the reason that Judas is so
intriguing is that—whatever he did and however the early and later Christian community responded to it—we as individuals face the same test as
Judas. How can the encounter with Jesus and the good news he proclaimed
be transformed into action? How do we relate to those who once were
faithful followers of Jesus who appear to turn against us when they or we
leave our community? Such an examination brings us to the very heart of
the message of Jesus. Specifically it raises the question: How does one draw
the inclusive and exclusive limits of the community of Jesus of Nazareth?

Notes

1. Vorster, "Gospel, Genre," *ABD*, 3:1077–1079, here 1079.
2. Dörrie, "Xanthippe," Pauly-Wissowa, *Realenzyklopädie*, 1335–1342.
3. On this topic, Talbert, "Biography, Ancient," *ABD*, 1:745–749. The impact of Socrates on the development of Greek biography is traced by Dihle, *Studien zur griechischen Biographie*. For evidence of the Jewish interest in "ideal figures," see Nickelsburg and Collins, eds., *Ideal Figures in Ancient Judaism;* on the broader picture, see Momigliano, *The Development of Greek Biography;* Stuart, *Epochs of Greek and Roman Biography;* and Cox, *Biography in Late Antiquity: A Quest for a Holy Man.*
4. Talbert, "Biography, Ancient," *ABD*, 1:747–749, here 749.
5. Guardini, *The Lord*, 351.
6. Mark 10:35-45//Matt 20:20-28. Neither Luke nor John has this incident but both deal with the same issue in more general terms (Luke 22:24-27; John 13:4-5, 12-17).
7. Weiss, *Die Schriften des Neuen Testaments*, 1:102. See Haugg, *Judas*, 10.
8. Blinzler, *Trial*, 60.
9. Grant, *Jesus*, 156. Such a conclusion is really quite astounding. Are we to assume that Judeans had less interest in a physical kingdom? Surely no profile of Judeans exists that helps us to understand Judas, even if we knew for sure that he did not come from Galilee. We do not know that the other eleven came from Galilee. We do know that the uniqueness of Galilee has been overdrawn. See S. Freyne, *Galilee:* "Galilean political attitudes were not at all so radical or sharply defined as has often been suggested" (392).
10. Manchester compiled eighteen volumes of carefully transcribed interviews. On the controversy surrounding its publication, see Corry, *The Manchester Affair.* The issue is far from resolved, judging from the controversy over Oliver Stone's documentary film *JFK*, released in 1991.
11. Tom Wicker, who covered the event for the *New York Times*, concludes, "I doubt that the truth about the Kennedy assassination has yet been told. It may never be." Ultimately, in his review of the Stone film (*International Herald Tribune*, Dec. 17, 1991), he concludes that it is a matter of faith about whose version one believes. Pheme Perkins also compares her research on Peter with the attempts to piece together the Kennedy murder (*Peter*, 23–24).
12. "In the beginning was the edificational, religiously understandable, interpreted and presented in the sense of a consideration of what is experienced in the proclamation (*Predigt*)" (Dibelius, "Die alttestamentlichen Motive," 222).
13. The first consistently to apply it is Vogler, *Judas Iskarioth*, followed by Klauck, *Judas—Ein Jünger des Herrn*, who, although separating the "triple tradition" from John, also has a concluding section in which the individual aspect of each account of the death of Judas is allowed to come forward.
14. Haugg, *Judas*, 69–72.
15. Haugg, *Judas*, 70.
16. Haugg, *Judas*, 72.
17. Haugg, *Judas*, 72.
18. Haugg, *Judas*, 72.
19. RV (1884), the RSV, NRSV, JB, and the *Gute Nachricht.*

20. The LXX has ἀποπομπαῖος, from the verb "to send away."

21. Dieckmann, *Judas,* 245–251; Girard, *Violence and the Sacred,* 250–273; idem, *Das Ende der Gewalt* (Herder, 1978), 180–230; and Perera, *The Scapegoat Complex: Toward a Mythology of Shadow and Guilt.*

22. See Girard, *Violence and the Sacred.* As far as I know, he deals with Judas only in his treatment of the "new sacrificial reading," the semiotic analysis of Louis Martin. See Girard, *Things Hidden,* 245–253, esp. 247. In a written communication to me (March 8, 1993), Girard states that, seen through the eyes of Matthew, Jesus made what Judas did "perfectly insignificant."

23. Schwager, *Must There Be Scapegoats?* 187, 190 (following Pesch, 190–191). All quotations and page references are from the German original (Munich, 1978).

24. Hamerton-Kelly, *The Gospel and the Sacred,* 42–45.

25. Plath, "Warum hat die urchristliche Gemeinde auf die Überlieferung der Judaserzählung Wert gelegt?" esp. 182–183. She notes the stories of the ancient past, Dante as well as some evidence from the twentieth century. See also Klauck, *Judas,* 143.

26. Abraham a Sancta Clara (Hans-Ulrich Megerle, 1644–1709), *Judas, der Ertzschelm.* See bibliography for title in detail.

27. Kann, *A Study in Austrian Intellectual History,* 90.

28. Kann, *A Study,* 92.

29. Herbert Cysarz, as cited in Kann, *A Study,* 97.

30. Kann, *A Study,* 114.

31. Santa Clara, *Judas,* 4:411–433, which he calls a funeral sermon, "Leichenpredigt." The sermons were, in fact, built on a medieval collection of apocryphal stories about Judas, the *Legenda Aurea,* as well as some scriptural materials. The sermons by Santa Clara were apparently translated into many languages. His complete works were published in twenty-one volumes from 1834 to 1954 and in a six-volume abbreviated edition in 1904–1907. See Grete Mecenseffy, *RGG*[3] (1957), 1:71–72. For critique, see K. Lüthi, *Geschichte,* 192–194; and Dieckmann, *Judas,* 36.

32. Springer, *The Gospel as Epic in Late Antiquity: The Paschale Carmen of Sedulius,* 1–2. The quotation is from p. 1.

33. The influence of Sedulius's epic is the more invidious because the epics were often made into hymns, and as such found to be "a more authentically Christian literary form and more truly 'original' than the biblical epic" (Springer, *The Gospel,* 7). In contrast to pagan writers, Christian epic writers claimed they were telling the truth (Springer, *The Gospel,* 16).

34. Von Dobschütz, "Legend, Legendary," *The New Schaff-Herzog Religious Encyclopedia,* 441.

35. Klopstock, *Ausgewählte Werke.* In the poem entitled "Der Messias" (263: II, 630–640).

36. Komroff, "Judas, Man of Doubt," in *Jesus through the Centuries,* 427–433. This quotation is from 427. According to Borges, "Three Versions of Judas," this became an important starting point for Nils Runeberg, a deeply religious Swede who followed de Quincey in reconsidering Judas from a radically different standpoint. In 1909 he published *Kristus och Judas.*

37. Quoted in Komroff, "Judas," 428.

38. De Quincey, as quoted by Komroff, "Judas," 431–433.

39. Cited from Dieckmann, *Judas,* 140, whose source is Ph. Wackernagel, *Kir-*

chenlied 2, 471, Nr. 625, from a hymnbook published in 1604. Lapide (*Schuld an Jesu Tod* [1989], 122) calls attention to a very similar hymn attributed to Luther:

> Twas our great debt
> Our heavy load of sin
> Jesus, True son of God
> Nailed to the Tree.
> So that we blame not you,
> In enmity, poor Judas,
> Or even more the Jewish throngs.
> The guilt, all of it, is ours alone.

40. D. S. Williams, "Rub Poor Lil' Judas's Head," *Christian Century*, 963.

41. Dieckmann, *Judas*, 227.

42. Dieckmann, *Judas*, 257.

43. Dieckmann, *Judas*, 277.

44. Dieckmann, *Judas*, 359 n. 19.

45. Books that use the standard redactional critical methods are Vogler, *Judas Iskarioth;* Klauck, *Judas;* and Haugg, *Judas,* which does so less consistently. This awareness that there are four Judases in the New Testament is apparent also in Elaine Pagels, *Origin.*

46. Brown, *The Death of the Messiah.*

47. Brown, *Death,* 1401 (his italics). In his discussion of Matthew, Brown notes that he dramatizes the "iniquity" of Judas, heightened even more by John (120–121).

48. Brown, *Death,* 261. The meanings of "otiose" are "idle," "indolent," "sterile," and "useless."

49. Brown, *The Epistles of John,* 367 n. 14, 364, 468, 486, 686–687. Judas is described as the only one whom Jesus lost, "but he belonged to the Evil One" (548).

50. Brown, *Death,* 29–30; 372–397; 835–837; 931–932; 1419–1434.

CHAPTER
TWO

THE NAME AND ITS
IDENTIFYING ROLE

Recent renewed concentration on the texts of the New Testament has turned
our traditionally Christian picture of Judas upside down. We discover that it
does not correspond to the New Testament. There Judas is certainly depicted
as a tragic figure, but not as the evil one.
                                                        —Wolfgang Feneberg, S.J.[1]

In trying to learn to know someone, we invariably begin
by being introduced to the name of that person. A name often tells us a
great deal about someone, particularly about his or her culture or ethnic
group. This certainly is the case with Judas Iscariot. His name is worthy of
some attention. In this chapter, I will examine the name of Judas in and of
itself, seeking clues for geographic significance and religious connotations
as well as any political proclivities.

Judas Iscariot

Judas Iscariot is mentioned twenty times in the four Gospels and twice in
Acts. Although he is designated as "one of the Twelve" in Matthew (26:14,
47) and in Mark (14:10) and is listed among the apostles in Luke (6:16) as
well as in Mark (3:19) and Matthew (10:4), Judas Iscariot does not play a
central role in any of the events portrayed and is described by one author as
"only a peripheral figure" (*Randfigur*) holding "no central place."[2] By contrast, Peter is mentioned some ninety times in the Gospels.

The name Judas Iscariot appears in five different forms:

1. The original name, Judas, the hellenized form of the Hebrew name,
yehudah יהודה, in Mark 14:43; Matt 26:25, 47; 27:3; Luke 22:47-48; Acts
1:16,25; and John 13:29; 18:2-5.

2. Judas Iscarioth, which is the Semitic form of Iscariot, in Mark 3:19;
14:10; Luke 6:16; and as a variant reading in Matt 10:4 and Luke 22:47.

3. Judas, the Iscariot (Ἰούδας ὁ Ἰσκαριώτης), in the Greek form, apparently to differentiate him from another Judas (Luke 6:16; Acts 1:13; John 14:22); and a reference to a member of the Twelve (Matt 10:4; 26:14; Luke 22:3; John 6:71; 12:4; 13:2, 26; 14:22). This name also appears as a variant reading in Mark 3:19; 14:10, 43; and Luke 6:16.

4. Judas, "the one called Judas Iscariot" (Matt 26:14; Luke 22:3; John 6:71).

5. Judas, son of Simon Iscariot (John 6:71; 13:2,26).[3]

Some of the forms are quite easily understood when we note differences in the Hebrew and Greek languages. While only a limited amount of light is cast on the personality of Judas through his name, what there is, is critically important.

The Name Judas

In the first century of the common era, two names were frequently given to young boys in Jewish families. In English, those names are Jesus and Judas. By the second century, the name Jesus hardly ever appears; among Christians, the name Judas starts to disappear. Today that name, in the form of Yehudah, remains a source of pride among Jews, especially Israelis, because it is the founding name of the Jews, linked to one of the patriarchs of the twelve tribes of Israel. Yet, most non-Jews would not think of naming a child Judas. As George Buttrick says, "We would not name a child, or even a dog, Judas."[4]

What has brought about the change from honor to disrepute? The answers are complex and elusive, yet increasingly scholars are concerned about answering this question. There are intense efforts to attempt to discover how the traditions about the historical Judas were shaped by the early and later church. These efforts can be rewarding not only in learning about the emerging church, but they can also cast light on the historical Judas.

The skepticism that rules among academics on the feasibility of such a quest is well known to me. When Dieckmann says, "The Gospel sources do not allow a precise conclusion on the historical figure of Judas because many Biblical statements about him are theological interpretations," he is, in part, correct.[5] The same can be said about Jesus and, indeed, about Socrates. That should not and does not lead us to hesitate to explore what is possible. In fact, we live at a time when scholarly confidence seems to run at an all-time high, and enormous energy is being spent giving various degrees of genuineness to sayings of Jesus. To cite just one example, John Dominic Crossan declares with a certain degree of confidence: "The historical Jesus was, then, a *peasant Jewish Cynic*."[6] In this definition the adjective and the noun are to be given equal weight. Indeed, scholars are far from

being unanimously agreed on degrees of skepticism or confidence about
what we can know about Jesus.

With some measured caution, therefore, we engage in our historical research about Judas. We know much about Jesus compared with other ancient figures. Most significant is the fact that our first Gospel seems to have
been drafted less than thirty years after the events they record and all of the
gospels were probably written by the beginning of the second century, less
than seventy years after Jesus lived. Eventful as those years were, it certainly
stands to reason that much of what the Gospels contain is historically reliable, even if theologically biased.[7]

In historical research, conclusions are never wholly precise, but they can
be informed and can point to historical probabilities. Among Christian
scholars, at least, a strong consensus has emerged that there was indeed a
Judas of history. For us, the quest for the historical Judas begins with an
analysis of his name, Judas Iscariot.[8]

There are eight men with the name Judas in the New Testament, as well
as one who wrote one of the epistles, Jude. They are:

1. Son of the patriarch Jacob and head of the tribe of Judah (Matt 2:6).
2. Judah, in the genealogy of Jesus, not further identified (Luke 3:30).
3. Judas, son of James, one of the twelve apostles (Luke 6:16; Acts 1:13;
John 14:22).
4. Judas Iscariot, twenty-two times.
5. Judas, the brother of Jesus (Matt 13:55; Mark 6:3).
6. Judas the Galilean (Acts 5:37).
7. Judas Barsabbas (Acts 15:22, 27, 32).
8. Judas of Damascus (Acts 9:11).

It is not clear whether Judas, the writer of the epistle that bears the name
Jude, is already included in this list, or whether possibly he is the same as
the brother of Jesus.[9] In any case, it is clear that it was a popular name in
first-century Palestine.

Josephus mentions nineteen men with the name Jude and thirteen with
the name of Judas, most of them leaders in the Zealot-Sicarii group. The
Zealots were believed by some not to have been constituted before the year
66 c.e. as a party, but others, myself included, believe they "formed a relatively exclusive and unified movement with its own distinctive religious
views . . . which had a crucial influence on the history of Palestinian Judaism
in the decisive period between 6 and 70 A.D. They were a group wielding
considerable influence especially among religiously committed Jews from
the time of the Maccabees (180–160 B.C.E.) onward."[10] Only people who
take this position would allow for the possibility that Judas belonged to
this group.

It is clear that Judas was a disciple of Jesus and a member of the inner circle, the Twelve. There is no listing of the Twelve that does not include his name. The fact that these lists were all written down after the crucifixion signifies an important degree of acceptance. Historically, it is a matter of the highest probability that a man by the name of Judas was a member of the inner circle of Jesus' disciples.

Given the popularity of the name Yehudah, it would be risky to infer too much from it alone. Nevertheless it is important to note that the name may have made it easier for those who handed on the Gospel traditions to recall certain parallels and analogies to the life of the patriarch Judah, especially the role that he played in handing over Joseph to the Egyptians. (See below, chapters 3 and 4.) In that sense Duncan Derrett may be right when he suggests that we need to pay more attention to the first part of his name, not simply to the second part, Iscariot.

The fact that the name Judas was used by patriots may have influenced Jews who were known as Zealots and Sicarii to use it as well. Moreover, the image of Judah the Patriarch in the first century, as well as the *Testament of Judah* in the *Testament of the Twelve Patriarchs,* may have had a bearing. If Judah represents the dimension of kingly rule, then had no disciple by that name emerged (three did) and had none come forward who had kingly ambitions, the Gospel writers would have had pressure to invent one. This was not necessary, however, and there is no reason to consider Judas Iscariot as an invention of the church.

In giving more attention to the first part of his name, we must not make the mistake of identifying Judas with all Jewish people. Disturbingly, this has been done throughout history—in recent times by such distinguished theologians as Karl Barth and Dietrich Bonhoeffer. Such analogies have done an enormous amount of harm. In a 1937 sermon, Bonhoeffer asks:

> Who is Judas? Shouldn't we ask here also about the name which he carries? "Judas," doesn't it stand here for that deeply divided people of Jesus' origin, for the elect people, which had received the promise of the Messiah and yet rejected it? For the people of Judah [*das Volk Judah*], which loved the Messiah and yet could not love him thus? "Judas"—in German the name means "Thank." Was his kiss not the thanks brought to Jesus by the divided people of the disciple and yet at the same time its eternal renunciation?[11]

Lest North Americans attribute such anti-Jewish sentiments to Germans only, we are reminded that the Glock and Stark study of anti-Semitism in the United States discovered that five times as many Protestants identify Peter, Paul, and other apostles as Christians rather than as Jews. When it comes to Judas, however, nearly twice as many identify him as a Jew rather than a Christian![12]

More disturbing is the general revulsion against his name. Yet the name

is honorable even when it is misused, as it was in the summer of 1994 when
former Soviet president Mikhail Gorbachev appeared in a Russian court to
testify and was met by a gauntlet of protesters shouting, "Judas!"[13] Prejudices as deeply ingrained as this cannot be easily removed. Perhaps, however, the day can come when we deal with real people and go beyond
hurling epithets. A name designates a person, a human being.

Judas acted as a human being. What he did has no more and no less of a
connection with the Jewish people than any of the other acts of the disciples—whether the beautiful anointing of Jesus by a woman or the crying
of Hosanna when the Son of man entered Jerusalem. Just as it would not
occur to us today to ignore the Jewishness of Jesus when we try to understand him, so also we must begin our search for the historical Judas with
one firm fact: like Jesus, he was a Jew of the first century. Whatever he did
must make sense in that context.

The Term Iscariot

The term Iscariot was not initially part of Judas's name but emerged to distinguish this Judas from many others. Over the years, a great deal of research—
and even more speculation—has focused on the meaning of this term.

Günther Schwarz lists nine interpretations of the term Iscariot and adds
another of his own.[14] These fall into four main groups:

1. Some hold that the term Iscariot indicates that Judas belonged to the
Sicarii, a term Josephus uses to disparage a group of dagger-wielding assas-
sins, perhaps a branch of the Zealots. Thus they concluded that Judas was a
member of the Zealots.[15]

2. Others suggest that the term is derived from the Hebrew *shachar* (שקר)
and designates the "false one." This highlights the character of Judas by
alluding in his surname to his act of deception and betrayal.[16]

3. Others believe that the word Iscariot designates his deed. He was a
"deliverer" (root *sakar* סכר), a simple translation of *(I)skariot(h)*. It has been
noted that the LXX of Isa 19:4 translates the pi'el of *sakar* סכר ("capture and
hand over") with the Greek *paradidōmi* (παραδίδωμι), the same word used in
Mark 3:19 to designate Judas *ho paradidous* (ὁ παραδίδους, "the one who
handed him over").[17] Morin takes the Markan designation to be a literal
translation of *(I)skariot,* "the one handing over."[18]

Some, while agreeing that it refers to the work that Judas did, conclude
that he was a red dyer[19] or a fruit grower.[20]

4. A number of scholars have concluded that the name "Iscariot" indicates hometown. Was Judas perhaps the only one of the Twelve from Judea,
from the village of Kerioth (Josh 15:25)? Paul Billerbeck[21] gives many cases
where the Hebrew *ish* (איש) is connected with a hometown and calls this

"the right explanation." Josef Klausner also assumed that Judas is from Kerioth (Isch-Kerioth) and that numerous disciples may have come from Judea and other places besides Galilee (Mark 3:7, 8).[22]

If so, where is this town to be located? Is it the Tel Qirrioth on the current map in the Negev? Or is it Askaroth or Askar, near Schechem, which has also been suggested?[23] There is no certain answer.

C. C. Torrey cited both Wellhausen's and Schlatter's observation that it is impossible to think of the Hebrew ish (איש) and then translate "Man from Kerioth." Such a construction, he reasoned, might exist among the educated who presumably spoke and wrote Hebrew but hardly among those who spoke Aramaic. Torrey and Wellhausen agree that the sobriquet would not have been formed by simple, uneducated people. Torrey, therefore, concluded that "there is no evidence that Judas was called Iscariot during his life time, or that the name was ever borne by anyone else." He judges "the probability is strong that the epithet was a reproach."[24] He concludes that the Jewish Aramaic epithet שקריא/שקריאי (shakrai, shakri), false one, hypocrite, liar, known from Talmud and Targum, continued in use for some time in the Christian Palestinian dialect; and the occurrence in Matt 7:5 of the very word that became Iscariot is a fact of no little interest.[25]

Those who repeat the arguments of Torrey are told that a wealth of new discoveries have rendered Torrey's objections invalid, so that it is quite possible to imagine this linguistic usage among the ordinary people of Palestine in the first century.[26]

Schwarz proposes that the original Aramaic of Iscariot yields the translation: "the man from the city" (i.e., Jerusalem). He supports this with evidence from the Targums, which came later, where the formula appears frequently in the plural form, "men from the city," and the word keriotha is often used to mean Jerusalem.[27]

Klaus Beyer, a writer on Aramaic in the first century, refers to countless ostraca or potsherds from Arad written in Hebrew until 588 B.C.E. but written in Aramaic after 400 B.C.E. From the third century on, the Old Testament was written in Aramaic script. There is even a report of the voice of God coming from the Holy of Holies in Aramaic. Not one word of Hebrew is found, he believes, in the New Testament; rather, the writers resort to Aramaic when citing the words of Jesus or early worship formulae.[28] No names combined with ben (Hebrew: son) appear; instead, the term bar (Aramaic: son) appears. He considers Iscariot an apparent exception, which is cited as proof at various places.[29] He then draws the surprising conclusion:

> The family (John 6:71;13:26) of the betrayer of Jesus must have chosen the Hebrew ish instead of the Aramaic da or men in designation of origin out of religious or political reasons, which may provide a clue for the reasons for the betrayal.

Can we really deduce from this evidence that the family of Judas chose this deliberately for religious or political reasons? I think not. People with the words *ben* or *bar* combined with their names do not necessarily come from a specific region and they seem to move to and fro between the usages.[30]

If those who suggest that the term Iscariot came into use only after Judas's death are right,[31] then it is also possible that not even the early evangelists knew what Iscariot meant.[32] Schwarz contends that is not the case. He concludes that Judas had been a Zealot before he was attracted to Jesus and that Jerusalem was Judas's hometown.[33]

Nearly a century ago, A. Plummer declared that "the meaning of 'Iscariot' is practically settled."[34] That view is not shared by many people today. We incline, rather, to the opinion that the last word has not been said or written about the meaning of this word. Although it seems plausible to interpret Iscariot as designating place of origin, no consensus has emerged regarding this interpretation or the place of origin to be designated.[35] Nor does it seem that one is on the horizon.

Regretfully we conclude that no clear light is shed on the personality of Judas by the word Iscariot. Moreover, the theories that try to explain Iscariot diverge so widely from each other that nothing can be built on them. Maccoby's view that Christian dogma cannot permit the logical view that the term points to his membership in the Zealot movement is disproved by the fact that so many Christian scholars have, in fact, argued for Judas's adherence to the Zealots or at least to their values.

One of the Twelve

In common usage the term "the Twelve" designates the inner circle of the disciples of Jesus. It occurs once in Paul, nine times in Mark, seven times in Matthew, eight times in Luke-Acts, and four times in John. There has been a considerable debate about whether "the Twelve" was a creation of the early church or goes back to Jesus.

The best treatment of this topic is by Robert Meye, who concludes that the Twelve as a group go back to Jesus.[36] At the same time, Gottfried Schille came to diametrically opposite conclusions. He argues that the expression "one of the Twelve" is best explained as a "current designation of honour [*Würdeprädikat*] for individuals."[37] The predicate, he argues, had its origin not in a fixed circle of people but from the church's recognition of the earliest followers of Jesus. The present state of research does not allow us to say with any degree of certainty what the situation originally was.

Judas's attachment to the group of the Twelve has posed theological problems since antiquity. These problems are even more acute if Jesus himself established this group and chose Judas to be a part of it.[38]

Typical of many scholars who have had great difficulty with the fact that Jesus chose Judas, Friedrich Schleiermacher finds it *"impossible . . . to think that Jesus deliberately chose his apostles."*[39] To do so presents the following dilemma: either Jesus was ignorant of what resided in the mind and heart of Judas or Jesus himself involved Judas in his deliberate destruction—in other words, he chose Judas to be "an apostle in order to destroy him, knowingly and intentionally."

Schleiermacher finds these alternatives unacceptable,[40] so he concludes that Judas entered the circle of the Twelve more or less on his own initiative. He saw Judas as one who opposed the way Jesus realized the messianic idea. Judas represented those who held fast to the political idea of the Messiah's function (to become a real king) and he never let go of that idea. "Judas' behavior can be understood and to some extent excused only on the presupposition that he held this wholly false conception of the Messianic idea and has never been able to overcome it, and his end makes his frame of mind to some extent comprehensible. Nevertheless the whole matter remains obscure."[41] Today we see other alternatives than the ones posed by Schleiermacher.

The earliest reference to the Twelve is found in 1 Cor 15:5 ("appeared also to the Twelve"). Since no reference is made to Judas by name either here or in 1 Cor 11:23 (where Paul refers to the arrest of Jesus), it is clear that Paul has no interest in the person of Judas or the role that he played. "The Twelve" is clearly a stereotyped phrase used by Paul, and it matters not one whit whether it actually meant eleven or twelve. Nor does Paul concern himself with the status of the Twelve, whether they were pillars of the community or not (Gal 2:2, 6, 9).

As the negative tradition about Judas formed, subsequent references mentioned only eleven at the postresurrection appearances.[42] Given the theological difficulties of including Judas among the Twelve, it seems highly likely that the tradition of his attachment to the Twelve rests on historical fact.[43] The more the community reflected on the capture and trial of Jesus, its interest in Judas's role increased, and the more critically it then judged his actions. The community was, however, unable to conceal his place among the Twelve.

Nevertheless, it is important not to ignore the strongest case that has been made against Judas being part of the Twelve, made by Philipp Vielhauer. He holds that "there is no doubt, one of the disciples did betray him. Nor is there any doubt that the church, living out of eschatological expectation, first fixed the number twelve for the disciples (1 Cor 15:5) and subsequently from another motive, created the legend of the betrayal."[44] Mark's intention is to highlight that a disciple who had been with Jesus for a long time betrayed him, according to Vielhauer. The theological postulate of the Twelve served that purpose but does not prove the existence of the Twelve before Easter.

Vielhauer admits that it is difficult to reconcile 1 Cor 15:5 with the Gospels. It is hard to imagine the invention of the Twelve, one of whom is a traitor. Because of its scandalous nature (in German, *Anstössigkeit*), the presence of a traitor among the Twelve could hardly be an invention. Thus the stories of Judas appear to provide support for the existence of a pre-Easter Twelve. In fact, however, they become a weighty argument against the correctness of 1 Cor 15:5. Nevertheless, Vielhauer maintains that the designated characterization of Judas in the Gospels "makes sense precisely with the presupposition of a post-Easter origin of the circle of the Twelve."[45]

Vielhauer has no doubt that one of the disciples betrayed Jesus, nor that the primitive church could handle this scandalous fact. As it did with the suffering and death of Jesus, so here it found the reason for the betrayal in the will of God, as indicated in scriptures: "The Son of Man is going the way designated for him in the scriptures; but woe to that man by whom the Son of Man is handed over!" (Mark 14:21).

The scandal of the apparent traitor was overcome, however, through Jesus' foreknowledge and reference to scripture. The scriptural proof consists in an allusion to Ps 41:18 in Mark 14:18, "one who is eating with me." Out of the psalm motif of a betraying table companion, one can explain the remarkable effort to bring the betrayer into the most intimate contact with Jesus: "one of you will hand me over, one who is eating with me" (Mark 14:18) and "it is one of the Twelve, who is dipping in the same bowl with me" (Mark 14:20). For Vielhauer, Judas's membership among the Twelve is a "theological postulate," but for him there is no historical evidence for the existence of the Twelve before Easter.[46]

Gottfried Schille[47] proceeds along similar lines. He notes that the Ebionite Gospel gives the list of nine disciples: Simon, John and James (the sons of Zebedee) and Simon, Andrew, Thaddaeus, Simon the Zealot and Judas, the Iscariot. In the call of Levi, it says:

> And you, Matthew, as you sat at the customs gate, then I called and you followed me. From now on I want you to be Twelve apostles as a witness to Israel.[48]

Schille asks:

> Can an enumeration more clearly deny any claim to be a genuine tradition of collegium [*Mitarbeitertradition*], i.e., to contain a memory of a genuine group?[49]

In dealing with John 21:2-13, Schille notes that it is really a list of seven apostles. The betrayer cannot be counted among the apostles by John because of John 13:16-18 (cf. also 6:70-71), where John designates Judas as

Satan. At the outset, Judas is designated as an instrument of the devil (13:2). For John's list of coworkers, Judas cannot be included, for neither in the stories of the call nor later is he drawn upon for the main purpose of enumerating the apostles. The Twelve as a group has no meaning, for in Acts, when Judas is replaced, of the Twelve only Peter is mentioned. Later, when Paul elects his coworkers, they are voted on by the whole assembly (Acts 15:37). Again the Twelve play no role. Klaus Dorn tries to reconcile 1 Cor 15:3b–5 with Acts and the Gospel accounts. He suggests that Matthias was one of the witnesses and so, technically, one of the Twelve. His strongest arguments consider Judas as one of the Twelve before the crucifixion, for the virtual nonexistence of the Twelve after Easter suggests there would have been no need then to invent them![50]

Observations

Modern writers have talked at length about Judas without fully recognizing him as a disciple of Jesus or as one of the inner circle. However, the most recent trend is to recognize that Judas was indeed, as Hans-Josef Klauck subtitled his book on Judas, "a disciple of the Lord."[51] It is from this perspective that Judas must be viewed. We do him a disservice if we do not take seriously the fact that he was a Jew of the first century who had decided to join the itinerant group of disciples who followed Jesus. What that meant precisely we do not know. But we can assume that Jesus was their respected teacher and that it was a considerable sacrifice for them to leave behind their friends, family, and, perhaps, business to take up with Jesus and his followers.

It is surely appropriate to assume that the teachings recorded as coming from Jesus were not merely intellectual ideas but formed something of a core of beliefs that became part of the glue that kept the band together. Central to that cluster of beliefs would have been the conviction that in Jesus the rule of God had broken upon the people of God in an unprecedented way.

We know now that the rule of God is established in individual lives and in corporate expression. It is seen most fully in the way a community lives together. Accordingly, there may be more kingdom realization in two or three Christians, whether clerics or laypeople, committed to living together for others than there is in all of Thomas Aquinas's *Summa Theologica,* Melanchthon's *Loci,* or Karl Barth's *Church Dogmatics* put together. Could there be more genuine discipleship in one act of loving one's enemies than in the most beautiful cathedral or Bach Cantata? This is not to diminish these glorious celebrations of homage to God, but it is a question, with all due respect, that has to be raised.

Judas was exposed, we can assume, to virtually all the messages and influences that we read about in the Gospels. So he knew about both the cost and the joy of discipleship. He had left all and followed Jesus. Judas had seen firsthand the power Jesus had shown to cure the demon-possessed and to restore the ill. The commission to go out and do that same work with other disciples, Judas had also experienced. As with the other disciples, he too had been baffled by the opposition that Jesus had aroused, and even more by the way Jesus responded to conflict. Yet he and many others stayed until the end, even though the form of their allegiance to Jesus expressed itself in different ways.

Since we have no evidence to the contrary, we must assume that Judas was in good fellowship with the other disciples. And even if we assume that the very worst things said about Judas are true, I cannot help concluding that Jesus, being true to himself, loved him to the end (John 13:1). Jesus could not teach about loving one's enemies and then decline to do it himself if, indeed, Judas betrayed him. To do so would have made his life a fraud and the cross a mockery.

Summary

For our purposes here, we conclude that Judas Iscariot was one of the twelve disciples of Jesus, possibly from Jerusalem, who probably served as treasurer of the itinerant group. His name always appears last in the lists of the Twelve, and, according to Jewish custom, this does not detract from his importance. He assisted the authorities in capturing Jesus by being an informer and leading them to him in the garden. His motive in doing so cannot be ascertained. It cannot, however, be ruled out that he understood better than any other disciple the need for Jesus to be "handed over" and was prepared to follow the directions of Jesus in this act as well. In any case, "a man whom the redeemer has thus distinguished merits the best interpretation we can give of his acts."[52]

So we begin our quest for the identity of Judas Iscariot with a name. A name carries with it an integral part of one's identity. For Judas we can register as fact that he was a Jew of the first century. Committed to a faith in God's rule, he had responded to the call to follow Jesus and was a devoted and trustworthy disciple of Jesus of Nazareth. He was in the inner circle, one of the Twelve. On that foundation we build our thesis and on no other.

Notes

1. Feneberg, "Ein neues Judasbild," 5, 2. From *Entschluss*, published by the Jesuit community in Germany, one issue of which was devoted to Judas. It was kindly made available to me by H.-J. Klauck.

2. Vogler, *Judas*, 9.

3. Vogler, *Judas,* 17; and Brown, *Death,* 1410–1413.

4. *IB,* 7 (1951): 582.

5. Dieckmann, *Judas,* 256.

6. Crossan, *The Historical Jesus,* 421. Can we really with confidence affirm that Jesus was both a Cynic and a Jew? Caution must be expressed that we do not slip into a non-Jewish Jesus. A procedure that retains the descriptive noun, Jew, for Jesus seems to me highly desirable.

7. My own approach is in sympathy with John G. Gager, "The Gospels and Jesus: Some Doubts about Method," but I do not share his skepticism about the results. Nor can I understand what he means when he says that "The Gospels are the final products of a long and creative tradition"(256). Surely in the transmission of literature, compared, say, with Homer, forty years is not considered "long."

8. On the name, see Klauck, *Judas,* 40–44; and Vogler, *Judas,* 17–24.

9. See Bauckham, *Jude and the Relatives of Jesus in the Early Church.*

10. Hengel, *The Zealots,* 5; still the best treatment of this group. The work was first published in German in 1970.

11. Bonhoeffer in a sermon of March 17, 1937, "Predigt am Sonntag Judika über Judas," in *Gesammelte Schriften,* 406–413, here 412. On Karl Barth's position, see below, pp 182–92.

12. Cited in Kirsch, *We Christians and Jews,* 50–61.

13. *Kitchener-Waterloo Record,* July 8, 1994.

14. G. Schwarz, *Jesus und Judas,* 6–12; and Brown, *Death,* 1410–1416.

15. Schulthess, 1922; Cullmann, 1956: 15; 1970: 21–23; and 1962: "Der zwölfte Apostel." Maccoby's detailed discussion (*Judas* [1992], 127–136) concludes: "Judas Iscariot means: 'Judas the Zealot'" (132). In 1991, "Who Was Judas Iscariot?" 13, he dismissed as "wrong" the theory of the historical Judas who was a Zealot, who was disappointed by Jesus' pacifism. It is not clear whether he considers both parts of the sentence as "wrong."

16. Torrey, "The Name" (1943); and Bertil Gärtner, *Iscariot,* but the interpretation goes back at least to Hengstenberg, *John,* 368.

17. G. Schwarz, *Jesus und Judas,* 7 n. 10.

18. Morin, "Les deux derniers des Douze: Simon le Zélote et Judas Iskariôth," *RB* 80:332–358.

19. Reading ‏סקר‎. A. Ehrman, "Judas Iscariot and Abba Saqqara," 572–574; and Y. Arbeitman, "The Suffix of Iscariot," 122–124.

20. Krauss, *Das Leben Jesu,* 199–207.

21. Billerbeck, *Kommentar* I (1922): 537; so also Haugg, *Judas,* 76; and Dalman, *Jesus-Jeshua,* 1929: 28–29.

22. Klausner, *Jesus,* 378.

23. Dalman, *Sacred Sites and Ways,* 1935: 213.

24. Torrey, "The Name 'Iscariot,'" 58.

25. Torrey, "The Name," 60–61.

26. Beyer, *Die aramäische Texte vom Toten Meer,* 57.

27. G. Schwarz, *Jesus und Judas,* 6–12. For critique, see Brown, *Death,* 1413.

28. Joseph Fitzmyer rightfully wonders about Hallelujah, Amen, to name just two!

29. The confusion goes back to antiquity. 2 Sam 10:6, 8; man of Tob becomes in the LXX *Istov* (Ιστωβ): Since Tob may not be a place at all, might not the Hebrew original *ish tov* (‏איש טוב‎) suggest a "good man"? So 1 Chron 7:18 ‏אישהוד‎ ("Ishod")

and LXX *Karioth* ("towns"), as in Hebrew the man from. . . . It is not at all sure that there is a village in South Judea called Karioth (קריות) (Josh 15:25). At any rate, the LXX makes it into the plural of cities, *poleis* (πόλεις). NT variants such as "from Karioth" (απο Καρυωτου), e.g., John 12:4, complicate the matter. There is no answer to this puzzle as yet, and Brown reminds us that derivations tell us little about a person (*Death*, 1416).

30. See Beyer, *Die aramaische Texte*, 57. Schwarz, although appealing to Beyer's book, does not use this page. There is nothing on p. 54, which Schwarz cites, pertaining to this subject.

31. Torrey, "The Name," 58; and Vogler, *Judas*, 1985.

32. Dalman, *Words*, 1902: 51–52.

33. G. Schwarz, 11–12, accepts Cullmann's conclusions but not his derivation of Iscariot from *sicarii*. So also Maccoby, *Judas*, 127–140, considers Judas a Galilean (130) and believes him to have been a Zealot (132). Originally, he believes, there was only one Judas and that "when he was chosen for the mythic role of the traitor" the good attributes of the historical Judas were shifted to a second Judas (134). Cullmann, too, from a careful analysis of the lists of the Twelve and the ancient variants, concludes: "The second Judas never existed" ("Der zwölfte Apostel," 220) but originated from a doubling of the names (222).

34. Plummer, "Judas Iscariot," *HDB* (1905), 2:796–799; see 796.

35. Klauck, *Judas*, 40–44.

36. Meye, *Jesus*.

37. Schille, *Die urchristliche Kollegialmission*, 118.

38. Luke 6:13//Mark 3:13-14//Matt 10:1-2.

39. Schleiermacher, *Life*, 413–414.

40. Schleiermacher, *Life*, 346.

41. Schleiermacher, *Life*, 346.

42. Matt 28:16; Luke 24:9, 33; Mark 16:14; Acts 1:26; cf. 1:13.

43. Philipp Vielhauer and Günter Klein have challenged this. See below and Robert Meye's response in *Jesus*, 205–209.

44. This summary of Vielhauer's position is based on his essay "Gottesreich und Menschensohn," 63. Sanders, *Jesus and Judaism*, 99–101, deals with Vielhauer's argument and acknowledges the strength of Meye's rebuttal.

45. Vielhauer, "Gottesreich," 63.

46. Vielhauer, "Gottesreich," 64.

47. Schille, *Kollegialmission*.

48. Epiphanius, *haer* 30/13. 2ff.; and Hennecke-Schneemelcher, *Neutestamentliche Apokryphen*, 1961, 102.

49. Schille, *Kollegialmission*, 35.

50. Dorn, "Judas Iskariot"; and H. Wagner, ed., *Judas Iskariot*, 39–89, here 66–73.

51. Klauck, *Judas*.

52. Nils Runeberg, as cited by Jorge Luis Borges, "Three Versions of Judas," *Labyrinths*, 97.

CHAPTER THREE

THE ACT OF JUDAS:
THE TRADITIONAL
POINT OF VIEW

There is no doubt that the Sages were not at all interested in the actual historical figures of the Bible, but with the lesson that renowned personalities could, or had the potential to teach the peoples of future generations.

For it appears that in their [the Sages] world there was no more boring and immaterial question than the question dealing with the need and utility of describing what actually happened in the past.

—M. D. Herr[1]

According to the unanimous testimony of the four Gospels, Judas was (a) a disciple of Jesus, (b) one of the Twelve, (c) the one who "handed Jesus over," and, according to John alone, the treasurer of the group.

In chapter 2 we concluded that whatever ambiguity may lie in the name Judas Iscariot, it tells us one thing for certain: he was a Jew who lived in the first century of our era. If a person is known by the name he or she carries, it is even more true that one is known by one's achievements. One's vocation or deeds become a part of one's identity. This certainly is true of Judas Iscariot. We now seek to arrive at some understanding of what Judas did when he "handed Jesus over."

In order to carry out this part of our work, we must engage in some analysis of the meaning of words. Our communication with ancient sources depends upon words; therefore fundamental meanings need to be reviewed. Words take on meanings of their own, so there is no foolproof way of accurately translating a given Greek or Hebrew word into modern languages. At the same time, there surely is a difference, for example, between saying that God is love and God is hate. We do not fully comprehend what it means to "love your enemies," and even though most scholars believe

Jesus spoke those words, we have not begun to obey them. The problem would be of quite a different order had Jesus said that his disciples were to hate and kill their enemies.

We begin with a review of what has traditionally been said about Judas and an examination of the foundations on which those judgments rest.

I. The Traditional Portrayal: Judas Betrayed Jesus

Judas Iscariot is invariably called "the Traitor," or the "one who betrayed." For most people, there is no debate regarding this point. Professor Ed Blair, writing in a standard biblical encyclopedia, summarizes what Judas did by calling him "the betrayer of Jesus," describing his act as one of "heinous treachery." The reason: "Nothing short of disillusionment over Jesus, from whom he had hoped so much, and a corresponding zeal to uphold the law and institutions of Judaism against the attacks of false prophets and messiahs would seem to explain a deed so radical." Blair judges the deed as even "more reprehensible if Judas participated in the holy sacrament."[2]

Judas is seen by many as the worst traitor that humankind has seen. Few have doubted the historicity of the betrayal, for who could have invented such a story? James Charlesworth, a vocal advocate of the Jewishness of Jesus, describes Judas's betrayal as "bedrock historical fact."[3]

Throughout the history of the church and even for most modern interpreters, the subject has been above argument. The four Gospels have set the precedent. All of them treat Judas as a member of the Twelve, and in all major modern translations of the Bible he is described as having "betrayed" Jesus. Presumably, the story of Jesus is enriched by this element. Much is made of the fact that in the very bosom of Jesus' inner group a traitor came into being. The ubiquity of betrayal is driven home by this fact. Furthermore, we are invited by some scholars to believe that a Judas lives in each of us and that to live is to betray.[4]

Most important, just as the figure of Socrates became more indelible if set against the foil of a supposedly shrewish wife, so it appears that the sacrifice of Jesus is more poignant if we posit a traitor as part of the scene. The ordinary understanding of the term "betrayal" means that Judas did something that Jesus did not want or expect. To many people Judas did something with malice aforethought toward Jesus, which came as a surprise to Jesus and the others around him. But what exactly did he do?

When we pursue this question beyond the traditional approach and ask what he betrayed, the answers are elusive. Albert Schweitzer already noted that for 150 years people have asked, "Why Judas betrayed his Master?" Few suspected that they should have been asking, "What he betrayed?" He concluded that there is something general (as he put it, "How can we—the

Romans, the high priests—get him into our hands?") and something specific ("How can we capture him without creating an uproar?"). But, Schweitzer believed, Judas betrayed Jesus by revealing the messianic secret. "Jesus died because two of His disciples had broken His command of silence: Peter when he made known the secret of the Messiahship to the Twelve at Caesarea Philippi; Judas Iscariot by communicating it to the High Priest."[5]

E. P. Sanders follows Schweitzer in the main, stating that "Judas betrayed . . . that Jesus and his band thought of himself as 'King.'" The more obvious explanation is that Judas conveyed Jesus' pretension to the chief priests.[6] "It was the final weapon they needed: a specific charge to present to Pilate, more certain to have a fatal effect than the general charge 'troublemaker.'"[7]

Fundamentally, Sanders follows many others in seeing Jesus as a renewal agent. He takes the Temple action seriously as a historical event that communicates to a small group that Jesus sees himself as "king," at least of the Temple, with a triumphal entry to Jerusalem, which may well have involved a large crowd. He also believes the "scandal" of Jesus may have been that he offered people inclusion in the kingdom (forgiveness) and did not require repentance as normally understood (restitution).[8]

It is hard to imagine that such a "scandal" brought Jesus to the cross. It also is highly doubtful that restitution was a burning issue. In any case, Sanders also noted that at least one sinner, Zacchaeus, offered to make restitution (Luke 19:8). Jesus is not reported as trying to persuade him otherwise. Nor must we assume that this is Luke's attempt to harmonize Jesus' practice with that of Judaism in regard to restitution.

Sanders, moreover, sees in the physical demonstration against the Temple, the "Temple action," a threat to public order, so that we "need look no further" for an act offensive enough to call for Jesus' arrest. "It was the combination of physical action with a noticeable following which accounts for and led immediately to Jesus' death."[9] Many factors help to account for his death. He lists Jesus' extraordinary self-claim; the gathering he attracted; the nervousness on the part of the Jewish leaders not to give the Romans occasion for collective punishment of the people; and the Romans' own anxiety about prophets and crowds at feast time. "The gun may already have been cocked but it was the Temple demonstration which pulled the trigger."[10]

Professor Sanders also ventures a guess on why Judas defected: "The defection of Judas may have stemmed from disappointment when it became evident that no such victory (a kingdom on earth with renewal of the world situation) was in the offing, and there may have been other defections."[11]

Bruce Chilton also defines Judas's betrayal as something he said, some information he conveyed to the Jewish authorities. Specifically, and here

Chilton is close to Herbert Preisker's position (see below), Judas revealed a feature (which he leaves unspecified) of the meals with Jesus after the Temple action. "Indeed the sense of these meals was the only substantial news Judas would have had to report to anyone; whatever Judas may have thought of the meals at that stage, his information to the priestly authorities of their ideology evidently caused them to act."[12]

A similar position was proposed earlier by Preisker, who held that Judas betrayed "what he had experienced with the disciples in the farewell dinner with Jesus." In this meal and specifically in his words over the bread, Jesus revealed himself as the Messiah and offered the disciples a part in the order of salvation of the kingdom that would begin with Jesus' death. In a decisive way he relates his person to the coming of that kingdom. It is "this celebration of the victory of the new kingdom and the special place which Jesus holds in that emerging kingdom which constitutes the central point of those last hours together. That gives the celebration its excitement, the uniqueness. And that is what Judas carried to the high priests."[13]

Martin Dibelius maintains that Judas "'betrayed' nothing except the meeting place; rather, he 'handed over.'"[14]

If we follow this line of thinking (this interpretation has the distinct advantage of being closer to the meaning of the Greek word used here), we still have to ask: How could Judas "deliver over" or "hand over" or "surrender" someone who surely did not belong to Judas? For the term παραδίδωμι (paradidōmi or "hand over") is used consistently in Josephus and other ancient literature to describe handing over prisoners of war or property. In other words, to hand something over, you must have it in your power. No clear text has surfaced in which the Greek verb means "to betray" (see below, pp. 47–52).

One point of vulnerability to every position that assumes Judas either betrayed or surreptitiously handed over Jesus is the strong self-confidence of Jesus that is communicated by the Gospels themselves. Jesus is clearly depicted as being in charge of his own destiny. Not Peter, not his mother, not his brothers or sisters, and certainly not any "betrayal" by Judas, takes that aura of confidence and clarity of purpose away from Jesus. It is consistently affirmed that his "handing over" was, "according to the scriptures," the will of God. Is the person who carries out that will of God therefore to be maligned, ridiculed, and abused?

A. E. Harvey has a fine treatment of this term and its "wide range of meanings, wider in fact than any comparable word in either Hebrew or English."[15] The two usages he explores are (1) the purely technical one of "handing Jesus over to the Jews, Pilate, to execution," and (2) the more mysterious and theologically significant use of the term. Here it relates to Isaiah, especially the LXX, which has the term three times in chapter 53:6,

12 where the Hebrew does not require it. Harvey's treatment is marred only by his insistence that "the same word used of Judas Iscariot clearly means, not just handing over, but *betraying*."[16]

But what if Jesus was "betrayed" by Judas and caught off guard? Again, the Gospel accounts are unanimous in telling us that Jesus predicted the action Judas would take. Indeed, they indicate that he selected Judas to do it, or pointed out that he would. This was found to be so difficult by some of the Gospel writers that they had to posit Judas's own action ahead of time. What is clear from the evidence, however, is that Judas is consistently a disciple of Jesus and that he did only what Jesus asked him to do—and that, only when Jesus was ready for it. The oldest accounts also indicate that, far from Judas being preordained to do this act, there was every possibility that any one of the disciples could have been selected for it.

It is, moreover, manifest that the task was to "hand Jesus over." What this entailed obviously needs to be analyzed. It could hardly have been much more than to bring about the opportunity for Jesus to be confronted by those who wished to take him into custody. Given the number of times that Jesus had eluded his captors before, there was no reason to think that, if he wished, he could not escape from them again.

The Gospel accounts also agree in affirming that not one of the disciples thought for a moment that Jesus would be crucified. There is, then, no reason to believe that Judas thought he would assist in bringing about Jesus' death when he brought Jesus and the authorities together. During his life and at death, Jesus carried full responsibility for himself. It may well be that Judas believed most strongly that in any confrontation between Jesus and his enemies, Jesus would triumph. We will never know.

What our earliest sources say is that Judas did nothing until Jesus told him to do it. Later, the final editors of the Gospels, beginning with Luke, Matthew, and John, found this possibility so difficult to swallow that they felt they had no choice but to ascribe dark motives to the actions of Judas. Yet they never imputed one saying to Jesus that actually criticized Judas, nor did they ever imply that Jesus considered what Judas was doing to be a sin. One author who shows no particular sympathy for Judas admits: "In all the scenes in which Judas meets Jesus we become aware of a great mildness of the Master towards his aberrant disciple and even when Jesus needs to admonish him he does it in a very reserved manner."[17]

If Jesus had suspected Judas of committing a grave sin—say, the sin of betraying the Messiah and forcing that Messiah to be killed against his own or God's will, or aborting his program—surely he would have rebuked Judas, as he did Peter, with the harsh command: "Get you behind me, Satan!" (Mark 8:33//Matt 16:23). Mark has the word *epitimaō* (ἐπιτιμάω), referring to Jesus rebuking Peter, which appears to be too strong for

Matthew here (although he uses it elsewhere seven times), but it is a word
that occurs elsewhere when Jesus is addressing devils or unclean spirits
(17:18). It is also used by Luke as the action to be taken within the community when someone sins (17:3). Given the frequency with which it appears
in connection with the behavior of the disciples, its absence in the Judas
narratives appears to be significant. Instead, Jesus calls him "friend," the only
disciple whom he ever addresses thus, and, according to Matthew and Mark,
fervently kisses him at the time of the arrest.

During the Last Supper and in the Garden of Gethsemane, Jesus addresses
Judas in the various passion narratives in the following words:

> Jesus said to Judas after Judas had asked him: "Surely it is not I, is it, Rabbi?"
> You say so? (Matt 26:25)

> Jesus then took the fragment, having dipped it, took and gave it to Judas, son
> of Simon Iscariot, and having received it, Satan entered into that one.
> Then Jesus said to him:
> What you are to do, do quickly. (John 13:27)

Then when they met in the garden, at the time of Jesus' arrest, Jesus said
to him:

> Friend, do what you have come here to do. (Matt 26:50)

In Luke's Gospel these words read somewhat differently:

> Judas, with a kiss you hand over the Son of man? (Luke 22:48)

Not only does Jesus speak to Judas with all respect and closeness, even the
later writers show what Karl Barth has called a "remarkable calm" in speaking about him.[18] If there is a reprimand in any of these statements, it has to
be inferred. Jesus' usual way of rebuking his disciples is clearly not followed
in his dealings with Judas.

In contrast, a doctoral dissertation by Roman Halas on Judas, written
four decades ago at a leading American university, allows no possibility that
Judas may have done anything less serious than "betraying" Jesus. The dissertation devotes nearly twenty pages to his "eternal lot."

The author believes that the prophecy of Judas's certain perdition was
infallible. Nor did the "false disciple" perish through a lack of care that
Christ was obliged to manifest toward him; he perished that the scriptures
might be fulfilled. Salvation was made impossible not by the crime itself but
because Judas was finally impenitent. He was "not deserving of divine
mercy and forgiveness, such as was granted the executioners of Christ."
Halas contends that because Judas despaired, he blocked the omnipotence
of God and refused to revoke his crime by the slightest sign of true contrition. He therefore deserved to be consigned to the everlasting torments of

hell, even though the mercy of God was willing to open for him the gates of salvation.[19] Certainly "Jesus was kind toward him and endeavored to dissuade him from the proposed betrayal on numerous occasions" (no texts are cited!).

The reason that Halas gives for Judas's consignment to hell— Judas did not "deserve" compassion—is especially revealing. This appears to come directly from Augustine. For Augustine, although recognizing that Judas was repentant, concluded that he despaired of God's mercy. Therefore, "He did not deserve mercy; and that is why no light shone in his heart to make him hurry for pardon from the one he had betrayed."[20]

Few scholars today would speak with such certainty about the crime and fate of Judas. Most would recognize that at the heart of Jesus' message is the affirmation that God loves even the undeserving, indeed especially them. One reason why the traditional viewpoint has been increasingly challenged is that the Greek word on which the condemnation appears to hinge— *paradidōmi*—cannot be translated simply as "betray."[21] We turn to an analysis of the evidence.

II. Judas "Handed Jesus Over": The Word *paradidōmi* (παραδίδωμι)

A. The Usage in Classical Greek

The standard lexicon for classical Greek, Liddell and Scott, gives these fundamental meanings for the word *paradidōmi* (παραδίδωμι):

1. To give, hand over to another, transmit, such as virtues from teacher to students, documents, give up an argument, etc.
2. To give a city or a person into another's hands, esp. as a hostage or an enemy with the collational notion of "treachery, betray."
3. To give oneself up to justice.
4. To hand over legends, opinions, doctrines.

The second meaning attributed to the word is critically important for this study. Upon closer analysis it turns out that in none of the following three references from the 1968 edition of Liddell and Scott is the meaning "betray" even possible as a "collational notion." To translate *paradidōmi* (παραδίδωμι) "betray" makes no sense in Xenophon, *Cyro* 5.4.51, where it clearly means "hand over or surrender,"[22] or in Pausanias 1.2.1, where it also means "surrender" and is accordingly translated.[23] And how can one "betray weapons" in Xenophon's *Cyro* 5.1.28? Again, the meaning is clearly to "give up, hand over, or surrender."

There remains, finally, the text that Bauer cites under the designation, "especially of the betrayal of Jesus by Judas," taken from Posidonius (sixth ed. 614). Granted that *paradotheis* (παραδοθείς) ("deliver up") appears in the Posidonius text (87, fgm 36,50 Jac), it is still clearly different from *prodosia* (προδοσία) or "betrayal" (F 247:134).[24] In a speech by Athenion in Athens, it is reported that a Roman commander by the name of Quintus Oppius had been "delivered up [to Mithradites] and was now following in his train as a captive" (Athenaeus 5.213). Here, too, the word *prodosia* (προδοσία) (betrayal or treachery) appears slightly later in a similar context and unambiguously conveys the meaning of betrayal (214, c).[25]

Not one ancient classical Greek text has so far surfaced in which παραδίδωμι (*paradidōmi*) means "betray" or has the connotation of treachery. Any lexicon that suggests otherwise is guilty of theologizing rather than assisting us to find the meaning of Greek words through usage. Nor is the word found with that meaning in the papyri.[26]

B. The Usage in the LXX

In the Greek translation of the Hebrew Bible, which is called the LXX, usually dated about 200 B.C.E., the word παραδίδωμι appears many times and renders more than twenty Hebrew verb forms. Often the idea of "handing someone or something" over to the enemy appears. Büchsel[27] states, it is surely a guess, that the Hebrew original of the New Testament usage is *masar* (מסר), a word that Koehler-Baumgartner list only once (Num 31:16) and describe as "dubious." Abraham Even-Shoshan's concordance lists two occurrences in the Hebrew Bible (Num 31:5, and in Num 31:16 where the ASV and RSV have "treachery," the LXX, *JB*, and NIV do not). In the first reference it almost certainly means "to draft" or conscript into an army. The fact that the word *masar* itself does not mean "betray" for the translator of the Chronicler (1 Chron 12:18 is clear from his addition of the words: "not in a truthful hand" [ovκ ἐν ἀληθείᾳ χειρός]). The word רמה (*ramah*) appears in Gen 29:25, where Jacob is deceived by Laban; in Josh 9:22, the trick of the Gibeonites; in 1 Sam 19:17, where Saul is tricked by Michal so that David escapes; in 28:12, when the soothsayer from Endor tricks Saul; in 2 Sam 19:27, where Saul's grandson, Mephibosheth, is deceived by his servant; in Prov 26:19 and in 1 Chron 12:17, where it clearly means to deceive or betray. In each case except Prov 26:19, the LXX uses the term παραλογίζω (deceive or betray). We conclude that the word "to hand over" does not have a negative connection in the Greek Bible.

There is, moreover, the evidence from the Pseudepigrapha. The concordance published by Albert-Marie Denis lists some forty-three occurrences of the verb παραδίδωμι, two occurrences of προδίδωμι, and two occurrences of προδότης. Not one of the occurrences of παραδίδωμι conveys the sense of betrayal or treachery. They range from a beneficial handing over to a handing over into enemy hands and handing over to death. Aseneth when handed over to Joseph to be his wife complains that she is being treated as a captive (*Jos.Asen* 4:8–9).[28]

We have noted that there is no precedent for translating *paradidōmi* (παραδίδωμι) as "betray" in any literature before the four Gospels. With regard to Greek literature, Wiard Popkes notes that there is not one case in which the word means to "betray a secret."

The most important appearance of this term for our understanding of the Gospel usage is in Isaiah 53 where it appears three times, even though it is not required by the Hebrew text: 53:6, 12 (two times).[29] With the exception of Luke 22:37, Isaiah 53 is never quoted by Jesus. Nevertheless, H. Walter Wolff has argued that in spite of its absence from his most striking sayings, one can see that Isaiah 53 played a dominant role in the personal decisions of Jesus as well as in instructions to his disciples. "With Isa 53 he went to his death." He sees the contrast between this strong influence of scripture upon Jesus and the lack of explicit scripture citations as part of the unique way in which Jesus related to scripture.[30] He did not need to quote scripture as part of his authority reservoir, since he seemed to live so fully within the value system of some of the prophets. Zechariah 13:6-9, with its plaintive motif of the prophet wounded in the house of his friends and the striking of the shepherd, may well have been in his mind during Jesus' last days.[31]

Nor should one forget that the theme of the abased leader who becomes exalted is not restricted to the Hebrew scriptures but also has a strong place in Cynic-Stoic thought. The idea that Jesus was entitled to kingly status may have been more attractive to Stoics and Cynics drawn to early Christianity precisely because of this theme of humiliation.[32]

C. The Usage in Josephus

Josephus, the most prolific Jewish historian of the first century, uses the word παραδίδωμι (*paradidōmi*) 293 times, but not once can one legitimately translate it employing the word "betray." For betrayal, Josephus has a perfectly good Greek word, *prodidōmi* (προδίδωμι) or *prodosia* (προδοσία), which he uses twenty-five times. The word for traitor is *prodotēs* (προδότης), which he uses about twenty-two times. Particularly interesting is his use of the verb παραδίδωμι (*paradidōmi*) in the Joseph narrative where Joseph's brothers are delighted that Joseph "by the will of God has been delivered into their hands" (*Ant* 2.20). Later, Josephus speaks about Pharaoh handing over an office to Joseph (*Ant* 2.89). In the same narrative, Jacob delivers Benjamin to the brothers (*Ant* 2.18) on Joseph's request and the same brothers "offer themselves up" for punishment to save Benjamin (*Ant* 2.137). But not once is the term used to describe Judah's betrayal of his father, or of Joseph or any other betrayals in that story.

Josephus, rather, uses the word *paradidōmi* (παραδίδωμι) to describe the handing over of slaves, territory, and property. In Josephus's own classical betrayal of his comrades and fellow Jews during the Roman siege at Yodefat, when he switched to the Roman side of the conflict, he prayed that he would "go not as a traitor [προδότης] but as your minister [διάκονος]."[33] Josephus is himself branded a betrayer (*JW* 3.439) and the term used is not ὁ παραδίδους, as in the Gospels, but rather προδότης. Ultimately Josephus sees God as the subject of "handing over" and reminds Vespasian that God is a better general than Vespasian, for he can deliver the Jews to the Romans without any exertion on their part (*JW* 4.370).

In a detailed study of the word, Ceslas Spicq has carefully classified many usages of the word. With the fourth category, however, he concludes that the predominant sense in the Old Testament is pejorative. When God does the handing over the outcome is generally bad. He further concludes that the New Testament "inherits this theology." But what is new for Spicq is that the term becomes a technical term in the passion of Jesus. "The term is to be taken first in its legal and judicial sense, but it conveys, moreover, a moral or psychological nuance and a theological value. *Paradosis* was also used for treason (*prodosia*). Judas Iscariot is always called *ho paradidous*, 'the traitor,' the one who betrayed or betrays Jesus."[34] Spicq states that the verb "rather often connotes this nuance of criminality . . . betrayal of someone's trust" and a footnote to Josephus claims to support that.[35] When Spicq then affirms that the early Christians saw Christ's death as less of pain and torture and more as "a result of perfidy" and that the whole "handing over" means that he was betrayed, he has departed far from his evidence. He insists that the shame of the cross was betrayal rather than torture, and again his conclusions may be right but they cannot be built on the evidence he cites. He has strayed very far indeed from lexicography.

Again no reference is made to the absence of this meaning in the papyri, and all the usages he cites from Josephus prove exactly the opposite. Apparently he hopelessly confuses the two words, *prodidomi*, meaning "betrayal," and *paradidōmi*, meaning "hand over." One can only say that theology here determines lexicography, not the other way around.

We conclude: Josephus often uses the verb παραδίδωμι, but on one or two occasions when it is translated "betray" it is an error.

D. New Testament Usage

The standard lexicon of the Greek New Testament (as distinct from classical Greek), by Walter Bauer, lists four meanings of παραδίδωμι:

1. To hand over, turn over, give up a person. "To hand over into the custody of: a) a thing b) a person."[36] *Especially of the betrayal of Jesus by Judas* with accusative and dative Matt 26:15; Mk 14:10; Luke 22:4,6; John 19:11" (my italics). Bauer gives no reason for his conclusion. Note that the lexicographer brings in the word "betrayal," which leads to an unusual rendering in the NEB in Matt 26:15: "What will you give me to betray him to you?"[37]

2. Give over, commend, or commit.

3. Transmit or hand over oral tradition, relate, teach.

4. Allow or permit.

The most commonly used New Testament word for the deed of Judas is *paradidōmi* (παραδίδωμι), which occurs 122 times in the New Testament, fifty-seven times in connection with the capture of Jesus. It appears eighteen times in the Gospels in the general passive sense; for example, "It is necessary for the Son of man to be handed over." Even though the verb is connected directly with Judas forty-four times and the KJV translates it "betray" forty times, the word is many-layered. It appears often in the New Testament without reference to Judas.

Judas is never mentioned by Paul, but he repeats the tradition of Jesus being handed over (1 Cor 11:23) without specifying who did it. The same verb is used by Paul in theological contexts as in Rom 4:25: "Jesus was delivered to death for our misdeeds." In Rom 8:32 it is God who delivers his own son and in Gal 2:20 Jesus delivers himself to death (so also Eph 5:2, 25).[38]

This widespread variation in usage of the term underscores that we commit an error to translate *paradidōmi* (παραδίδωμι) as "betray." As noted earlier, this translation is misleading and is, at most, quite peripheral in biblical literature.[39] The oldest occurrence of the word in connection with Jesus' capture occurs in 1 Cor 11:23b, where Judas is not mentioned by name. Since the text does not say who handed him over, we conclude that the tradition of Judas as betrayer was not found in Paul or in the earliest layers of the tradition.

It is important to emphasize that for the early Christian community the two key actors in the arrest, trial, and death of Jesus were Jesus and God. What they did is central; what others did is framework. To focus on what Judas might have done or not done and, most important, to spend any energy on decrying what he did is to miss the point of it all.

In order to protect Jesus and Judas from making serious mistakes of judgment several scholars have even conjectured that Judas was taken captive by the high priests during the time of the Temple action and he was then forced to reveal where Jesus could be apprehended.[40]

Because the church has focused so much on the perceived evil of Judas, it has lost sight of the marvelous saving grace of God at work even in him.

Even more important, the church has lost sight of the earlier appearances (as in Paul and in the Gospel sources) of the word "to hand over," ignoring its theological roots in Isaiah and its christological roots in the life of the historical Jesus.

Those earliest occurrences clearly indicate that in modern versions of the fifty-nine occurrences of *paradidōmi* related to the death of Jesus, twenty-seven are translated "hand over" where Judas is not mentioned and thirty-two times translated "betray" when Judas is mentioned. The identical word!

Undoubtedly a stage of development is missing here. An analysis of the earlier forms of the prediction that Jesus will suffer and die supports the idea that Jesus could well have used a tripartite formula:

- I will need to suffer and be rejected by Torah powers.
- I will be handed over into the hands of men.
- Behold, I am being handed over to the Torah powers and they will hand me over to the Gentiles.

These three predictions, the core of which could well go back to Jesus himself, occur in:

- Mark 8:31b-d//Matt 16:21b-d//Luke 9:22b-d.
- Mark 9:31b-d//Matt 17:22b-23b//Luke 9:44.
- Mark 10:33-34//Matt 20:18-19//Luke 18:31b-33.

Several writers have noted that the theme of the suffering of the just is embedded in these sayings. But it is most important to note that it is God who hands over the suffering servant into the hands of sinners. As Pesch concludes: "The dark word picks up a sharpened expression of the theology of the suffering righteous one and indeed perhaps concerning the suffering servant, from which Judaism shies away: God deserts the just (Gott gibt den Gerechten preis)."[41] Lumping together the religious authorities with the political Roman authorities, they are simply called "sinners." According to both Matt 26:45 and Mark 14:41, Jesus turned himself over to "sinners" as part of his resignation to God's will knowing that the end of this process could only be death. Commentators at times try to adjudicate the measure of guilt; so, for example, R. H. Lightfoot concluded in commenting on John 19:11 that the "chief Priests were more guilty than Pilate; and Judas, we may believe, was more guilty than the Jews."[42]

What remains critical for our topic is that the announcements of Jesus' suffering most often have as their earmark the word *paradidōmi*. The term is generally unspecified and in the passive voice, which can only lead to the conclusion that God will be the main actor. There is no reason to believe that Jesus did not himself formulate it like that. Mark, for the most part, adheres to this formula, and it is only as the later church seeks to translate this formula into Greek and to make sense of the suffering and death of Jesus that the "evil men" and the Gentiles are more closely defined. For Jesus, it was all summed up in the words:

"I [the Son of man] am destined to suffer much."

After some struggle, Jesus accepted the will of God and obeyed it, according to Christian belief. In his perfect obedience, all other obedience and disobedience find their proper perspective. It is likely that Jesus increasingly saw himself as engaged as God's divine warrior and that "being handed over" did not follow the traditional formula of God handing over the enemy into Jesus' hand. Rather, God's own nonviolent warrior, the suffering servant, was handed over, or better said, handed himself over into the hands of his enemies to let them do with him whatever they wanted. To add to the irony, it was Judas, a close friend of Jesus, who played a critical role in informing the Jewish authorities and then "handing over" Jesus, thereby serving as God's instrument in the path of obedience for Jesus. This is not the usual way to wage a war and certainly not the conventional way to win it!

In the first section of the holy war stories, there is a "handing over" formula (see LXX, Judg 4:7, 14 for a formulaic use of the expression, "I will hand him [the enemy] over into your hand."[43] The inverted form appears in the Gospel tradition as "The Son of man will be handed over into the hands of men"[44] or into the hands of sinners.[45] Only Luke repeats this holy war formula as a postcrucifixion reminder to the disciples by the men at the tomb (Luke 24:7).

It is nevertheless possible that if Judas was thinking in terms of the holy war, he and the other disciples understood Jesus' talk about "handing over" to mean that one of them would, as God's servant, hand over "the enemy" to Jesus.

It is especially Matthew's community that formulated Jesus' philosophy in the second discourse of Jesus at the time of his captivity. Jesus reminds them that all who take the sword will perish by the sword. His disciples are not to match the aggressive action of the arresting party with violence. "Don't you think I am able to call upon my Father, who will immediately supply me with more than twelve legions of angels?" (26:53). Lohmeyer-Schmauch note that the choice of "legion," with its connotations of Roman might, is deliberate. In addition, the number of angels is very large indeed. The number twelve could well have a bearing on the number of apostles. Furthermore, the statement rules out "all use of violence and demands nonviolence on every occasion."

Beyond the details, the kernel of the statement is decisive: "The one who stands captive among his captors knows that the power of heaven stands beside him. In the presence of that power the paltry power of the world dissipates like smoke, and out of that awareness Jesus permits that power to run its capricious course. He denies himself a request for help. . . . The intimate closeness which this one has with God does not express itself in the triumphant help of heavenly powers but in the nonviolent submission to worldly power."[46]

Here we are at the heart of primitive Christian Christology and a totally new view of the Messiah and his rule.

Nearly thirty years ago, a study basic to this discussion was published by Wiard Popkes. It has not entered the discussion about Judas's act to the extent it deserves. Given the very inadequate treatment of the word "to hand over" in the standard encyclopedias, the treatment by Popkes is all the more needed. It is especially valuable in providing material on the Greek-speaking world and Jewish usage.[47] What emerges is that the term "deliver over" acquires nuances in the New Testament not found anywhere else. The most serious mistake is simply to settle for the meaning "betray," which has no basis in the original meaning of the word. Yet it appears in all standard Bible translations and in most commentaries.

It is worth our while to look at some of the places where Judas is not mentioned. For example, παραδίδωμι is used of the chief priests who deliver Jesus to Pilate[48] and to describe his being delivered over to the "Jews" (John 18:36), and by the contemporaries of the apostles (Acts 3:13). Pilate "hands [Jesus] over" to be crucified.[49] It would be foolish to translate the underlying Greek word as "betray" in these cases.[50] At the same time, virtually all translators consistently translate παραδίδωμι as "betray" when Judas is the subject of the action.

According to Schwarz's tabulation, the verb appears fifty-nine times in connection with the death of Christ in the Gospels, and thirty-two (see above) times it is related to Judas:

Matt 10:4; 26:15, 16, 21, 23, 24, 25, 46, 48; 27:3, 4.
Mark 3:19; 14:10, 11, 18, 21, 42, 44.
Luke 22:4, 6, 21, 22, 48.
John 6:64, 71; 12:4; 13:12, 11, 21; 18:2, 5; 21:20.

In all of these places, modern translations (RSV, NEB, *JB*) present the word wrongly as "betray." It is particularly noteworthy that in the following places where the same act is mentioned, but Judas is not, the word is translated "hand over."

Matt 17:22; 20:18, 19; 26:2, 45; 27:2, 18, 26.
Mark 9:31; 10:33(bis); 14:41; 15:1, 10, 15.
Luke 9:44; 18:32; 20:20; 23:25; 24:7, 20.
John 18:30, 35, 36; 19:11, 16, 30.

This is, in the first instance, a serious mistranslation of the Greek word, which does a considerable injustice to the writers of the Synoptic Gospels, who are made to say things in translation they have not said in Greek. Not least of all, it is a serious injustice to Judas himself.[51]

First and foremost, it is bad practice to distort the use of a word just because so many people believe that Judas was a traitor. It is noteworthy how often scholars admit that the verb does not mean betray and yet go on to treat what Judas did to Jesus as, in fact, a betrayal.

Yet perhaps this distortion is understandable. One notable aspect of the Gospels is that Judas is never mentioned without some reference to the handing over; apart from it, Judas has no recognizable identity. The fundamental meaning of the Greek word must guide us, then, in determining his act—not some church dogma or tradition. It is relatively easy to say what the verb does not mean; what, then, is its real meaning?

In Luke 6:16, the noun προδότης ("traitor") stands in the place of the word ὁ παραδίδους ("the one who handed over"), and in Acts 1:16 Judas is designated as the hodēgos (ὁδηγός), the one who pointed the way to those who sought to take Jesus captive. Most often, Judas is simply noted as the "one who handed him over," the meaning of which it is our duty to explore. Ever since the New Testament has been studied critically in the original Greek language, it has been recognized that "the rendering 'betray' adds something to the force of the original word. The exact word 'traitor' (προδότης) is applied to Judas only in Luke vi.16. Elsewhere the word used of him is some part of the verb 'to deliver up' (παραδιδόναι), and not of the word 'to betray' (προδιδόναι)."[52]

If we explore a broader context, for example, in Matthew 10, the word appears four times in a parallel usage in which strife and tension among the family is described. In two of the four usages translators are wont to render it "hand over." In the other two, it is consistently rendered "betray," once for Judas (Matt 10:4) and once for what brothers do to each other (10:21). In the other occurrences, it is translated either "hand over" or "arrest" (10:17, 19). It makes perfectly good sense in the passage to translate it consistently as "hand over," and there is inherently no reason to assume betrayal or treachery in any of the acts described. Indeed, Jesus (if these words are genuine) could well have been describing an enactment of the laws of Deuteronomy (13:1-18) where not only the "prophet or dreamer" but even "your brother, your father's son, . . . or your dearest friend," if they should entice you, "shall be delivered to death and you are to be the first to cast the stone." In short, in both ancient Hebrew society and the society of Jesus' time, these words had a quite different ring than they do for us. We should not read "betrayal" into a word unless the context clearly demands it, especially since a different word meaning betrayal was ready at hand for the first writers.

There is only one case where the context seems to permit an undercurrent of betrayal: Matt 24:10: "Many will lose their faith; they will hand one another over [betray?] and hate one another." But perhaps the notion of betrayal is introduced by translators because the notion of "delivering up" appears already in verse 9: "You will be handed over for punishment and execution."[53] The Greek has the same verb and could well be translated "and hand one another over" in verse 10.

Popkes, in his thorough study of this concept, offers four possibilities for the translation of παραδίδωμι in connection with Judas:

1. Judas, in a very general sense, handed Jesus over to his death.
2. Judas surrendered Jesus to the authorities in a legal sense.
3. Judas denounced Jesus or informed against him by reporting some infraction on the part of Jesus.
4. Judas betrayed Jesus. He broke faith with Jesus.[54]

Of these, we are convinced that the evidence weighs in the direction that if we combine some elements of the first three, we attain the closest proximity to the reality. The last, the one that has been almost universally accepted, has the lowest degree of probability.

What seems most unusual is the progressive blaming of Judas even among the writers of the second-century church, despite the fact that the Greek word "to deliver over" (not "betray") is used to describe the deed of Judas. Later English translators (starting in the sixteenth century) have brought in the negative meaning of betrayal.[55] By contrast, an analysis of the usages of παραδίδωμι in the earlier writings reveals that the word retains its neutral character.[56] The word has no inherently negative connotation. It definitely does not carry the connotation of treachery, deceit, or stealth.

So what, then, was the act of Judas? There are a number of possibilities. He may have served as a connecting link between Jesus and the powers that sought to arrest him. If, along with the other disciples, Judas believed that unusual powers had been bestowed upon Jesus and that he had nothing to fear from people like Pilate and Caiaphas (who ruled, after all, under the sovereignty of God), then the commission that he received from Jesus to make a connection with them was one that Judas could fulfill with integrity.

At the same time, Jesus' warning that things would not go well with Judas is understandable in the light of his awareness that the act likely would be misunderstood and misrepresented. Never was a prophecy more accurate!

There is, however, another possibility of defining the nature of Judas's act more closely. Again, we must begin with a historical fact: Judas is a Jew of the first century who belongs to a band of disciples who have attached themselves to a rabbi. It may have become increasingly clear in his relationship to Jesus that the path Jesus keeps hinting at is different from any traditional messianic one, and there is mounting friction between Jesus and the religious establishment of his time. This friction would not be surprising, given that Jesus had made no effort to study Torah in the recognized institutions of his time (except for routine studies as a child). Yet he seems to show not the least reluctance to make authoritative statements about the Torah and how it is to be observed.

Most threatening of all, Jesus does not confine himself to teaching about Torah; nor does he, like the Essenes and the community of Qumran, withdraw from the mainstream of Judaism. Indeed, his major base of operation whenever he comes to Jerusalem is the Temple itself.

He gathers people together who are serious about living together in a new divine family under the rule of God. Those who are commissioned to assist in monitoring Torah observance become increasingly nervous about Jesus, not least because there is evidence that an increasing number of people are following Jesus, or at the very least giving him a hearing. The entry into Jerusalem and a prophetic action in the Temple are clear indications that both the political and economic structures of the Temple are not beyond Jesus' criticism. His renewal program began with the people in Galilee. Now it had to come to Jerusalem, where he focused on the holy Temple.

Summary

Let us review our evidence so far. It has been shown that there is no linguistic basis—in classical Greek, in the Greek translation of the Hebrew Bible, in Josephus or patristic sources—for a translation of "betray" to describe what Judas did. Only one text in the New Testament (Luke 6:16) describes his act as one of "betrayal." By using the same word to describe what the Jewish leaders did to Jesus ("You have betrayed and murdered him," Acts 7:52; cf. Acts 3:13: "handed over and disowned"), Luke signals his intention of knitting together Judas's deed, by then seen as evil, with that of the Jewish people through the actions of their leaders. The absence of the Greek word for "traitor" or "betray" applied to Judas in the earliest sources (except once, in Luke) and, indeed, throughout the New Testament is an unassailable witness to the fact that whatever Judas did, the earliest Christians did not view it as a betrayal of Jesus or of their faith community.

We shall now consider a possible option for Judas of several open to him. The one that may have been attractive to him is called the $m^e sira$ (מסור). In popular parlance this is called an "informer" and often classed among "heretics, apostates and high-handed sinners" who are excluded from the blessings of the future life.[57] In the next chapter we turn our attention to that possibility.

Notes

1. Herr, "The Conception of History," 138, 142, quoted from Joseph Milikowsky, "*Seder Olam,*" 1981 unpublished manuscript. I thank David Flusser for making this available to me.

2. Ed Blair, *IDB,* 2:1006–1007. This quotation is from 1007.

3. Charlesworth, *Jesus within Judaism,* 14. Later, Charlesworth avers that Jesus suffered through the betrayal of Judas, which, along with the denial of Peter, appears among a list of items that are "relatively trustworthy" (169). No clue is given on how we know that Jesus suffered on account of the betrayal or what indeed the word "betray" means in the case of a disciple doing what the Master said he would do. So also Borg, *Jesus: A New Vision,* 177: "He had been betrayed by one of his own."

4. Teichert, *Jeder ist Judas: Der unvermeidliche Verrat.*

5. W. Montgomery's translation, *Quest* 1948: 394.

6. Matt 26:14//Mark 14:10//Luke 22:4.

7. Sanders, *Jesus and Judaism,* 309. Cf. *Quest,* 396.

8. Sanders, *Jesus and Judaism,* 206.

9. Sanders, *Jesus and Judaism,* 304.

10. Sanders, *Jesus and Judaism,* 305.

11. Sanders, *Jesus and Judaism,* 230.

12. Chilton, *The Temple of Jesus,* 151.

13. Preisker, "Der Verrat des Judas," 154.

14. Dibelius, "Judas und der Judaskuss," 277. Many others have followed Dibelius in this specification of the meeting place without noting his caveat about the meaning of the word παραδίδωμι. He explicitly states that "the actual meaning of the word which we usually translate 'betray' is to 'surrender or extradite'" (273).

15. Harvey, *Jesus and the Constraints of History,* 22–29, here 23.

16. Harvey's italics, 23.

17. Haugg, *Judas,* 111. He finds admonitions to Judas in Mark 14:43-45 and in John 6:70; 12:7-8; 13:2-30. In the first reference, Jesus says nothing at all to Judas, and the parallel accounts certainly do not criticize Judas. The silence of Jesus toward Judas in the Johannine references is the more striking considering the animosity John has expressed toward Judas.

18. Barth, *Church Dogmatics* II, 459.

19. Halas, *Judas Iscariot*, 190–191. Halas's work, until Maccoby's book was published in 1992, is the only critical book-length study on Judas to appear in English.

20. Halas, *Judas*, 198. For Augustine, see *City of God* 1.17 and *Sermon* 352.3.8 (*PL* 39: 1559–1563).

21. Possibly the first scholar writing on παραδίδωμι who does not list "betray" as one of its meanings in a scholarly reference work is F. Büchsel, "παραδίδωμι" preferring *Auslieferung*, surrender or "deliver"(*KTWBNT*, 2 [1935]: 171–174). Strangely he, nevertheless, concludes that 1 Cor 11:23b "without doubt" refers to Judas. My article "Judas Iscariot," *ABD*, 3 (1992): 1091–1096, refuses to use the word "traitor" in connection with the deed of Judas.

22. See Walter Miller's translation, LCL, 1961.

23. W. H. S. Jones, LCL, 1959.

24. See W. Theiler, *Poseidonius*, 1982: 181, 182. Bauer's parenthetical statement: "To be sure, it is not certain that when Paul uses such terms as 'handing over' 'delivering up,' 'arrest' [so clearly Posidon.: 87 frgm. 36, 50 Jac παραδοθείς] he is thinking of the betrayal by Judas" (614), is puzzling. Does he mean that in contrast to Paul, where there is some uncertainty, there is none in Posidonius, where it "clearly" means "betray"? If so, this is misleading, as anyone who checks the Posidonius text must agree.

25. Κόιντος Ὄππιος παραδοθεὶς ἀκολουθεῖ δέσμιος...καταγαγὼν θρίαμβον as cited in Edelstein and Kidd, *Posidonius: The Fragments*, 223, line 79 citing (F 36 Jac) Athenaeus 5:211D–215B. For the contrast with προδοσία (betrayal), see p. 225, line 134.

26. See J. H. Moulton and G. Milligan, *The Vocabulary of the New Testament Illustrated from the Papyri* . . . . (London: Hodder & Stoughton, 1914–1929); Friedrich Preisigke, *Wörterbuch der griechischen Papyrusurkunden* (Berlin, 1927); Hans-Albert Rupprecht and Andrea Jördens, *Wörterbuch der griechischen Papyrusurkunden* (Wiesbaden: Harrassowitz, 1991), who provide not one instance where it might mean "betray." So also R. H. R. Horsley, *New Documents*, 4:165.

27. παραδίδωμι, *KTWBNT*, 2:172.

28. In one instance (*T.Benj* 3:8), clearly a Christian interpolation, the Greek has παραδίδωμι and Howard Kee translates it, incorrectly, "betrayed." It clearly means "handed over."

29. Popkes, *Christus*, 27–36.

30. Wolff, *Jesaja 53 im Urchristentum*, 69.

31. G. Schwarz, *Jesus und Judas*, 88.

32. Höistad, *Cynic Hero and Cynic King;* and D. Aune, "Heracles and Christ, Heracles Imagery in the Christology of Early Christianity," in *Greeks, Romans, and Christians*, ed. David L. Balch et al. (Minneapolis: Fortress, 1990), 3–19.

33. *JW* 3.381; 3.354; 2.360.

34. *Theological Lexicon*, 3:13–23, here 21.

35. Not one of the texts that Spicq cites supports his case. Three are, however, worthy of comment. The first, *Ant* 5,131, recounts the classic case of betrayal based on Judg 1:25. The LXX has no word here meaning "betrayal." During the capture of Bethel by Ephraim one of the town's inhabitants leaves the town to look for food and is captured. "They gave him their word that if he would betray [*sic!*] [παραδίδωμι] the city, they would spare his life. . . . and he on these terms swore to deliver it [ἐγχειριεῖν] into their hands. So he by treason (προδούς) saved himself. . . ." The

translators (Thackeray and Marcus) do not distinguish between the two terms here. Josephus does. On another occasion (*Ant* 6, 344–345) in discussing Saul's bravery Josephus uses both terms: "Saul . . . determined . . . not to betray [προδίδωμι] his people to the enemy . . . instead he thought it noble to hand himself over [παραδίδωμι], his household, his children to these perils, and along with them, to fall fighting for his subjects." A third example is a mistranslation that occurs in Spicq's rendering of *BJ* 4:523 (Spicq, 22 n. 46). Josephus introduces the section by speaking of the "treachery" [προδοσία] on which James is meditating. Describing it in detail, however, he uses the term παραδίδωμι "hand over" (523, 525) and not "betray," a fact not reflected in Spicq's translation. This illustrates that Josephus was conscious of the difference between the two terms. Spicq, however, citing Josephus, concludes: "To say that Jesus was handed over, then, means that he was betrayed" (22). *Caveat lector!*

36. Bauer, *Lexicon,* trans. Arndt and Gingrich, 4th ed., p. 620. In the sixth ed., p. 614, the same misleading phrase appears: "Esp. of the betrayal of Jesus by Judas," although adding, "It is not certain that when Paul uses such terms as 'handing over' . . . he is thinking of the betrayal of Judas." Indeed not. Should we not say that it is certain that he is not? (See above, endnote 24.)

37. KJV and RSV have "deliver"; *Gute Nachricht* has: "Wenn ich ihn euch in die Hände spiele?" (help someone gain something without anyone knowing it). In Mark 14:10 and 11, they all have "betray"; except GN, which has first "in die Hände spielen" and then in v. 11 "verraten." In Luke 22:4, 6 first use: "Put Jesus into their power"; second use: "to betray him," the same verb used in Greek. In John 19:11, "the man who handed me over to you" (NEB).

38. Gärtner states that according to "primitive Christian understanding, Judas and the Jews were the instruments by which were fulfilled those plans of God indicated" in the servant songs of Isaiah 53 (*Iscariot,* 25). The Jews were probably not included in those allegations until after the year 70.

39. Klauck, *Judas,* 45. Note also Klaus Dorn's frank admission that the meaning "betray" can be advocated "von der Sache her" but has no other foundation ("Judas," 63–66). If I understand this, it means that we translate it "betray" because that's what the text says, a classic circular argument.

40. Crossan, *Who Killed Jesus?* 81, which he describes as a guess. He needs to find a linkage between the Temple event, Judas's treachery, and the arrest. Myllykoski also conjectures such an arrest, *Die letzten Tage Jesu,* 146.

41. Pesch, *Das Markusevangelium* II, 99. See G. Schwarz, *Jesus und Judas,* 96–97.

42. R. H. Lightfoot, *St. John's Gospel,* 306.

43. Jones, "The Concept of Holy War," in Clements, *The World of Ancient Israel,* 299–321, esp. 311–312.

44. Matt 17:22//Mark 9:31//Luke 9:44.

45. Matt 26:45//Mark 14:41//Luke 24:7.

46. Lohmeyer-Schmauch, *Matthäus,* 365.

47. Popkes, *Christus Traditus.* See the analysis and critique in Feldmeier, *Die Krisis,* 220–229.

48. Mark 15:1, 10; Matt 27:2, 18; Luke 24:20; John 18:30, 35.

49. Matt 27:26; Mark 15:15; Luke 23:25; John 19:16.

50. The problem is well illustrated in W. Swartley's assertion: "Mark's Gospel

shows Jesus' death as a *betrayal*. It is first a betrayal of Jesus by Judas (one of the twelve disciples) to the Jewish leaders (14:10, 11, 18, 21, 41, 42, 44). Second, it is a betrayal of Jesus by the Jews to the Romans (15:1, 10). And, third, it is a betrayal of Jesus by Pilate (the Romans) to death (15:15). The same Greek word (παραδίδωμι, meaning 'to deliver over' or 'betray') is used in all ten instances" (*Mark,* 183).

51. G. Schwarz, *Jesus,* 24.

52. Westcott, *The Gospel according to St. John,* 192.

53. Popkes, *Christus,* 90–93, noted often by writers, at least as early as Schläger, "Ungeschichtlichkeit" (1914): 53–55. See also N. Perrin, "The Use of (παρα)διδοναι in Connection with the Passion of Jesus in the New Testament," 204–212. He divides the usages into three categories, as a technical term for the Passion, an apologetic use by referring to OT passages, and its use to develop a soteriology of the cross rather than an apologetic. He shows no interest in dealing with Judas.

54. Popkes, *Christus,* 218.

55. The OED entry under "betray" links Judas with this word as early as 1300 and Wycliffe seems to be responsible for the connection, while Tindale made it standard. D. Moody Smith has called my attention to the fact that in Old English, the word "betray" had no connotation of treachery but simply meant to hand over, coming from the Latin *traiere,* from which we presumably get our English word "tray."

56. Lampe lists "betrayal" as the last meaning for the word in *A Patristic Greek Lexicon,* 1013, but even the references he cites do not unequivocally mean betray.

57. Montefiore and Loewe, *Anthology.* As a class they have no place in the life to come (xlviii, 601) and one is allowed to hate them since God hates them (469). Even Elijah, the proverbial peacemaker, had difficulty associating with them (256).

CHAPTER
FOUR

JUDAS AS AN INFORMER

The word *masor* was behind the description of Judas Iscariot, "who also betrayed him" (Matthew 10:4).

—David Daube[1]

It is not a question of Jesus condoning, still less conniving, at Judas's action. But this did not mean that he did not welcome it.

—J. D. M. Derrett[2]

I. The Act of Informing: The מסירה (*mᵉsira*)

A. Informers among the Romans

In the first century, informers were known not only among Jews. Tacitus, the Roman historian, writes about the state of the empire during the Augustan period, about 32 C.E.: "It was, indeed, a horrible feature of the period that leading senators became informers even on trivial matters—some openly, many secretly. Friends and relatives were as suspect as strangers, old stories as damaging as new. In the Forum, at a dinner party, a remark on any topic might mean prosecution. Everyone competed for priority in marking down the victim. Sometimes this was self-defense, but mostly it was a sort of contagion, like an epidemic."[3]

According to Tacitus, informing was popular during the time of Jesus because Caesar took the side of the accusers and instituted a reward system that covered even an informer who had committed suicide. "Thus the informers, a breed invented for the national ruin and never adequately curbed even by penalties, were now lured into the field with rewards."[4]

B. Informers in Judaism

In chapter 3 it was demonstrated that the word describing the action of Judas, παραδίδωμι (*paradidōmi),* cannot rightfully be translated "betray." At the very least no text has surfaced in which it clearly means "betray." It is now our task to review some possibilities of Hebrew and Aramaic words that could have been underneath the description of this deed and that might have made possible the negative spin that the deed of Judas eventually received.

One intellectually defensible suggestion about the meaning of the term *paradidōmi* and the possible action of Judas is to relate it to the original Hebrew or Aramaic of first-century Judaism and to the usage of the LXX and intertestamental literature and the role of the informer, the מסור.[5]

It has been noted that the root מסור (*masor*), found infrequently in the Hebrew Bible, becomes more common in later Hebrew.[6] Jacob Levy lists one meaning of מסר as being to surrender a hostage and cites the discussion (in *J. Ter* 8:46b) of what to do if Gentiles take a caravan hostage and request one person to be surrendered to them, otherwise they will kill everyone. Even if all are killed, the Jews are not to give up one Israelite. If, however, the Gentiles name one person in particular whom they want delivered over (cf. 2 Sam 20:21-22), then the Jews must deliver that person up so that the others' lives are spared. Offering a different set of circumstances, *B. Qam* 93a deals with the hypothetical situation of reporting on one's neighbor, actually referring his or her legal status (i.e., guilty or not guilty) to God. The person who does so will be punished first, just as Sarah died first because she accused Abraham before God of having wronged her when the handmaid Hagar became haughty after conceiving Abraham's child (Gen 16:5).

Levy cites another text (*Men* 64b), which describes how an old man who spoke Greek delated his people to Rome during the siege of Jerusalem. He told them that as long as the Jews could carry out their sacrifices they could not be conquered. Consequently, the Romans offered them pigs instead of lambs, so they would be unable to perform sacrifices.

There is also a discussion that indirectly relates to one aspect of the Judas story concerning the money an informer received. Since informers to Gentiles are killed, the question is raised, What should be done with the money the informer received? One sage says it can be deliberately destroyed, for if you are allowed to kill a person, how much more one should be allowed to destroy his belongings. Another rejects that argument because the informer may have children who should inherit his goods (*B. Qam* 119a).

One text says that the Messiah will not come until the denunciators multiply (*Sanh* 97a). Even the question of someone being voluntarily "handed over" (as was the case with Jesus) is discussed. R. Josua hands over a refugee fleeing from the Romans. Even though he is permitted to do so, since the refugee had agreed to it, Elijah asks, Does such an action accord with the teaching of the Hasidim?[7]

The מסור (*masor* or *maser*) hands over a person or property from the inside to the outside, or from the inner circle to the outer. An act such as this may be accompanied by betrayal or treachery, but neither is implied in the word. The best English translation of this word may well be placed on a continuum from delator or denouncer to informer. An informer need not, however, have anything to do with betrayal and may, in fact, render an essential service. Police officers, a relatively new invention of civilization, are paid informers in that it is their duty to report infractions of the law or anything that threatens society to those who can do something about it. Accordingly, from ancient times, they have been called "peace officers."

C. Informers in Hebrew Scriptures

One biblical example of the *masor* occurs in the Joab-Sheba confrontation recorded in 2 Sam 20:1-22 in the city of Abel, where Sheba had gone for additional allies in his rebellion against David. Standing before the gates, a wisewoman pleaded with Joab, David's general, not to attack. Instead, she said the townspeople would hand over the leader of the rebellion to Joab, and the city could be spared. This incident, Derrett states, was cited in the second century "to justify the surrender of a named member of the group; that is not *m⁻sira* (denominative of מסר) in the technical sense, it is not a crime, for necessity knows no law. . . . If the individual betrays his group to the aliens that is *m⁻sira*."[8] David Daube declares that "the word [מסר] was behind the description of Judas Iscariot, 'who also betrayed him'" (Matt 10:4), but for some reason Daube has Judas dealing with non-Jewish authorities.[9] Although Daube often translates the verb as "betray" and describes it as a "terrible action," he also gives evidence that certain circles wanted to protect God from being a *masor*. He notes that "in other contexts *masar* is frequently employed in a neutral or good sense."[10] The Tosephta in the second half replaces it with the more innocuous *nathan* ("to give"), thus removing any suggestion that handing over a person under all circumstances could be looked upon as treachery.[11]

The fundamental rule that Derrett enunciates is "that no individual should place a fellow Jew in the power (physically or financially) of the alien ruler."[12] He cites the Temple Scroll:

- A man has informed against his people, and has delivered his people up to a foreign nation, and has done evil to his people (line 7).
- You shall hang him on the tree and he shall die. On the evidence of two witnesses and on the evidence of three witnesses (line 8).
- He shall be put to death, and they shall hang him on the tree (line 9).[13]

Baumgarten believes that during the early Hasmonaean age, Jews began to be concerned about defining treason. Thus, they may have been influenced by Roman definitions. He mentions the case of Menelaus, who delivered the Temple and his priestly countrymen into the hands of Syrian King Antiochus. He is therefore called a traitor, *prodotes* (2 Macc 5:15), both to the laws and to the fatherland. During Judah's campaign against the Idumeans, two officers who were accused at a gathering of the leaders of the people of accepting bribes and allowing people to escape were subsequently slain for having turned traitor (*prodotes genomenous,* 2 Macc 10:22). It is important to note that the informer in this instance went to the "foreign nation."

By contrast, those who serve as informers to Jewish authorities (e.g., Temple authorities) are regarded as essential to the health of the Jewish community. Each member is responsible for the corporate life of the Jewish people, and the righteous informer "who tells the Jewish court of the misdeeds of his coreligionist is a benefactor. [But] the one who delates a fellow Jew to the gentiles is to be punished under their laws as a מסור."[14]

One such case is Razis, referred to in 2 Macc 14:37-46. Razis was informed on by a fellow Jew, unjustly so. The word used in this case is *menuō* (μηνύω), another word used in Greek for informer.[15] It is often used in a legal sense, "to serve as an informer" (μηνύτηρ), and the information laid is called the μήνυμα. It is used thus by the Fourth Gospel when the author reports that the chief priests and the Pharisees had given orders that anyone who knew where Jesus was should give information (μηνύω), so that they might arrest him (John 11:57).

The term used here has to do not only with stating where Jesus might be found but also with providing the Jewish authorities with evidence that could constitute a legal basis for arresting Jesus.[16] It is used of Moses giving solemn testimony in Luke 20:37: "That the dead are raised is attested by Moses."[17]

This alternative of viewing the action of Judas as informing is rejected by a former Israeli chief justice, Haim Cohn, who believes that Caiaphas, and presumably Judas, would not have survived had they engaged in such a dangerous activity. His reasons are unpersuasive. Although he argues convincingly that Caiaphas does not fit the category of informer—for he doubts that such "traitors and collaborators," "informers or quislings" would have escaped lynching—he seems open to treating Judas in this category.[18] In the final analysis, it is as traitor and not as informer to the Temple hierarchy that Cohn treats him. He has, therefore, no option but to conclude "that the whole tale of Judas' treachery is so unlikely, so incongruous, regardless of who his fellow conspirators might have been, that it merits no credence." Granting that the story may have theological significance, he rather thoroughly demolishes any historical probability for Judas's act. He concludes: "[Our premise is] there was no conspiratorial arrangement with Judas . . .

and the episode reported in the Gospels provides no clue to the question,
. . . Who prompted the arrest of Jesus?"[19]

The greatest *masor* of Jewish legend was Joseph the Righteous (Gen
50:21). Joseph was an informer against his brothers (Gen 37:2), "bringing
their father a bad report." They in turn hated him (37:4) and became increasingly jealous of him (37:11). When the brothers had an opportunity to
get rid of him they agreed to do so, haggling about whether to kill him
outright or to hold him hostage and send him into captivity themselves.
They agreed to sell him to a caravan going to Egypt after Judah, invoking
the simple profit motive, asked: "'What profit [מה בצע, *mah besa*] is it if
we kill our brother and conceal his blood? Come, let us sell him to the
Ishmaelites, and not lay our hands on him, for he is our brother, our own
flesh.' And his brothers agreed" (Gen 37:26-27).

For our understanding of Judas, it is not irrelevant that the decisions
about Joseph were initiated by Judah and were made during a meal. Later
tradition has it that his brother Simon negotiated the deal for thirty pieces
of gold. He and Gad kept ten pieces for themselves and showed the rest to
the others, an interesting legendary detail divulged by Gad on his deathbed
(*T. Gad* 2:3).

The ambiguity of the *mᵉsira* was nowhere more apparent than here. This
corrupt act arose from the basest of motives, personal greed and fraternal
hatred (*T. Gad* 1:8-9; 2:1, 4), and was directed at a relatively blameless person; yet it led ultimately to the preservation of God's chosen people.

In several attempts, Derrett has sought to bring to our notice the parallel
position of Judah and Judas.[20] Certainly the characteristics of Judah and his
place among the Twelve brothers are well known. He is "the Lion's Whelp"
who returns from the kill with pride in his achievements (Gen 49:8-12).
But any detailed parallel founders on the fact that the figure of Joseph, like
the figure of Phineas (both of whom are of keen interest to first-century
Jews), held no discernible interest for any New Testament writers, as far we
can see.

D. Judas as Informer to the Temple Authorities

We shall never know precisely what role Judas played. What is suggested
here is that it is perfectly logical to assume that, just as Jesus availed himself
of the Temple as a place to teach, so also Judas would avail himself of the
institution of informing to the Temple authorities. To what extent Jesus was
apprised of this, we will never know. Perhaps he knew more than we are
told and perhaps he even discussed the matter with Judas.

It is possible, of course, that Judas had one game plan and Jesus quite
another. Or perhaps Jesus had none. Perhaps he preferred to wait for God
to act. Judas was a collaborator, not only with the Temple hierarchy but

also possibly with God. Judas had every reason to believe that the rulers in the Temple served by the appointment of God, if they did not in fact carry out God's will. Whether he believed, along with the Zealots, in the partnership in God's war (*symmachia, συμμαχία*), we do not know.[21] He could well have, since it is a fundamental affirmation of Judaism that God works together with humans to achieve divine purposes.

Of highest importance is the recognition that Judas collaborated with Jesus himself to bring about what Jesus wanted to have done: God's will. He did not want to die; he displays no death wish at any point. But he had to hand himself over into the power of those charged with doing the divine will, the religious authorities. What the outcome of that would be no one knew, although Jesus had reason to suspect the loss of his own life. His struggle in Gethsemane revolved around the question: Could Jesus entrust himself into the hands of the ones delivering him over—God, Judas, Caiaphas, Pilate—all of whom were carrying out God's intention?

It is possible to depict the events of the Passion Week with the best of motives on the part of all people involved and still end with the tragedy of Jesus' crucifixion. There is reason to believe that Judas profoundly regretted what happened, that the last idea that would have entered his head was that his action might lead to Pilate's court and Jesus' death. He was surely convinced that Jesus had not been guilty of anything deserving death (cf. Matt 27:4). He would have found it hard to imagine that anyone had death in mind for Jesus. Like all the other disciples, Judas could not fathom that Jesus foresaw a literal death on a cross. That, after all, is not the conventional way in which messiahs establish their kingdoms.[22]

Indeed, Jesus had hardly sorted out the matter of his fate himself; otherwise, he would not have suffered the time of agony in the Garden of Gethsemane. There is, then, abundant reason to give Judas the benefit of the doubt. Schleiermacher may be right that Judas's major role was to move the Temple authorities from vacillation to action. "The actual historical significance of Judas's 'betrayal' is that it brought the vacillation of the Sanhedrin to an end."[23] In their state of indecision, Judas's assistance seems to have given them the final impetus they required. If they had rejected Judas's offer when he made it, they would have compromised their faith seriously, for Judas was only obeying their order to reveal where Jesus was.

The juxtaposition of the narratives of anointing and Judas's decision suggests the evangelists saw a connection. Raymond Brown notes that at the anointing, "Readers . . . learn from Jesus' own lips that the efforts of the authorities to kill him will be successful. In confirmation of this (and perhaps as part of a stubborn rejection of Jesus' condoning the waste), Judas . . . goes to the chief priests and helps their plot by offering to give Jesus over, a betrayal for which he is promised silver."[24]

This is not the place to judge Judas's act, because it is very difficult—and, indeed, inappropriate—to make such a judgment. In one sense, he merely obeyed the order of the Sanhedrin. The larger question is: What led Judas, as a member of the inner circle, to approach the Jewish leadership? Was it something that Jesus said at the supper when he was anointed in Bethany? Was it Jesus speaking distinctly about his coming burial that caused Judas to act and to reveal Jesus' whereabouts? By Judas's action, both parties were inexorably drawn together; the rest could safely be left to God, who had appointed both parties to their respective roles. There is no plausible evidence to make us think that Judas Iscariot operated from any other base.

Schwarz is correct when he says that it is time for the words "betray" and "traitor" to vanish from the translations of the New Testament in connection with Judas's deed.[25] Brown has done it and set a fine precedent in his translation of the passion narrative.

Whatever it was that Judas did, once Jesus was in the hands of his captors, events began to move very quickly. The only one who was even partially prepared was Jesus. He remained serenely calm through the trial process, refusing to cooperate with the authorities, thereby possibly hastening his death. He was even remarkably poised through the agony of his death. Indeed, as some aspects of the Lukan tradition have it, his first thoughts on the cross in Luke were for others (perhaps for Judas?) as he prayed: "Father, forgive them, for they know not what they do (Luke 23:24)."[26]

Judas committed a serious act; deadly serious. The immediate outcome, whatever Jesus or Judas hoped for, was devastating. It is suggested that his act of informing may have been done with the finest of motives, but it may also have been done with base motives. Most likely, being a human act, it was mixed with both. The act may also be judged by its outcome, immediate and long-range. Moreover, we must consider the role that Jesus had in asking Judas to do what he did. We can hardly conceive of it as betrayal if Judas did what Jesus wanted him to do. What are we, for example, to make of the serious charges that Barth levels against Judas, that he interrupted a career on the rise and that Jesus could have done so much more good had not Judas intercepted with his "vile betrayal"? Surely that kind of thinking cannot help us to understand the significance of the Judas act. Rather, the act of Judas and the handing over of Joseph, and perhaps the act of Josephus as well, share a wholesome outcome—the eventual survival or triumph of the very people whom they were presumably "betraying."

Let us summarize our conclusions about the nature of Judas's act:

1. Judas officially met the high priest and his associates and agreed to assist them in meeting Jesus.

2. Both parties wanted to minimize the risk of open conflict in any show-

down between Jesus and the authorities, a showdown that appeared more and more inevitable.

3. It is certainly possible that Judas became convinced, after discussion with Jesus himself, that an opportunity to meet with the high priest and those in authority in the Temple needed to be arranged. Jesus' own teaching had stressed that when a fellow Jew sins, one speaks to him directly about it (Matt 18:15-20//Luke 17:3). Jesus had practiced this manner of collegial rebuke with his disciples, most notably with Peter (Matt 16:23), but also with James and John (Luke 9:56).[27] Had the time come for him to confront the high priest? Perhaps Judas knew the high priest well enough to be able to arrange such an encounter, or had the courage to bring together two of God's appointed leaders. Possibly he assumed that such an encounter could and would resolve their differences. If Judas was indeed a disciple concerned about financial matters, he would have been sensitive to the financial needs of the Temple in a way that Jesus might not have been. He may have thought that, by meeting Temple authorities, Jesus could become better disposed toward the traditional way in which changes were made in the Temple and that Caiaphas could get a better understanding of the reform program Jesus had in mind for the renewal of Israel.

4. Judas would have no difficulty justifying this approach on the basis of Jewish practice, which not only allowed but also encouraged such an approach, if not an informer system. The high priest needed to know what Jesus was teaching, especially if threats, even veiled threats, had been made against the Temple or the establishment that ran it.

5. Judas brought to the high priests the message that Jesus himself was now ready for an encounter and that he was speaking more often about his impending "handing over" to death. Having been told by Jesus to do what he had to do quickly, Judas could have assured the high priests that Jesus would not offer resistance, nor would he encourage his followers to resist his arrest.

A remarkable book written more than sixty years ago by Frank Morison details his perception of the events that transpired between the departure of Judas from the supper and the arrest. He is convinced that nearly five hours elapsed between these two events and suggests that the high priests needed that time to consult with the members of the Sanhedrin and indeed with Pilate himself. His arguments are persuasive that Judas brought the news that Jesus was ready to allow himself to be handed over and that Judas had been authorized by Jesus to help do so. It may also be that a pact did not exist between Jesus and Judas. As Morison puts it: "Jesus was a master of psychology, and His irrevocable determination to deliver Himself to His accusers that night was accomplished by infinitely subtler means."[28]

Most important is the consistent witness of the Gospels, even of John, that Judas acted, if not on the orders of Jesus, at least with his full knowledge. Whatever it was that he did was under the control of Jesus himself. It is important, precisely in this connection, to remember that the disciple is dependent upon what the Master does.[29] Such words as treachery or betrayal simply do not apply. They can be invoked only when it is clearly demonstrated that Jesus had other things in mind. Instead, we have, it is most likely, a disciple following the will of his master.

Judas needs neither our defense nor attack. All historical actions are ambiguous. They are particularly hard to evaluate when we have emotional ties to the main players or a stake in the outcome. Acts such as the reporting of irregularities to authorities are especially open to misinterpretation. Judas's act was very vulnerable in this regard. Even today the informer or whistleblower has a hard lot, especially when governments are involved. What is of critical importance in the evaluation of Judas's act from the perspective of first-century Judaism is the fact that "Judas did not go to the Romans. He felt like a Jew."[30] As a Jew the decision of what to do with Jesus had to be made not by one individual but by the priests charged with that decision.

II. The Whistleblower Today

It is important that we remove all prejudices from this term. Before modern police forces were established, societies placed a very high level of importance on informers. When government rules by power instead of consensus, when it breaks down or is perceived to be threatened, informers flourish. In Canada, for example, it was revealed in 1992 that a former Quebec cabinet minister for many years had served as a paid informer to federal police at the height of the Quebec independence movement. Despite some cries of outrage, it is amazing how calmly this news was received by his erstwhile colleagues twenty years later.

In the United States, Congress passed a statute in 1986 that provided handsome rewards to whistleblowers who save the government money by detecting graft and overspending by defense contractors. One award of $13.4 million was given to Chester Walsh, whom a judge cited for "performing a service to the United States" when he alerted the United States government to alleged fraud by General Electric in sales to the Israeli military.[31] Another award of $7.5 million was given to Christopher Urda for blowing the whistle on an item overspent by $77 million.[32] One can imagine such people as heroes from the government side, while those in industry consider them traitors.

The use of police informers is, of course, very widespread. Understandably, they enjoy certain protection from the courts. Nevertheless, the Supreme Court of Canada correctly notes: "As long as crimes have been committed, certainly as long as they have been prosecuted, informers have played an important role. . . . Whatever their motives, the position of the informer is always precarious and their role fraught with danger."[33] In the United States, it was observed, "Often they are punished more harshly than the wrongdoers themselves."[34]

One classic case involves policeman David Durk, who informed on his own police department in New York City over many years. He first received great public recognition and then became increasingly ostracized.[35] Criminal defense lawyer Lawrence Goldman, who knew Durk's work well, described Durk as a "'zealot,' but a non-zealot could never have done what he did." He also paid tribute to his work for New York: "In terms of the history of this city, he made a tremendous difference, and how many people can you say that about? It's societally wrong what happened to him. Somebody, somewhere, should give him some money and say, 'Durk, go be Durk.'"[36]

Another classic case of "informing" or "whistleblowing" is that of Peter Buxtun, a Jewish social worker–lawyer, who became aware of the U.S. government using black prisoners as human guinea pigs in syphilis research without actually treating them. He could not let the matter rest. At great personal sacrifice, he exposed and subsequently wrecked the study that had gone on for forty years. Was he a traitor to the medical research group, indeed to the U.S. government? He was clearly an informer, but he betrayed neither his own conscience nor the powerless blacks who were victims of the experiment.[37] Who would be prepared to say that he betrayed the government—or the American people?

An intriguing case from modern Israeli history is that of Mordecai Vanunu, who moved to Australia and handed over secrets relating to Israel's atomic weapons industry to a London newspaper in 1986. The Israeli government understandably considered him a traitor, kidnapped him in September 1986, and after a secret trial imprisoned him (in strict solitary confinement) for eighteen years. Vanunu believed he was making the world a safer place, arguing that he was also acting in the best interests of Israel, contending that its ultimate security could only be threatened by the amassing of atomic weapons.

One does not have to take sides to see how complex such issues can become, especially when people have the courage to act on their consciences. The matter is complicated when the informers switch to a different religion or ideology, as Vanunu had done by moving to Australia and becoming a Christian prior to his abduction and arrest by Israeli authorities.[38]

But one reviewer, Paul Foot, concludes: "Vanunu is a constant deterrent to all the other potential informants who could enrich and democratize the world by passing on secrets which should not be secret at all. [He] did the world an enormous service by telling the truth about his country's nuclear arsenal."[39]

To betray someone, according to the Oxford Dictionary, is to "give up treacherously (a person or thing) to an enemy."[40] It can also mean to be disloyal to a friend, to lead astray, or to reveal treacherously. In those terms, it is hard to conceive how Judas could have betrayed Jesus.

If we want a modern example of a betrayal, surely it is that of a parent or stepparent who abuses a child, sexually or otherwise. Or a politician elected to guard the environment who abuses that trust and encourages exploitation for purposes of greed. Or spouses who do not live by their marriage vows. Or the tens of thousands of fathers who ignore support payments and thumb their noses at court orders to care for their children, and instead desert them.

Betrayal involves doing something contrary to what the rules of the relationship demand. Is there not a far deeper betrayal in the action of one supervisor, police officer, professor, pastor, priest, nun, or rabbi who uses a position of power to physically and emotionally abuse a student, parishioner, or client than in anything Judas did? Since Jesus knew it was going to happen and even according to some accounts designated the one who would hand him over, it hardly can be called a "treacherous" act.

In the area of church life, Joseph Parker suggests that church bureaucrats and politicians who try to alter the direction of the church without concern for the spiritual side are as guilty of betraying Jesus as was Judas. "The spiritual kingdom of Christ has suffered severely at the hands of men who have been proud of their diplomacy and generalship . . . of elaborating intricate organizations." He inveighs against the "policy of dexterous managers" in the church.[41]

A Contractual Relationship

It is my hypothesis that Judas abided by the implied contractual relationship established in the Jesus community as fully as any other disciple. The earliest sources show no evidence that he violated this contract more flagrantly than did any other disciple. At the very least, the burden of proof is on those who believe he did violate this covenant. That proof cannot content itself with generalities; it has to spell out specifically how Judas betrayed Jesus by doing something that Jesus did not want to have done and that he did not anticipate. As far as the early Christian community is concerned, Judas did one thing that hurt them deeply: he left and did not return. Peter left, too, as did every one of the group. But they returned. Judas did not.

Recent interpreters of Judas have taken various approaches to his act. To say that all people are, in fact, betrayers of one sort or another (and therefore it behooves us not to make too much of Judas's betrayal) is a truism that is not helpful to an understanding of what Judas did and why.[42] Then there is the approach of Werner Vogler, who concludes that the so-called betrayal was merely a breach of trust. Each of the disciples is guilty of this breach, but Judas was the first in the chain, as Karl Barth put it. Vogler pinpoints the deed of Judas as leaving Jesus before any of the other disciples did. Judas eventually went over to the other side, to the opponents of Jesus, where he was when Jesus was captured. "That and only that could have been the historical deed of Judas."[43] Vogler's position, however, does not take seriously enough the fundamental meaning of the word "to deliver over."

Klauck comes close to sharing that point of view. He insists that the historical kernels of the Judas traditions in the New Testament are: "Judas turned away from Jesus, outwardly and inwardly, and in the events surrounding the capture of Jesus played in some way an unpraiseworthy role. What he did qualitatively separated him from the desertion and failure of the rest of the disciples."[44]

Klauck also ventures into the darkest chamber of all, speculation about Judas's motives. He rules out the possibility of bribery, greed, and/or the desire for money, and certainly rules out the possibility that Judas was, from the beginning, a hypocrite. He concludes:

> Independent of all that he might have become he was in the first place this: a disciple of the Lord, like the others, a faithful and loyal travelling companion [*Weggefährte*] of Jesus. The least speculative seems still that explanation which traces his deed back to an inner journey in which he became deeply disillusioned with preconceived Messianic expectations. This disillusionment must have been the more acute, the more things came to a head in Jerusalem, the more clear it became that everything was heading for a catastrophe and the less hope existed for a powerful inbreaking of the messianic Kingdom.[45]

Summary

Neither Judas nor Jesus was prepared for God's new way of achieving victory, but each of them carried out their part and God's purpose was achieved through them. It is unfair to blame Judas for the role he played, just as it would be to blame Jesus for his. Each played his part with an uncertain script and with no assurance of how the drama would come out. Just as Jesus in the last analysis obeyed his father, so Judas also obeyed his master. Their integrity and the integrity of their actions is not for us to judge, since we are the beneficiaries of their actions. Both Judas and Jesus made an unparalleled contribution to human emancipation by transcending the ambiguity of their actions.

What precisely was Judas's contribution? I submit that in the grand scheme of things, it was quite modest. In discussions with Jesus, he had often heard Jesus criticize the Temple hierarchy. When Judas reminded Jesus that his own advice had always been to rebuke the sinner directly, Jesus may have said that an occasion to confront the high priest directly had not appeared. Perhaps at that point Judas offered to arrange it, hoping that the process of rebuke would work. At the same time, he may have questioned Jesus about his own faithfulness to his mission. All of this could have led to a plan whereby Judas would arrange a meeting with Jesus and the high priests, each agreeing to that meeting on their own terms and with their own hopes for the outcome. This role in the "handing over" was later transformed into a more sinister one, especially after Judas died at his own hand. Whether the reader is able to accept this interpretation of the earliest traditions available to us, I submit that it is at least as plausible as the very negative view of Judas that still pervades the church but rests on a very shaky foundation.

Notes

1. Daube, *Collaboration with Tyranny in Rabbinic Law,* 8.

2. Derrett, "The Iscariot," 15.

3. Tacitus, *The Annals of Imperial Rome,* trans. Michael Grant, 203, 205.

4. Tacitus, *The Annals of Imperial Rome,* 4.30, trans. C. H. Moore.

5. Büchsel concludes: "Hebrew equivalent is מסר" (*KTWBNT,* 2, 172:7).

6. Derrett, "The Iscariot," 2–23. Brown-Driver-Briggs give only three references to it in the Hebrew Bible: Num 31:16; Num 5:6; 2 Chron 36:14 for certain, and one possible one (Num 31:5). In none of these cases is it certain that we are dealing with the word as it was used later.

7. See Levy, *Neuhebräisches und Chaldäisches Wörterbuch über Talmud und Midrasch,* 176–179; and Ginzberg, *Legends,* 4:212–214. In contrast, Jastrow, *A Dictionary of the Targumim, the Talmud,* 810–811, has only a few entries. A thorough study of these usages and the practice itself is much needed. A beginning has been made by D. Flusser, "Some of the Precepts of the Torah."

8. Derrett, "The Iscariot," 9.

9. Daube, *Collaboration,* 8. His first two chapters provide a fine summary of this matter. See also the very helpful article on "Informers" by various authors in *JE,* 3 (1971): cols. 1364–1373 and also in *EnJ,* 9 (1905): 42–44.

10. Daube, *Collaboration,* 19, 25.

11. Daube, *Collaboration,* 25–26. David Flusser kindly read this section and comments: "מָסַר never means to betray, but always 'deliver,' '*ausliefern*' [his italics]. If Jesus has commanded Judas to do it, there is no blame in it. Naturally if one 'ausliefert' a man to the enemy (or to the colonial power), then it is a crime for which there is no pardon" (personal letter, July 25, 1993).

12. Derrett, "The Iscariot," 4.

13. Text quoted from Baumgarten, "Hanging and Treason in Qumran and Roman Law," *Eretz-Israel*, 7–16, here 11.

14. Derrett, "The Iscariot," 5.

15. Used more than sixty-eight times as a verb by Josephus and about twenty-three times in various noun forms. During the Augustan period, informers flourished. (See above, 62.)

16. The same term is used in Acts 23:30 in the case of Paul. For full evidence, see Bauer, *Lexicon*, 6th ed. Also see Liddell and Scott.

17. The difficulty of this reading is evident from the variant introduced.

18. Cohn, *The Trial and Death of Jesus*, 36–37.

19. Cohn, *The Trial*, 79, 83. He introduces the element of "treachery" and on those terms he is right.

20. Derrett, "The Iscariot," 8; idem, "Miscellanea: A Pauline Pun and Judas' Punishment," 132–133; and idem, "Haggadah and the Account of the Passion," *DRev* 29 (1979): 308–315, esp. 313. Joseph's brother Reuben is also rejected as an informer, Ginzberg, *Legends*, 1:415.

21. See the section on the expectation of the divine *symmachy* in the later Zealot battle for Jerusalem in Schwier, *Tempel und Tempelzerstörung*, 156–170. I see no reason why these same hopes and dreams could not have been alive in the hearts of many, if not all, of Jesus' disciples and indeed in Jesus himself.

22. As Windisch put it, "The death of the . . . Messiah is the proof of his deception and the demise of his cause," *Der messianische Krieg*, 33.

23. Schleiermacher, *Life*, 388.

24. Brown, *Death*, 119–120.

25. G. Schwarz, *Jesus*, 26. In Lindsey's *A Hebrew Translation of the Gospel of Mark*, whenever παραδίδωμι is connected with the action of Judas, the word in Hebrew is מסור (*masor*). The NEB provides illustrations of bad translations, e.g., Matt 26:15: "What will you give me to betray him to you?" and good ones: Matt 27:4: "I have brought an innocent man to his death," and 27:18: "For he knew it was out of malice that they had brought Jesus before him." In each case the same verb, παραδίδωμι, is used.

26. In some manuscripts, at least. The assumption that Judas is not included in this prayer must be rejected. For he, above all, along with the other disciples, had no comprehension of what he was doing. See against, among others, Halas, cited above. This text is dealt with below, 124–27.

27. See the excellent treatment of this point in Kugel, *In Potiphar's House*, 214–246. I am grateful to Krister Stendahl for alerting me to this book.

28. Morison, *Who Moved the Stone?* here 37. This immensely popular book, written by a layperson, has made a deep impression, for it is closely reasoned and sensibly argued. Note that through translation into German (1961) it has also had an impact on German scholarship; see Schwarz.

29. Schlatter, *Matthäus*, 738.

30. Schlatter, *Matthäus*, 737.

31. *Globe and Mail*, Dec. 7, 1992.

32. See *New York Times*, July 19, 1992, "Week in Review," 2.

33. *Globe and Mail*, Sept. 8, 1992, A22.

34. *New York Times*, June 13, 1993, "Week in Review," 6.

35. James Lardner, The Whistle-blower," *New Yorker*, July 7, 1993: 52–70, and July 12, 1993: 39–59.

36. Lardner, *New Yorker,* July 12, 1993: 56.

37. The story is well told in the book by J. H. Jones, *Bad Blood: The Tuskegee Syphilis Experiment.* Myron and Penina Glazer studied sixty-four whistleblowers, *The Whistleblowers,* 1989.

38. See *Globe and Mail* (Toronto), "Prisoner of Conscience," by Mordecai Briemberg, Sept. 30, 1988: A7, and the story of the film made on Vanunu's act in *Jerusalem Post,* Jan. 3, 1990, 2, and *Globe and Mail,* Jan. 3, 1990. See also the book by Cohen, *Nuclear Ambiguity: The Vanunu Affair.*

39. *London Review of Books,* Oct. 22, 1992: 11.

40. Webster's has four meanings: (1) To lead astray, esp. seduce, (2) to deliver to an enemy by treachery, (3) to fail or desert, especially in a time of need, (4) to disclose unintentionally or in violation of confidence.

41. J. Parker, *The Inner Life of Christ,* 3:351–352, here 352.

42. See the remarks about this approach in Dieckmann, *Judas,* 322.

43. Vogler, *Judas,* 35.

44. Klauck, *Judas,* 54.

45. Klauck, *Judas,* 55.

CHAPTER FIVE

JUDAS AS SEEN
THROUGH THE EYES
OF MARK

In sober reality, the word ascribed in the later account in many manuscripts of Luke, "Father, forgive them; for they know not what they do," is in strict accord with Mark's theological appraisal of the reason for the senseless and stupid acts of both friends and foes. . . .

The Gospel of Mark is very far from being pure history untouched by theology. Rather it is theological to the core, rivalling the Fourth Gospel for that distinction.

—M. S. Enslin[1]

The Gospel of Mark is the earliest written Gospel still extant. Generally it is dated around the year 70 C.E. and attributed to an unknown person, written at an unknown place. The author shows no interest in historical questions of the usual sort (What happened, when? What relation does event A have to event B?) but rather seems keenly interested in telling the reader something about the identity of Jesus as both Son of God and Son of man. The Gospel stresses that the disciples were not aware of Jesus' true nature, although the author also seeks to describe the foreknowledge of Jesus. His knowledge of the suffering that was to befall him has a strong place in this Gospel. Mark also describes the mighty acts that Jesus performed in "making all things good" (7:37). But perhaps most keenly, it is irony that pervades Mark's story.

At the heart of this irony lies the rejection of Jesus by humankind, beginning with his immediate family circle (Mark 3:21; cf. 31–35) and extending to his closest disciples. It is important that we allow Mark to speak his own words. For if we stay with the meaning of the word παραδίδωμι (*paradidōmi*) as we defined it in chapter 4, we note with some surprise that the foreknowledge of Jesus is not invoked to designate the one who is to "hand

over Jesus." Nor does Mark exploit the irony of a "betrayer" coming from
within the inner circle. This can only mean that, for Mark, there was no
tradition of a traitor as we have generally understood it.[2] Amazing as it may
seem, in Mark "Jesus does not identify Judas as the traitor, but contents
himself with a veiled allusion, couched in the language of scripture."[3]

This analysis of Mark's portrait of Judas Iscariot seeks to avail itself of the
pertinent results of all the modern tools for Gospel research: literary criticism, form criticism, and redaction criticism.[4] Regrettably, within the limited scope of this work, it will be impossible to do a detailed study of each
of the Gospels. Our focus will be on what each Gospel says about Judas.

The high point of Mark's Gospel is the passion narrative. The path of
Jesus goes from Galilee to Jerusalem, from his mighty works among the
masses to his complete humiliation by crucifixion in the city of Jerusalem.
Scattered throughout the narrative are Mark's indications of the suffering
that lies ahead of the Son of man;[5] and indeed there are several indications
that Jesus himself foresaw this suffering as part of divine necessity, speaking
the word openly (παρρησία, 8:31) although, at the same time, asking the
disciples not to speak about it.[6]

In any case, the disciples are consistently too dense to discern the nature
of Jesus' kingdom concept or too devoid of faith to accept the shape that
Jesus' mission is taking. On one occasion, Mark gives the disciples the benefit of the doubt by saying that they could not understand the prophecy
(ῥῆμα) he was telling them but were afraid to question Jesus (9:32).

Theodore Weeden concludes that "Mark's polemical master stroke was
his character assassination of those whom his opponents claimed as mentors,
the disciples."[7] Jesus teaches and encourages an inclusive, suffering discipleship commensurate with an open, suffering messiahship. The disciples, by
contrast, appear as advocates of a divine man (θεῖος ἀνήρ) Christology: they
"hold in contempt" the humiliation Jesus teaches, and instead parade their
own exclusive superiority over others. Throughout the Gospel, "Jesus and
the Twelve remain at loggerheads" over the proper understanding of messiahship and discipleship. "It is a Christological controversy that is never resolved," says Weeden.

Consequently, Mark is intent on totally discrediting the disciples and is
"assiduously involved in a vendetta against them." Even though the disciples
are specially selected to extend Jesus' ministry, and though they are pecu-
liarly well placed as confidants of Jesus and recipients of special revelation,
their position relative to Jesus progressively and precipitously deteriorates
throughout the Gospel. One can see it moving from unbelievable imper-
ceptiveness (1:1—8:26), through ever-widening misconception (8:27—
14:9), to complete rejection (14:10—16:8).[8] "Surprisingly," says Weeden,
"*Judas plays only a subordinate role in these proceedings; the real villain of the*

piece, the figure in whom is crystallized all of the disciples' obtuseness and hostility, is Simon Peter."[9]

The turning point of the Gospel, the point at which the disciples' true colors are unfurled, occurs at 8:27-33 at Caesarea Philippi. Peter, acting as spokesman for the Twelve, confesses Jesus to be a Messiah of the divine man (θεῖος ἀνήρ) type, an ascription flatly denounced by Jesus (=Mark) as satanic.[10]

From this it has been concluded that Mark's congregation did not have a theology determined by the cross.[11] Perhaps its members found a loftier Christology more to their liking. Other scholars make a detailed comparison of Peter and Judas and refer to John 13:20 as the "final sifting" of the disciples. Judas is sifted out, and Peter comes dangerously close.[12]

Judas is hard to fit into the Gospel writer's view of what Jesus represented. It is therefore no surprise that Mark says very little about Judas and attributes no particular motive to his actions. It may also be that at this stage, the early church had little interest in Judas' role.[13] The earliest Christians seem to have been captured by the conviction that what had happened with Jesus was willed by God and was directed solely by the divine force of love.

Heinz Gunther challenges the position that Jesus had already summoned a group of twelve and forecast Judas's betrayal as a pre-Easter event. Gunther instead follows Vielhauer in concluding:

> It is important to note that it was a psalm (Ps 41:9) which enabled the later church to overcome apologetically the embarrassment which Judas' betrayal of Jesus must have meant for the community's Christology. Jesus' allegedly intimate relationship with Judas (a relationship first prompted [sic] by Ps 41:9) was later worked back into Jesus' earthly life.[14]

To consider the "association of Judas with the twelve as a theological postulate" with no historical proof may be within the acceptable confines of current scholarly method, but it defies all common sense. What earthly reason would the Gospel writers have to invent Judas as a member of the twelve? A review of the Markan evidence on the role of Judas is in order.

For Mark and his community, Judas is of little direct interest; he is simply the one who "handed over" (3:19; 14:10, 43). By name he appears only three times. Nevertheless, three parts of the Judas tradition that Mark appropriated from an earlier source are traceable:

A. Mark 14:43, 46

> Then Judas, one of the twelve, appeared, and with him a crowd[15] with swords and clubs from the high priests; . . . they laid hands on him and captured him.[16]

Here, in what is perhaps the oldest layer of redaction (in other words, a pre-Markan source), it is simply reported that while Jesus was speaking, Judas, one of the Twelve, appeared[17] with an armed group that had been sent by the chief priests, lawyers, and elders, who seized Jesus and held him fast. The designation "Iscariot" is missing and the verb παραδιδόναι (*paradidonai,* "to hand over") is not attached directly to Judas (v. 44 not being a part of the pre-Markan tradition), thus attesting to the antiquity of the tradition. At the same time, his source tells us that Judas, whom the reader presumably knows, comes with the arresting party to the garden to apprehend Jesus. No explanation is given as to what Judas's role is and why he is there. The verb "to be present" or "appear" is deliberately bland. Most remarkable of all is the abrupt way in which Judas appears at the arrest when he has not figured in the table discussion at all. The reader is not prepared for this abrupt appearance.

In the final edited form, the text also informs us that "the scribes and elders accompanied the delegates from the chief priests." Mark also provides additional information: the means of identification was a kiss. (See excursus at the end of chapter 6.)

B. Mark 14:18 and 14:21

Slightly more recent pieces of tradition make up the two reports in 14:18 and 14:21. The section is entitled "Jesus Foretells His Betrayal" in Kurt Aland, *Synopsis.* The standard commentaries and also the German heading in Aland when they speak of the designation of the betrayer, or the "exposing" (*Entlarvung*=unmasking) of the betrayer, misread this text. As Schenke observed, the name of Judas does not appear in this context, nor is there even an indication of a specific disciple. "There can be no reference to an unmasking or exposure of the traitor."[18]

i. Mark 14:18

And as they were reclining and eating Jesus said: "Truly I tell that one of you will deliver me;[19] one who eats with me."

It has generally been assumed that we have here an allusion to Ps 41:10 (LXX Ps 40:10) and its lament that even a bosom friend, literally, "the person of my peace" (ὁ ἄνθρωπος τῆς εἰρήνης μου), can turn against one. Taken in that way, this may be an allusion to the self-designation Jesus gave his disciples in Luke 10:6.[20] They were children of peace, with all that term implies, and one of those children of peace—specifically one who ate with him—would separate from the disciple group. Some explanation for their sadness must be given and this pericope seeks to provide it. The peace that

Jesus admonishes his disciples to pursue especially through eating (Mark 9:50) is not a reality.

The structure of this sentence in Mark is awkward. Nevertheless, it is not necessary to assume that the story of the deliverer/informer arose out of the Old Testament text, as Bultmann holds.[21] Matthew's reluctance to use the Old Testament text, in this instance, may have come from his general reluctance to use the psalms;[22] we can then safely attribute the insertion of the words from the psalm to Mark's final editing. The other Gospels may have wished to avoid it in order to avoid duplicating references to the supper.

Eating was a bonding event even more in first-century times than it is today. For the Jesus community, it must have been a time of great joy and celebration, especially since there is evidence that the community did not always have food, which therefore meant they could not take eating for granted. The meals around Passover would have been especially intimate and joyous. The note of sadness that Jesus introduced needed to be placed into perspective. Mark, by selecting this psalm, tries to do so. His overall approach to the Old Testament is quite different from that of Matthew and Luke. Mark is aware of a vast time differential between the Old and the New Testament and he seeks to overcome that by "re-presenting the past in the present."[23]

Thus this pericope reports that as the disciples sat at supper, Jesus predicted that one of them now eating would be the critical divine agent of handing over. He does not reveal who that person is.

ii. Mark 14:21

Because the Son of man goes just as it is written about him. Too bad for that man through whom the Son of man will be handed over. Better for him if that man had never been born.[24]

This woe pronounced by Jesus upon the one who will deliver him has been a strong factor in the negative portrait of Judas. Most research, however, deals with the woe form in the Hebrew prophets. There is, consequently, no agreement on its meaning in the New Testament. Some scholars assume it is equivalent to a curse. Nevertheless, one writer concludes: "In the New Testament οὐαί expresses sympathetic sorrow rather than condemnation."[25] The sequence of woes upon the scribes and Pharisees in Matthew 23 is considered denunciatory, but the "undertone of sorrow is not absent." And "the woe concerning the fate of Judas (Matt 26:24; Mark 14:21; Luke 22:22) has acute sorrow uppermost: 'alas for that man.'" But the divine wrath is also an element, for the expression "that man" applied to one still in the supper room suggests that severance from Christ had, in effect, already taken place: "Judas was putting himself outside of God's mercy."[26]

In New Testament sources, the woe formula appears first in Paul. "Woe is me, if I preach not" (1 Cor 9:16). Surely in Paul's case the meaning is not that God would punish him if he did not preach; so why is the woe for Judas seen as putting him outside God's mercy? Why not take the word as an "interjection of pain, lament and above all a warning or a threat"?[27] It appears in the triple tradition: Mark 14:21//Matt 26:24//Luke 22:22.

What is the significance of this cry of woe? Does it support the notion of perdition or damnation for Judas? Matthew uses the term "woe" some eleven times in his Gospel, with heavy concentration in chapter 23 where Matthew's Jesus is lamenting the present state of Jewish leadership. Luke uses it only in materials he owes to Q and to Mark, with the exception of the Sermon on the Plain and here. Luke uses it a total of ten times. Mark uses it only twice, here and in an apocalyptic context in Mark 13:17.

The cry of woe never appears in John's Gospel but frequently does in the Apocalypse. The clue to its understanding is to be found in the prophetic oracle and lament.[28]

Waldemar Janzen, who has made a thorough study of this word in the Hebrew scriptures, notes that the woe cry "can undergo a metamorphosis from grief and mourning to accusation, threat and even curse." This metamorphosis is visible in the Old Testament itself "so that we are able to trace an unbroken continuum in the function of the woe-cry, a continuum which, in arc-like manner, spans those *hoy*-words clearly expressive of funerary lamentation and those which are hurled against a slayer, literal or metaphorical, in a spirit of bitterness and revenge."[29] The potential of the *hoy* formula is to express contrast, reversal from an acceptable life situation to gloom and darkness.[30]

Hillers notes that the cry is sometimes impersonal, but he tries to argue for a more personal character of these oracles, a "prominent vocative element." Sometimes the woe or *hoy* passage could contain direct address, but no threat is directed to the evildoers (Isa 5:11-12.18-23).

H. W. Wolff, however, argues for a more impersonal tone. "The person threatened is never addressed; he is never characterized by a name, but always only by his deed."[31]

The usage here in Mark has to be related to the context. Clearly it is an impersonal usage and pronounces, at least in Luke, simply the regret and pain that Jesus feels toward the one who has been chosen to carry out this role. That person remains unidentified here in all three texts, although an editorial addition in Matthew leaves the reader in no doubt as to who it is. Like Paul, who cried a woe to himself if he did not proclaim the gospel (1 Cor 9:16), so Jesus pronounces a woe on the one chosen to deliver him up.

He does not say why. It could be because of the misunderstanding that inevitably would arise from the act. The woe may have been expressed out of sympathy for the rejection that the informer would experience from his fellows. It could also be that Jesus knew that whoever carried out the deed would need the intellectual strength and spiritual maturity to be able to think through its implications. Doing the will of God, as Jesus himself knew well, was not easy. If he himself was so misunderstood, how much more so would be the informer.

We must guard against any equation of the woe with a curse.[32] A woe in ancient Judaism was an expression of love. Just as the prophets spoke their woes to the people of Israel in ancient days, so Jesus spoke his woes to those who would live with the reversals the kingdom brings. He had a special concern for the informer, without whom apparently he could not carry out his mission, but whose participation most certainly would lead to woes. Any reading of this saying other than a cry of compassion from the master on behalf of one of his disciples is a serious misreading of the text. Rudolf Schnackenburg notes that the woe is "an ancient prophetic stylistic form meant to warn and threaten. . . . Its sharpness must not promise the traitor eternal damnation, for it is a Jewish manner of speaking, seen elsewhere as well, and a hyperbole similar to Mark 9:42."[33]

Rudolph Pesch sees this whole passage as determined by the theme of the suffering of the just person, the *passio justi* theme. Woe cries are evident among the traditions of the just man.[34] The woe cry is then particularly poignant because of the question: If this is what happens to a just person, what will happen to the world, where there are so many unjust people (Luke 23:31)? The woe presupposes an apocalyptic insight on the part of the speaker. But we do not need to accept the idea that "the man who had better not been born is cursed."[35]

To assume that Jesus curses Judas confuses the very clear words employed by the New Testament to describe curses. One need only compare the blessings and curses of the New Testament with those found at Qumran to see the precise and extensive difference that exists between the communities. Jesus instructed his disciples to "bless those who curse you" (Luke 6:28); it would hardly be the case that he would curse one of his own disciples. He no more curses "the deliverer" here than he does the women who are expectant with child or suckling during the hard times, connected with the abomination of desolation (Mark 13:17).

That Mark and each of the Gospel writers interpreted this scene parenetically, that is, as a warning to the reader, is assumed.[36] That the one handing Jesus over participates in the holy common meal and is an intimate member of the community makes the primitive church's theme of woe plausible. For in the presence of the substitutionary atoning death of Jesus (14:22–25) we have the judgment that threatens Judas. Perhaps Pesch is right when he sees the inspiration of the spirit of Jesus working through the narrator of Mark and later in the evangelist, in the fact that a curse is not carried out.[37]

No doubt both Mark and Matthew helped later readers to misread earlier texts by adding: "It would have been better for *that man* not to have been born." For both the formula "that man" (ὁ ἄνθρωπος ἐκεῖνος)[38] and the expression "better not to have been born" have a note of despair about them that does not really fit the woe itself. Luke omits these words from his record and thus refuses to condemn Judas.

The woe is meant to bring someone to repentance.[39] Its very passionate cry is meant to awaken people to the reality of their condition. In this case, what complicates the matter is that we are dealing with an event that has been forecast long ago. It is "according to the scriptures." Those who are called upon to bring scriptures to fulfillment cannot, lamentably, at that time be called blessed.

Perhaps Jesus' perceptive powers into human nature led him to speak these words. For just as he doubted that Peter would stand the test that lay ahead, so he had even more serious doubts that the disciple entering the troubled waters of handing him over, or informing, would be able to live with the consequences of his action.

Mark portrays Jesus' own death as necessary but devastating for the person who hands him over. This tradition promotes the view that the death of Jesus was no accident, that Jesus had a premonition of it, and that, indeed, it was according to the divine plan revealed in scripture. For both Mark and Luke, the words are, as Enslin stated it, a "theological appraisal of the reason for the senseless and stupid acts of both friends and foes" (see above, beginning quote). There is an unbroken chain with three links in the course of Jesus' being handed over beginning with the inner circle of his friends whose faithfulness falters as they all desert him, his own people in the person of Caiaphas, and the worldly powers of Rome. Thus Jesus is torn from the soil that nourished him, and the community that sustained him handed him over to the powers which intended to protect him, Rome, but which ultimately condemned him to death. But above all, Jesus handed himself over.[40]

To summarize, the curse is a distinct literary type that should not be confused with the woe oracle.[41] To interpret the woe as a curse, as has been traditionally done,[42] is a serious misunderstanding of the text. A prophetic woe is more like the lament cry. It is quite different from a curse, which invokes divine power against the one being cursed and therefore is, in effect, a prayer for the mobilization of divine power toward that person's destruction. To take this woe spoken by Jesus as a curse against Judas lies deeply embedded in Christian history. The reader will have to decide whether that is truly the case in the earliest strata of the Gospel tradition.

C. Mark 14:10-11

A later development is evident in Mark 14:10-11, where mention is made of a financial reward offered by the leaders. The text says simply:

> And Judas Iscariot, one of the Twelve, went off to the high priests in order that he might deliver him over to them. And they, having heard it, rejoiced and promised to give him silver; and he sought an auspicious time when he might deliver him over.

This text reveals a tradition that maintains that the high priests were on the lookout for an informer. They found one in Judas and they offered him money, as was the custom in such cases. The promise of payment of money made it a binding agreement and gave it validity.

As Klauck says, because Mark refrains from psychologizing here, seeking to explore Judas's rationale, "the motives of Judas are left in the dark; the theological background of his action shines more brightly and allows us to understand 'that the actual activity lies with some one else, namely with God.'"[43]

The final redaction of Mark contains a solemn declaration by Jesus that the informer will be "one of you" (14:18), strengthened by the "amen" (ἀμὴν λέγω ὑμῖν) formula and the fact that Jesus was with the Twelve in a solemn Passover meal (14:17). His prediction comes as they are reclining for a meal. Mark heightens this historic aspect by stressing the meal component and also especially by quoting "one eating with me" (Ps 41:10).

The Hebrew form of that text speaks of the closest friend as "my man of peace." Jesus uses this psalm, which illustrates the deepest alienation that can come to the closest of friends. It has been suggested that this is a deliberate contrast between the generosity of the anonymous woman and the deal Judas made with the chief priests. "Jesus is to be delivered up to death by his 'brother' in the family of God, one who was appointed to be with him (3:14)."[44] His mother and brothers reject him as crazy or beside himself (3:21). Even his new family cannot accept him.

The disciples' reaction to his announcement is one of λύπη: deep sorrow, pain, shock, and regret. It is the way Peter felt when Jesus asked him the third time, "Do you love me?" (John 21:17). It is the verb Mark uses to describe the feelings of the ruler who could not become a disciple (Mark 10:22), and it is the feeling Matthew attributes to Jesus in the Garden of Gethsemane (26:37).[45]

Their dismay led them to question, one after the other: "μήτι ἐγώ, Not I, surely?" In this way Mark drives home the point that any one of the disciples could possibly have served as informer. Each had reason to go to the Temple leadership to blow the whistle on Jesus, for each was baffled by the direction of Jesus' work and had no idea where it was heading during those last hectic days in Jerusalem. There is little doubt that more than one disciple believed that what Jesus was doing in some way represented a potential threat to the Temple and its hierarchy. In any case, from this point onward "Mark as good as suggests that the disciples as a whole are little better than Judas."[46]

To their question, "Not I, surely?" Jesus replies: "One of the Twelve, the one who dips with me in the bowl" (Mark 14:20). Again, reference is made here to the closest of relationships, the sharing of a meal, even of a dish. Just as Judah and his brothers were eating when they decided to sell their brother Joseph, so Jesus during a meal expressed his premonition that there was enough unhappiness among the disciples about his mission that one of them would certainly communicate his concerns to the people in charge.

D. Mark 14:41-42

And he came again a third time and said to them, "Still sleeping? Still taking your rest? The matter is settled. The hour has come, behold the Son of man is to be delivered into the hand of sinners. Arise, let us go forward; behold, the one who delivers me has arrived."

Virtually the only word unique to Mark in this unit is the word ἀπέχει, which I have translated as "The matter is settled." It has been argued by Klaus Müller that it should be translated: "(The cup of wrath) has been poured." Müller provides an excellent survey of the positions taken and the difficulties and strengths of each. He concludes that the verb *apechei* (ἀπέχει) is here to be taken as the third person singular of the imperfect derived from the verb *apochein* (ἀποχεῖν), "to pour out," and connotes the notion that God poured out his anger of judgment in the cup Jesus saw before him. The hour of judgment has begun.[47]

Boobyer sees the verb applying to Judas, who in this dramatic hour faithfully fulfills his duty. "It was the hour for the (deliverer) to receive and hand over the Son of Man to death from which he would rise to universal sovereignty!"[48] Suhl follows Feldmeier in concluding: "*apechei* can only mean the remoteness (*Fernsein*) of God and should accordingly be translated, 'he is remote.'"[49] This basic experience of God's remoteness in prayer when one's need is greatest, Israel shares with other religions of the ancient Orient.

Others have seen in it a reference to Judas and his financial reward, for the term can be used to state that an account has been paid in full.

It is important to note the threefold desertion of the disciples whom Jesus brought to assist and accompany him during this heavy hour. None are of any help to him. As Jesus prays that the cup of wrath may be removed from him, his prayer cannot be answered. While the three leading disciples sleep, Judas carries out his mission. His arrival signals Jesus' call to the slumbering disciples to move on to the fulfillment of obedience of God's will.

The irony of Mark comes to its fullest flower here. The Son of man, who is to come in judgment, must first of all himself be delivered into the hands of sinners. Before administering the cup of wrath in judgment, the son must himself drink it. In both references to what is to happen to him, the word "hand over" or "deliver" is used. In the first case, God is the instrument—as the passive of the verb would suggest. It is Judas, however, who is God's agent of deliverance. Mark does not, of course, speak of him as a traitor. Later English translators gave that false lead. But the irony is still there. One of the Twelve serves to hand over the Son of man to the high priests, as had been predicted.[50] What is striking is the reference to "sinners or evil men." This reference to "sinners" is also part of Mark's irony. Originally the reference began as a prediction that the Son of man would be handed over to men;[51] then it becomes "into the hands of sinful men."[52] Apart from these three usages, the idea of turning Jesus over to sinful men does not occur elsewhere. In fact, the place where one might expect it— in the sermons in Acts—the act is excused on the grounds of ignorance: "Jesus, the same Jesus whom you handed over and then disowned in the presence of Pilate after Pilate decided to release him" (Acts 3:13).[53] The phrase about sinful men can be traced back to the Greek version (LXX) of the Psalms where the prayer to be rescued from the hands of sinners is frequent (71:4; 140:4). Rescuing the poor and vulnerable from the hands of sinners is seen as part of the character of God (82:4; 97:10). Above all, the psalm writer requests (140:8) that God not "hand me over to the sinner because of my uncontrolled desire" (μὴ παραδῷς με, κύριε, ἀπὸ τῆς ἐπιθυμίας μου ἁμαρτωλῷ). In early Christian discussion about the crucifixion, one earmark is clearly that Jesus was delivered into the hands of sinful men (Luke 24:7), but not in the earliest layers.

My translation of Mark 14:41-42 seeks to reflect the decisive steps Jesus now takes. He does not shrink back or seek to escape but meets Judas and the crowd resolutely and decisively. The agony of the garden is behind them and the crucial hour has arrived.

E. Mark 14:43-49

And immediately while (Jesus) was speaking, Judas, one of the Twelve, came on the scene accompanied by a crowd with swords and sticks sent from the high priests, the scribes, and the elders. The informer gave them a sign, previously agreed to by them, saying, "The one whom I will kiss, that's the one.

Bind him and take him away safely." And when he had arrived he came forward, saying to him: "Rabbi" and affectionately kissed him. But they laid
their hands on him and bound him. . . .

    Jesus replied, "As a thief you come out to take me with swords and sticks?
Daily I was with you teaching in the Temple and you did not arrest me. But
let the scriptures be fulfilled."[54]

In the present form of Mark, the capture of Jesus has some distinctive
features that bear on our understanding of the role of Judas. There is no
dialogue between Jesus and Judas. Judas speaks only one word, "Rabbi,"
and kisses Jesus.

    It is not clear what the word "Rabbi" signifies in this context. Was it a
word even in use at the time of Jesus? No scholarly consensus has emerged
on this topic and it could be taken here simply as a form of polite address,
"My teacher," without any hidden meaning or particular signification of
respect. Both Mark and Matthew have Judas address Jesus as "Rabbi," the
only word Judas speaks to Jesus in this context; indeed, in all of Mark. The
word "Rabbi" occurs in Mark three times (once as Rabbouni in Mark
10:51). It is always on the lips of Jesus' closest disciples: Peter twice (9:5;
11:21) and Judas once (14:45).[55] It appears another seven times in John (once
ῥαββουνί, 20:16), generally used by Jesus' disciples or by those inquiring
about discipleship.

    By using it, Mark suggests that Judas expressed his respect for Jesus: "All
four instances [in Mark] convey a sense of Jesus' particular greatness."[56] Matthew, who adds the word "Hail" (χαῖρε) to the address, goes his own path.
As John P. Meier puts it, "Strange to say, to address Jesus as 'Teacher' or
'Rabbi' (in the vocative) is for Matthew, the sign of an unbeliever, or at least
of someone not yet a true disciple. Such an address indicates that the speaker
sees Jesus merely as a human teacher and nothing more."[57] In Luke and
Matthew, Judas says nothing to Jesus except in the latter, "Hail, Teacher!"
but Jesus says something to him. John has no words pass between them at all.

    In Mark's final edited form, the text also informs us that "the scribes and
elders accompanied the delegates from the chief priests." Mark also provides
additional information: that the means of identification was a kiss.

    The kiss, Mark's editorial comment suggests, was an agreed sign desig-
nating Jesus to the arresting party. It may have had the additional advantage
of being a practice that Jesus had introduced into the group of his disciples,
for we find it later in the early church as a characteristic of the community
of believers.[58] It is an act that fits into the communal life fostered by Jesus
and his disciples.[59] Later in the church, Paul and 1 Peter admonished the
church to practice the "holy kiss" or the kiss of love (1 Peter 5:14). Jew and
Gentile came together in one community in the church and the kiss was a
public sign of their oneness in Christ. Among the disciples it also was a

symbol of the new family Jesus was seeking to bring into being. Only later in Luke is the appropriateness of this symbol for this occasion questioned. (See excursus at the end of chapter 6).

Austin Farrer, in his study of Mark, concludes that a needless mystery surrounds the role of Judas. In fact, he believes there is no mystery at all. The high priests, since they had no detective corps, wanted someone to guide their men so that they could seize Jesus without fear of a crowd gathering to rescue him. They required someone who knew his way around. Judas would do, but he was hardly irreplaceable. Had they not found Judas, they would have found someone else.

There might be a mystery about Judas's motives if his "treason" was responsible for the capture of Jesus. But Jesus' arrest was coming, one way or another, and when it was to happen was not the critical issue. According to Farrer, Judas put himself on the safe side by taking his action.

Nor is the money the critical factor. He received a fee, which one could argue aggravates the loathsomeness of his act, but John first offers the suggestion of cupidity as a motive. For Farrer, it is sufficient to see in Judas the man who made a job of being a coward. "St. Peter's premeditated heroism succumbed to danger. Judas premeditated the policy of safety."

Mark does not need to impute motives of any kind to Judas, because the most commonplace of all motives, personal safety, suffices. Those who find Mark's story unintelligible and say it is necessary to invent a whole novel to explain it find no support from Farrer. "For myself I understand Judas by looking into my own heart. I hope that I would behave better, but I see what the temptations might be." [60]

The difficulty with Farrer's approach is that "the policy of safety" could be as easily used to explain the disciples' wholesale defection. It is therefore really no explanation, and makes an even greater riddle (if not mystery) out of the role of Judas in Mark's narrative regarding what happened between Jesus and Judas during those fateful days.

What Is Missing in Mark?

In the light of what is reported in Matthew, Luke, and John, it is perhaps worth noting what does *not* surface in Mark.[61]

Mark does not refer to Judas by name at all in the story of the anointing of Jesus (Mark 14:3–9). Vociferous objections were raised by those assembled (v. 4: ἀγανακτέω) to the prodigious waste (ἀπώλεια) of this act, and the suggestion was made that the three hundred denarii be given to the poor. The woman herself was assailed (ἐμβριμάο, 14:5). The people who spoke out are referred to simply as "some of them" (τίνες), and their objections were first voiced among themselves. It is clear that Jesus strongly defended Mary's action. As far as the account in Mark is concerned, Judas does not figure in it. He may have been included in the "certain ones" of verse 4, but Mark gives us no reason to think so.

Mark makes no connection between Judas's act and the demonic. In Mark's Gospel, Jesus is engaged in a battle against the demonic and Jesus is winning. It could have served Mark's purpose as much as Luke's or John's to invoke Satan in explaining Judas's action. The fact that he did not allows us to consider the possibility that the chorus of condemnation had not yet begun its litany of rejection of Judas at the time Mark composed his Gospel.

Missing also in his record of Jesus' cry of woe is the name of the one who will hand him over (Mark 14:21). Once the identity of that person has been revealed and once Jesus has been crucified, the community—unable to deal with the complex issues involved—changed this compassionate cry of Jesus into a negative statement (indeed, a threat) and directed it against Judas, thereby beginning the process of making him a scapegoat. The irony of this process is that the original saying of Jesus specified that it was the will of God (i.e., "according to the scriptures") that Jesus himself become the sacrificial lamb.

Judas as a Member of the Jesus Community

With respect to the Jesus community, Mark makes the point that Judas was not just any false brother who had deviously moved himself into the inner circle of the Twelve but that he was chosen by God and by Jesus Christ. Judas had a place in the community, even participating in the Last Supper. He belonged to the core of the church.[62]

We know all too little about the nature of this group. But we can suggest that it reached as high a quality of community life as that which existed at Qumran, where study, worship, and deep care for one another were closely blended.[63] In such a community, the question of what happens to erring and disaffected members is a critical issue. Qumran had its own way of dealing with such members, which in cold print appears brutal and harsh. Those who were excommunicated were left to die in the desert. What the Jesus community did is not clear, unless the story of Judas provides some clue. If Judas is, in fact, the first to leave or be expelled from the community of Jesus, it is hard to conceive of a harsher or more severe rejection of "those who have left us."

Furthermore, Mark's portrait of Judas warns his community that as Jesus and his circle of disciples could not protect themselves from the defection of Judas, neither can the church protect itself from defectors. Strictly speaking, Mark knows none of this and shows no interest in making Judas look worse than any of the other disciples.

Moreover, as the church is not certain that there will be no defectors, so the individual believer is never certain whether he or she may not ultimately become a defector. The question: "Not I, surely?" (14:19) leads the readers of Mark to ask this critical question of themselves: "Am I the one you have chosen to do the will of God?" Jesus had, of course, indicated that every one of them would be scandalized by what Judas would do (Matt 26:31// Mark 14:27). Even the Fourth Gospel makes it clear that Jesus expects to be left utterly alone as each one of the disciples flees to his own house. Only God will not leave Jesus alone (John 16:32).

Finally, defection embodies changing one's loyalty, and leads, at the very least, to a woe (14:21). Perhaps this defection can even be connected with the anathema of the early church toward Judas. In the later church, the term "kiss of Judas" refers to any act of defection.[64]

Summary

What, then, may we conclude about Mark's portrait of Judas? Clearly, Judas is known to Mark and comes to him in the tradition that he uses. He appears last in the list of the Twelve offered at the beginning of the Gospel. There we have the addition "Iscariot" as well as the words "the one who handed him over."[65]

Mark is at the beginning of the written tradition of Judas. As such, he confirms that originally there was only one Judas as a member of the Twelve. His role was an ambiguous one, open to several interpretations. Compared with Peter or with the other disciples, Judas comes out relatively well. Mark provides us with no evidence that there was any alienation between Judas and Jesus. Judas was a faithful disciple of Jesus, he was one of the Twelve, and, as such, he obeyed Jesus. As a fellow member of the family of God, "one who was appointed to be with him" (3:14), he delivered Jesus up into the hands of God's appointed servants, the priests of God.[66]

Notes

1. Enslin, "How the Story Grew: Judas in Fact and Fiction," 123–141, here 138–139.

2. For a general discussion of Mark's Gospel, see Paul J. Achtemeier's article, "Mark, Gospel of," in *ABD*, 4 (1992): 541–557. In addition to the specialized studies noted below, I am indebted to Erich Auerbach, *Mimesis: A Portrait of Reality in Western Literature;* Frank Kermode, *The Genesis of Secrecy;* and Helen Gardner, *The Business of Criticism,* 101–126.

3. Vincent Taylor, *Jesus and His Sacrifice,* 113.

4. In addition to the careful work done by Hans-Josef Klauck (1987): 33–69; W. Vogler (1985, 1st ed. 1983), 39–56; and G. Schwarz (1988): 35–200, in their books

on Judas, I am also indebted to form-critical analyses of the passion narratives, in the case of Mark, in particular Schenke, *Studien zur Passionsgeschichte des Markus,* 199–280.

5. Mark 2:20; 3:6; 11:18; 12:12; 14:1–2.

6. Mark 9:9, 12, 31; 10:32–34; 14:41–42.

7. Weeden, *Mark: Traditions in Conflict,* 34 and 50.

8. C. C. Black's summary and sharp critique of Weeden's position in *The Disciples according to Mark,* 154.

9. Weeden, *Mark,* 50.

10. The summary is of Theodore Weeden's *Mark,* 34 and 50. Weeden cites G. Klein as using the term "character assassination of Peter" (the words are Weeden's), attributing it to "factions in the early church" (Klein, *Apostel,* 312). Klein speaks of a "fierce resentment against Peter (*grimmiges Ressentiment gegen Petrus*) in circles which were predisposed against him" (324). Weeden himself says: "I conclude that Mark is assiduously involved in a vendetta against the disciples. He is intent on totally discrediting them. He paints them as obtuse, obdurate, recalcitrant (51) men who at first are unreceptive of Jesus' messiahship, then oppose its style and character, and finally totally reject it."

11. Schenke, *Studien,* 279.

12. Quast, *Peter and the Beloved Disciple,* 61–62, and his discussions of G. F. Snyder, "John 13:16 and the Anti-Petrinism of the Johannine Tradition," and A. H. Maynard, "The Role of Peter."

13. Some scholars question that Judas was from the beginning a member of the Twelve. Gunther, *The Footprints of Jesus' Twelve in Early Christian Traditions,* suggests that "most likely Luke removed the Q numeral (δώδεκα) in order to avoid any allusion to Judas' possible participation in the divine judgment. Judas was apparently not part of the Q Twelve, which makes them into a post-Easter group different from the pre-Markan Twelve" (45 n. 101). Crossan accepts as "historical the treachery of Judas, who was a follower of Jesus but not one of the Twelve, an institution that did not exist until after Jesus' death," (*Who Killed Jesus?* 81).

14. Gunther, *The Footprints,* 50 n. 134.

15. ὄχλος ("mob"), a term used by Mark 38 times, Matthew 49 times, and Luke 41 times; all three Synoptic Gospels have the word here and Matthew adds "large."

16. In order to make it easier for the reader to follow, the complete text being discussed will be cited. In these first texts from Mark, we are working with the oldest traditions as they have been isolated by redaction critics. See Vogler's detailed argument, 39–56. Hyam Maccoby (34–49) treats Matthew and Mark together and, although he notices that Mark has only one Judas, his lack of interest in the historical Judas makes it difficult for him to see Mark's unique role in the formation of the Judas traditions. The best treatment of Mark's passion narrative complete with extensive bibliography is Raymond Brown, *Death,* 46–57, 77–85.

17. Only Mark has the rather innocuous verb παραγίνομαι (draw near), which occurs only here in his Gospel. It appears elsewhere relatively frequently in Matthew, Luke, and John. Its usage here is overlooked in Arndt and Gingrich's translation of Bauer's fourth edition (1957).

18. Schenke, *Studien,* 209.

19. Schenke states that the word παραδίδωμι ("hand over") here is devoid of theological reflection and that it may have been suggested by the earlier formation

of Mark 14:21b. He notes that the usage of the term here is different from the rest of Mark (*Studien*, 270 n. 1).

20. See W. Klassen, "'A Child of Peace.'" Its direct rootage in the psalm is rejected by Schenke, *Studien*, 211.

21. Bultmann suggests three phases: (1) the Lukan formulation without any OT influence (Luke 22:21), (2) the Markan form with a latent influence of the OT, and (3) the Johannine form with an explicit OT text cited (13:18) (*Geschichte*, 284). As Suhl has noted, there is a contradiction in the argument. If Luke is original, then we would surely expect a reference to the OT there. There is none. Alfred Suhl, *Die Funktion der alttestamentlichen Zitate*, 51.

22. Suhl, *Funktion*, 51.

23. Suhl, *Funktion*, 167.

24. Daube's essay "Black Hole" provides parallels to this sentence.

25. Hillyer, in *NIDNTT*, 1051–1054. This quote is from p. 1052. E. Gould says, "This is not a malediction . . . but a solemn announcement of Divine judgment" (*St. Mark*, ICC, 1912: 263).

26. Hillyer, in *NIDNTT*, 1053.

27. Balz, in *EWNT*, 2:1320–1322. Collins, *ABD*, 6:946–947, states that the word denotes "pain, discomfort, or unhappiness."

28. Waldemar Janzen, *Mourning Cry and Woe Oracle*; and Delbert Hillers, "*Hoy* and *Hoy*—Oracles: A Neglected Syntactic Aspect." NT scholars seem never to have analyzed the more than thirty usages in the NT and try to ascertain what they might signify. There is, e.g., no article on it in the *IDB*. The word does not even appear in the index of Kittel's *TWNT*.

29. Janzen, *Mourning Cry*, 39.

30. Janzen, *Mourning Cry*, 87.

31. Cited in Hillers, "*Hoy*," 185.

32. Vincent Taylor, *Jesus and His Sacrifice*, 112: "The 'Woe' (Mk. xiv.21) is not a curse, (cf. Mk. xiii.17) but an expression of deep sadness and of warning."

33. R. Schnackenburg, *Markus*, 2:240. See Limbeck, "Judasbild," 97.

34. Five in *EthEn* 92; 91:1–10; 18f., 94–105. L. Ruppert, *Gerechte*, 139, assumes that there is a collection of such woe oracles that anticipates the suffering of the righteous and their martyrdom. See R. Pesch, *Das Markusevangelium* (Herder, 1980), on Mark 14:21.

35. Pesch, ad loc., cites Job 3:3ff. and Sir. 23:14, which make the opposite point. See, however, Billerbeck, *Kommentar*, 1 (1922): 989ff.

36. Against Pesch, ad loc.

37. Pesch, *Markus*, 353.

38. Lev 17:4, 9; 20:3, 4, 5 (LXX).

39. So rightly Schürmann, *Das Lukasevangelium*, 1:338–341. Swete writes: "The woe is not vindictive, or of the nature of a curse; it reveals a misery which Love itself cannot prevent" (*St. Mark*, 314).

40. Gerhardsson, "Jesus." "The 'handing over' by Judas (a regular or proper 'betrayal') is completed by the disciples of Jesus as all leave him in the lurch and draw back from him, all defect, desert him and flee" (271). One only asks how he can be so sure that the act of Judas is based on "falsehood and enmity" and that it was a genuine betrayal, especially since his nuanced treatment of *paradidōmi* and its antecedents in the Hebrew Bible does not lead to that conclusion.

94   J U D A S

41. In addition to Delbert Hillers, and above all the thorough study of this literary type by Waldemar Janzen, cited above, see R. E. Clements, "The Form and Character of Prophetic Woe Oracles," 17–29. In the article "Woe in the NT" in *ABD* 6:1992: 946–947, R. F. Collins unfortunately does not treat this occurrence of the woe at all.

42. Schenke refers to it as a "banning curse": *Bannfluch, Studien,* 264.

43. Klauck, *Judas,* 49, citing J. Gnilka, *Das Evangelium des Markus* 2 (1979): 229.

44. Tolbert, *Sowing the Gospel: Mark's World in Literary-Historical Perspective,* 274–275, who also sees the woman as good soil, Judas as the rocky ground.

45. Mark does not use it in the garden scene; he prefers the stronger verbs, ἐκθαμβέομαι (horror), which appears only in Mark (9:15; 14:34; 16:5.6), and ἀδημενέω (dismay). Then follows "a sorrow which well-nigh kills" (Swete, *St. Mark,* 322) in v. 34. Hebrews 5:7 ("loud cries and tears") is equally picturesque.

46. Schillebeeckx, *Jesus,* 322.

47. Klaus Müller, "ΑΠΕΧΕΙ (Mk 14 41)—absurda lectio?" 99–100.

48. G. H. Boobyer, "'ΑΠΕΧΕΙ in Mark XIV.41, 47."

49. Suhl, "Gefangennahme," 298, citing Feldmeier, *Krisis,* 212–215.

50. Mark 8:31;9:31;10:32–34.

51. Mark 9:31//Matt 17:22//Luke 9:44.

52. Mark 14:41//Matt 26:45//Luke 24:7.

53. Notice the accurate translation of *paradidōmi* (παραδίδωμι) in the *JB* translation.

54. This formula, καθὼς γέγραπται, appears with slight variations some twelve times in Matthew, four times in the passion narrative, twice in Mark, only in the passion narrative, twice in Luke, never in the passion narrative (4:21; 24:44). It occurs some six times in John, three times in the passion narrative.

55. For the statistics on the Greek term διδάσκαλος ("teacher"), Viviano, *Study as Worship: Aboth and the New Testament,* 161, notes that the word appears as follows: Matthew, 12; Mark, 12; Luke, 17; John, 8; and Acts, 1. Vocative, Matt, 6; Mark, 10; Luke 12; John, 3. It refers to Jesus directly 10 times in Matt; 12 times in Mark; 14 times in Luke; and 7 times in John.

56. Hayim Lapin, *ABD,* 5 (1992): 601.

57. *ABD,* 4:637. Lapin also notes the polemical use of the term in Matthew and that Judas is the only one to address Jesus as such in that Gospel (ibid.).

58. See excursus at end of chapter 6 below. There is no reason to view the kiss as "treacherous" or demonic. Certainly no text implies that. M. Dibelius, "Judas und der Judaskuss," is correct in describing the Judas kiss as "not an especially malicious kiss of love, but the usual greeting" between a master and student. Although he bases it on K. M. Hofmann's monograph, *Philema Hagion* (Gütersloh, 1938), he overstates the frequency of the kiss and has no basis for stating that it is a kiss on the cheek.

59. Viviano, *Study as Worship,* 143–152. I believe that the place of Torah study, fellowship at table, and the procedures used to hold each other accountable at Qumran are particularly close to what Jesus and his disciples experienced.

60. Farrer, *A Study in Mark,* 195–196.

61. My last four points are adapted from Vogler's summary at the end of his discussion of Mark; see Vogler, *Judas,* 55–56.

62. Klauck, *Judas,* 63.

63. Kee, *Community of the New Age,* 1988.

64. Vogler, *Judas,* 55–56. Cf. also Klauck's conclusions.

65. "Iscariot" appears twice in Mark as the grecized form of the Hebrew, Ἰσκαριώθ (3:19; 14:10), and once in a poorly attested reading in the formula Ἰούδας ὁ Ἰσκαριώτης in 14:63.

66. Tolbert, *Sowing the Gospel,* 275.

CHAPTER SIX

JUDAS AS PORTRAYED BY THE GOSPEL OF MATTHEW

Those who, looking beneath the surface of the Gospels, discern a layer in which Judas was not a traitor but an advocate of an earthly messianic kingdom, think that they have discovered the true historical Judas. But they have only uncovered an earlier layer of the legendary Judas, at a time when he represented the Jerusalem church in its contemporary conflict with the Pauline church.

—Hyam Maccoby[1]

The Gospel according to Matthew is considerably longer than that of Mark. With respect to the passion narrative, it has been estimated that four-fifths of the Matthean passion story is identical in vocabulary and content with its Markan counterpart.[2]

At the beginning of our treatment of the various Gospels we observed that, although both the first two have extensive materials on the passion of Jesus, Matthew provides more material about Judas than does Mark. In spite of a striking degree of overlap between Mark's and Matthew's passion narrative, Matthew provides significant new material on Judas. He offers an intriguing case study of how the tradition on Judas developed.

It has been argued persuasively by Raymond Brown that Matthew is using materials from a popular tradition. This material is "marvellous, vivid, and imaginative" in those sections of Matthew (passion narrative, birth narratives) where he is not dependent upon Mark or Q.[3] He also notes that it is distinctly more anti-Jewish.

Matthew does not show as much interest in the Twelve as does Mark. In terms of frequency of usage, Matthew uses the expression "twelve disciples" and the Twelve virtually equally: "twelve disciples" four times,[4] the expression "twelve apostles" only once (10:2), and the expression "the Twelve" three times.[5] Mark, on the other hand, uses the term "the Twelve apostles" only once (3:14) and the term "the Twelve" eleven times. He never uses the numeral with the word "disciples." Luke uses the term "the Twelve" seven times in his Gospel.

Matthew describes Judas as one of the Twelve on two occasions (26:14, 47), as does Luke, in addition to listing his name among them in 10:3. Mark does so three times. The Fourth Gospel, while not providing a list of the Twelve, describes Judas as one of the Twelve only once (6:70).

Moreover, it has often been noted that many of the pejorative incidents or reactions attributed to the disciples in Mark are altered or omitted in Matthew.[6] Matthew neither idealizes nor criticizes the disciples; that does not seem to be part of his view of discipleship, nor does it fit his objectives. Matthew depicts Peter's weaknesses in the passion narrative and presents the disciples as "not ideal Christians but representative ones."[7]

In five places, where it is not in his sources, Matthew includes a reproach for the weakness of the disciples' faith.[8] Nevertheless, Judas is not singled out and the term παραδιδόται, the passive form of "hand over," becomes almost a technical term in Matthew's passion narrative. It is used "almost exclusively for the handing over of Jesus to his death."[9]

There are five accounts of Judas in Matthew:

1. The core narrative, which points to Matthew's suffering servant (παῖς) tradition and the Son of man (26:14-16).

2. Announcement of handing over (26:20-25).

3. Arrest of Jesus (26:47-56).

Neither of the last two has the word Iscariot; rather, they use the addition, "the one who handed him over," ὁ παραδίδους (26:25, 48; cf. John 18:2, 5).

4. Account of Judas's remorse (27:3-5).

5. The account of the disposal of the money (27:5-10) and Judas's death (27:5) shares characteristics with that of Luke: the Old Testament flavor and basis, the absence of the name Iscariot, tied to a place-name in Jerusalem. Both seem to be independent and unattached.

Matthew offers nothing by way of tradition that is not found in Mark, but the redactional development is notable and he has made the passion narrative "a more memorable story."[10] Three texts (26:15, 25, 50) are taken from Mark but are developed in more detail. In one of them, he quotes Judas directly (26:15). Matthew thus livens up the narrative and provides Judas with some new features. To each of the three texts he has added new materials of an editorial nature.[11] We shall look at each in turn.

A. Matthew 26:14-16

Then one of the Twelve, the one called Judas Iscariot, went to the chief
priests and said: "*What are you willing to give me if I hand him over to you?*"[12] *But
they weighed out*[13] *thirty pieces of silver.* After that he sought a good time when
he might report him to them.

Matthew adds the detail that Judas asked for money as reward for turning
Jesus in.[14] What in Mark shows up as a gleeful initiative offered by the
Temple hierarchy becomes in Matthew a bargaining point initiated by Judas. For Matthew, "silver" becomes a major motif, if not the dominant
motif that brings coherence to his narrative.[15] There is no explanation of
the reason why Judas asked for money and there is no haggling or negotia-
tion. The sum of thirty pieces has been much discussed.[16] Connections are
drawn between it and the thirty pieces of silver that were the wages of the
shepherd in Zechariah 11 and that the Lord commanded him to throw into
the Temple. While this may have had a bearing on Matthew's account of
Judas's demise, the message of the Zechariah story surely does not apply
here. There are, moreover, other biblical stories about thirty pieces of
money.

According to Exod 21:32, for example, thirty shekelim was the price one
had to pay if one's ox gored a slave (male or female), no matter what the
slave was worth or how beautiful he or she was. According to rabbinic
regulation, if a free man was gored, recompense had to be paid according
to the scale in Leviticus 27:1-8. There valuations are fixed according to the
sacred shekel:

GENDER	AGE	WORTH
Male	1 mo.–5 yrs.	5 sh
Female	"	3 sh
Male	5–20 yrs.	20 sh
Female	"	10 sh
Male	20–60 yrs.	50 sh
Female	"	30 sh
Male	60+ yrs.	15 sh
Female	60+ yrs.	10 sh

Other concerns have been raised. It has been noted, for example, that
silver coins were minted by then and did not need to be weighed. However,
the Greek verb also can mean "counted" or "measured." Pinchas Lapide
has also questioned the reference to a type of coin that had not been in
circulation for nearly three hundred years.[17]

All of these are valid concerns deserving discussion. However, for Matthew, it is important that money was part of the Judas transaction. Indeed, while John makes no mention of money passing hands, and Luke (22:5) merely mentions it, for both Matthew and Mark the exchange of money was important, although only Matthew mentions the amount and suggests that Judas took the initiative in asking for payment. John has made a point of Judas being a thief but does not attribute the deal with the authorities to greed. A strong incentive to see that as the clue to Judas's behavior is provided by John Chrysostom.[18] His considerable oratorical powers, as those of Abraham Santa Clara later, were directed at making the sin of greed responsible for what he considers a despicable act.

Whoever sees evidence here of Judas's insatiable greed should note that the amount is small indeed. Yet, if or when greed is involved, amounts are not necessarily determinative. Recently a premier of a Canadian province, who reputedly is a millionaire several times over, fell from power as a result of questionable dealings over a mere $25,000. Most important for the Judas story is the fact that Matthew constructed his own version of the story. The needs of his community determined what went into it once the basic outline of the story had been formed. The outline was given to him by the tradition of the early Palestinian church. That Judas stood in that tradition as one who had a key role in the passion of Jesus, we take as a given. That he "betrayed" Jesus for money is simply not found in those sources.

In Matthew's treatment of Judas, we need, above all, to consider the role of the Hebrew Bible. Here we do well to heed the caution of Nepper-Christensen against the "concordance method" of finding parallels. He suggests instead that we pay careful attention to a style of the Bible that carries over from the Hebrew Bible to the early Christian writings.[19] In addition, caution is recommended when suggesting that the Hebrew scriptures actually "generated" stories, such as the death of Judas.[20]

Matthew has a special interest in tracing Judas's act to a pecuniary motive, although he does not go nearly as far as John does. In the anointing story, Matthew states that "the *disciples*" were indignant at the waste (26:8), while Mark has "*certain of those present.*" But Mark escalates their anger (or perhaps Matthew softens it) by mentioning it twice (14:4, 5) and gives no indication that Judas might be driven by love for money. Matthew by implication does, although one should note that, even for Matthew, the matter of money is almost routine. There is, of course, nothing in the text as it stands which condemns this act. The negative connotation arises only when we mistranslate the word παραδίδωμι (*paradidōmi*) as "betray."

B. Matthew 26:21-25

And while they were eating with him, he said: "I solemnly tell you (i.e., please, believe me) that one of you will hand me over." And being *deeply* distressed, each one of them began to ask him, one by one: "Surely it is not I, is it, *Lord?*"

But he answered: "The one who puts *his hand* with me in the dish; that one will hand me over." [Then follows the woe, see above, [81–84].

And Judas, the one who delivered him, answered him and said: "Surely it is not I, is it, Rabbi?" He said to him: "You say so."[21]

Under the traditional interpretation that παραδίδωμι means betrayal, Judas is portrayed here as an unscrupulous man. Although he has already put into action his plan to hand over Jesus—and has already gone to the high priests, asking them how much they would give him if he handed Jesus over to them (26:14), and therefore should not even be with Jesus—in the hearing of the others, he asks: "Could it be I?" Only in Matthew, Jesus openly says to Judas: σὺ εἶπας ("You say so?").[22]

We probably do Matthew a disservice if we view Judas as being hypocritical here. Lohmeyer-Schmauch remind us that the Gospels nowhere try to psychologize Judas and that this fragment probably was formed without any knowledge of a previous meeting with the high priests, which came into the sources later.[23]

The meaning of this response and its significance are worthy of consideration. Matthew's preference for direct discourse and dialogue signifies something about his literary style, but it is also a mark of early Christian literature, especially the Gospels. According to Erich Auerbach, the literature of the New Testament deviates in this respect from ancient historians, signaling thereby that it is "written from within the emergent growths and directly for everyone. Here we have neither survey and rational disposition, nor artistic purpose."[24] It also signifies the antagonism between sensory perception and meaning that was integral to the early Christian view of reality. I shall attempt to explain how what is happening between Jesus and Judas in this discussion has a deeper meaning than what we initially perceive.

It is noteworthy that Matthew has Judas ask the question, "Surely it is not I, is it, Rabbi?" No other Gospel portrays any relationship between them whatever. We would not be fair to the text in Matthew if we see any deviousness here, on the part either of Jesus, Matthew, or Judas. There is no reason to think it improbable that Judas could have been one of the disciples who asked, "Is it I?" Nor is there any reason to assume that Jesus could not have replied as he did. Matthew has Judas address Jesus as the enemies of Jesus address him, not like the other disciples as "Lord" (cf. Matt 26:22) but as "rabbi," or as "teacher." But what was the meaning of Jesus' reply? For more than a hundred years there has been a great deal of discussion about Jesus' response.[25] A definite solution to this complex question is not in sight.

If we seek to locate the saying in its original Jewish context, three options present themselves:[26]

1. We can take σὺ εἶπας ("You say so") to mean an affirmative reply: "It is as you say." Accordingly, Jesus is saying: "You are the man" (σὺ εἶ ὁ ἀνὴρ ὁ ποιήσας τοῦτο), as Nathan said to David (2 Sam 12:7).

This option raises at least two problems: Jewish practice does not ordinarily rebuke someone so directly. There is a gentler way of allowing people to arrive at answers to their questions, especially when those questions have to do with one's judgment about oneself. Could Jesus have so directly charged Judas with "handing him over"? All Gospels agree that none of the disciples knew who was to do the assignment. In John, Jesus selects the one by giving him a morsel. He also portrays Jesus as "deeply troubled" on three occasions: on the death of his friend Lazarus (11:33), when the Greeks come to see him (12:27), and here when he announces that one of them must deliver him up (13:21). Only John describes Jesus in such non-stoic terms here. In Matthew and Mark it is a grieving moment for the disciples (Matt 26:22; Mark 14:19).

The second problem relates to the meaning of the phrase or similar phrases that appear in Greek or the Hebrew equivalent. In none of these cases does it mean an unequivocal affirmative. Nor does it here. Lohmeyer-Schmauch state quite bluntly: "Jesus' answer is neither a yes nor a no. Until now he has avoided a clear designation of the traitor. And so he does here." But since only Matthew singles Judas out by name and since he himself asks after the woe has been spoken, the reader is led to believe a veiled yes.[27]

2. We can take it as either equivocal or obscure, certainly not affirmative.

This approach fits more clearly into the way in which Jesus often dealt with people, certainly with his closest disciples. The obscurity, like the parable method of teaching, makes it possible for people to reflect on the answer and to arrive at their own judgment. Like a competent Jewish rabbi, Jesus allows the insights to come from the disciples, who learn to think for themselves and to draw their own conclusions. He seems more comfortable with questions than he does with answers.

3. Third, we can decide to equivocate but lean toward the negative. This point of view is championed by the first Jewish scholar to give major attention to this expression, Daniel Chwolson, who became ever more convinced that the saying was intentionally ambiguous.[28]

David Catchpole cites Chwolson as taking the phrase to mean that the inquirer has to make the judgment, the speaker will not; that is, don't blame the speaker for rendering the verdict, whatever it may be.[29] This approach does not suggest a direct affirmation but merely a rejection of the blame that might arise from imparting bad news. A later conclusion by Chwolson renders the translation, "Whether the matter is as you say, I allow to remain open, but I did not say it." Chwolson suggested that it is, in fact, ultimately an indignant denial that one would suggest that such a statement had been made.[30]

One of the difficulties of interpreting this response is that it has been contaminated by another text in which Jesus responds with similar words when Pilate asks him if he is King of the Jews. To Pilate's question Jesus replies: *su legeis* (σὺ λέγεις) (Mark 15:2//Matt 27:11//Luke 22:3). The high priest (only in Matthew) adjures him by the living God to say whether he is the Christ, the Son of God, and Jesus says to him: "σὺ εἶπας" ("You say so?") (Matt 26:63). Luke writes: "You say that I am" (ὑμεῖς λέγετε ὅτι ἐγώ εἰμι) (22:70), and Mark has simply: "I am who I am" (ἐγώ εἰμι) (14:62) when, at his trial, Jesus is asked whether he is indeed the Messiah.

Catchpole, for example, introduced Matt 26:25 to argue against Chwolson. Certainly Jesus did not say expressly that Judas would betray him, but this is the only respect in which σὺ εἶπας here is less than a clear affirmative. "Judas asks with the others, (22) μήτι ἐγώ εἰμι; 'It is not I, is it?' and receives the unexpected answer, 'σὺ εἶπας' [you say so?]."[31] Catchpole feels it would jar the context hopelessly to take it otherwise and so concludes that it is a clearly affirmative answer here. "In Matthew 26:25 σὺ εἶπας contains an affirmation modified only by a preference for not stating the matter *expressis verbis*."[32]

But where does that "preference" come from? For the trial narratives he concludes: "affirmative in content, and reluctant or circumlocutory in formulation."[33] This writer believes that his conclusion is incorrect with respect to the Judas interchange, as it is for the trial narrative. The best translation still is: "It is you who have said it."[34] Jesus does not judge Judas, but invites Judas to examine or pass judgment on himself; in this case, to decide for himself whether to accept the divine commission to be the agent of God who hands him over.

C. Matthew 26:47-56

And as he was speaking, behold, Judas, one of the Twelve, came with a *large* crowd with swords and clubs from the chief priests and elders *of the people*. But the one who was to turn him in gave them a sign saying: "The one whom I shall kiss, that's the one, bind him." And immediately coming to Jesus, he said, "*Hail*, Master," and he kissed him. But Jesus said to him, "*My friend, do that for which you have come.*" *Then they came forward*, laid their hands on Jesus and captured him.

And *behold, one of those with Jesus stretched out his hand*, drew his sword, and struck at the lieutenant of the high priest and lopped off the *earlobe*.

Jesus said to him: "Return your sword into its place. For all who resort to the sword,
die by the sword. Or do you think that I am not able to call upon my Father and he
even now will supply me with more than twelve legions of angels? How then would the
scriptures be fulfilled which say that this must be?"
    In that hour Jesus said to the crowds: "Why do you come after me with swords
and sticks as if I were a bandit? Did I not *sit as* a teacher daily in the Temple
and you did not capture me? *All of this has happened* in order that the scriptures
might be fulfilled." *Then all of the disciples* fled, leaving him behind.

Matthew portrays Judas as outgoing, decisive, and able to take the initiative. He highlights this character trait when Judas forthrightly meets Jesus
in the garden with a kiss and the appellation: "Hail, Master." In Mark, Judas
greets Jesus with the word "Rabbi," and in all three Synoptic Gospels Judas
kisses (or in Luke is about to kiss) Jesus. In Matthew, the ruthless Judas
carries out his act, seeks repentance by trying to return the money (Matt
27:3-5), throws it down in the Temple, and goes out and hangs himself
(27:5).

To heighten this dark picture of Judas, Matthew draws sharp contrasts
between Judas's behavior and that of others around him: the woman who
anoints Jesus' feet (26:6-13), the disciples at the table (26:20-35), and finally,
the contrast between Judas and Jesus himself (26:47-56).

And yet, Matthew's account stands alone when, after noting that Judas
discovers that Jesus is condemned to die, he describes Judas's remorse (27:3),
his declaration that Jesus is innocent (27:4), and his efforts to make restitution (27:3). Unlike Luke, Matthew does not pass judgment on Judas as
demon-possessed or ascribe any ulterior motive to his deed. The money is
too small an amount to be considered a motive and, in any case, is routine
for an act of informing.

In Matthew, Jesus relates to Judas with gentleness during these last days.
This is evidenced especially by his greeting in the place called Gethsemane.
According to Luke, Jesus addressed him by name, saying: "Judas, do you
hand over the Son of man with a kiss?" (Luke 22:48). Matthew has Jesus
addressing Judas as "friend," which he uses for no other person in direct
address: "Friend, what are you here for?" (Matt 26:50). The Greek word
ἑταῖρος ("friend") occurs only in Matthew and each time as direct address;
twice in parables (20:13; 22:12) and once here. In two cases the one addressed is committing an ungrateful action against the one who has been
generous. Here it highlights the relationship of trust that exists between
Jesus and Judas.[35] Whereas the term was used by Matthew in a context of a
subordinate who was in the wrong, "it has a deeply profound meaning that
the master who spoke a word of woe towards the betrayer (26:24), in the
moment of the betrayal addresses him with the name of a trusted member
of the inner circle," *a chaber.*[36]

The possible meanings of the words Jesus spoke to Judas in the garden

(Matt 26:50) are still debated. The words ἑταῖρε, ἐφ᾽ ὅ πάρει? may be translated variously as follows:

1. Friend, for this then you have come!
2. Friend, why you have come, I know! (a kind of *aposiopesis*).
3. Friend, why have you come?
4. Friend, have you come for this?
5. Friend, do what you have come for.[37]
6. Friend, let that be done for which you have come.
7. Friend, is this what you came for?

It appears that Matthew seeks to stress that Jesus knew in advance not only about the handing over and who would do it but also that it would be accompanied by a kiss. Of all of the possibilities mentioned above, the one suggested by F. Rehkopf makes the most sense. Since there is no doubt that the relative pronoun *ho* (ὅ) refers to the kiss, he suggests that a translation such as, "Friend, this is what you are here for!" either as an exclamation or as a question is grammatically correct. However, because of the context, he prefers the sentence in the form of a question. After extensive discussion of the various options, he concludes that the best translation in this context is: "Friend, is this what you came for?"[38] Thus it agrees with Luke fully, both in content and in tone. Neither Matthew nor Luke is dependent upon the other. They have separate oral traditions which must be old, since the formulation in Luke is pre-Lukan.

It is important to note the ambiguity of what Jesus says to Judas. Here, too, the tradition behind Matthew's text shines through and leaves us with a Jesus who does not condemn Judas. Indeed, if we take his statement here to be an exclamation of surprise, it may indicate that Jesus was surprised that the only disciple who could be counted on to do what Jesus asked of him during these dark days was Judas. Only he allowed himself to be used as an agent to achieve the divine will. It may be a recognition of true friendship and acknowledgment that the purpose for which Judas has come is the same goal that Jesus wrestled to attain in the garden: the will of God.

> These words [of Jesus to Judas] place the seal to that revelation of God, Jesus himself provides his signature, he himself knows and wills and works together to further the end toward which Judas has come, therefore he calls him his friend.[39]

In Matthew, it is only after Jesus has said these words—in effect, given his approval—that the captors come forward to take him.[40] Matthew's portrait of Judas is based on traditions found in Mark's Gospel, except for the account of his death preserved in 27:3-10. Matthew's redaction of the Markan

materials is noteworthy. The narrative becomes more lively by the introduction of direct address in 26:15, 25, 50. More important, Matthew has added
new dimensions to the portrait of Judas by introducing direct discourse. In
26:14–16, he offers additional information by providing the amount of
money Judas bargained for and received. In another passage (26:20–25), Jesus
expresses a cry of lamentation over Judas: "It would have been better for
that man if he had never been born" (v. 24; cf. Mark 14:20–21; Luke 22:22).
In Matthew's account, the ambiguity of Judas's deed is heightened by the
fact that he has already taken steps, as one of the Twelve, to hand Jesus over
(26:14–16), and despite this, joins the others in the final meal where he takes
his turn to ask, "Is it I?"

Matthew's depiction of Judas serves as an example to the community.
The transgressor or the informer is openly exposed. Peter weeps bitter tears
and finds his way to genuine repentance,[41] whereas Judas, in spite of his
remorse, exercises the final judgment on himself. This has traditionally been
seen as representing a considerable escalation of the debt laid on Judas.

At the same time, Birger Gerhardsson has demonstrated what a profound
theology of the passion is found in Matthew.[42] The themes of justice and
righteousness are central to this Gospel. It therefore comes as no surprise
that Pilate's wife in Matthew acclaims Jesus as a just man (δίκαιος, 27:19), a
verdict that Pilate, according to a strong textual tradition, confirms when
he takes some water, washes his hands, and says to the crowd: "I am innocent of this man's blood, see to it yourselves" (27:24). This signifies that, for
Matthew, Jesus suffers as a just man who carries the sins of others. Ironically,
it is both Pilate and Judas—as the only disciple who bears this testimony
from within the community—who affirm Jesus' innocence ($\dot{\alpha}$θῷος, 27:3,
24).

One of the cardinal elements of Matthew's theology is his concern for
community and for life within that community. Accordingly, we must ask
whether Judas is being treated as a member of the community in accordance
with instructions attributed to Jesus on how to deal with the group's own
members. An illuminating attempt is made by Una Maguire to apply the
rules of "group dynamics" to the Last Supper. She sees Judas in some ways
as "the heart of the group" but never having been recognized as such by
the others. After he left, he was not missed. "Nor did they try to find him
to have him in their group's centre on such a night. One gesture from, one
movement on the part of any of them might have prevented Judas from his
feeling of exclusion and isolation. No such gesture is recorded. . . . The
apostles left him with the burden when they should have gone to help
him."[43]

Although love is seen as being operative within his own community,
Jesus apparently does not conceive of people loving only those who are

within the fellowship. It needs, therefore, to be asked whether Judas is treated as one of the fellowship, as one of the least of them, or instead as an enemy. Whatever one decides, in each case Judas is eligible for the love of Christ and of the community that strives to live according to the teachings of Jesus. For it is precisely in the neighbor and in the brother or sister that God visits people—especially the one who is being tempted to sin or does in fact commit sin.[44]

It is important to note that Matthew joined Luke in reporting that Jesus taught his disciples to love their enemies. He also reports that Jesus was true to himself and to God's love covenant in his dealings with Judas.

Conclusion

To do justice to Matthew's account, we must note that he is the only writer who describes the demise of Judas as part of the Jesus story. Luke defers it until he tells the story of the emerging church. What this means for our understanding of Judas is not at all clear. Further attempts to understand it will be made when we deal with the death accounts. For now, it is simply observed that Matthew's view of community—especially his need to sharpen the lines of difference between Christians and Jews during the early life of the church—may have been a factor in the way Judas is portrayed. Nevertheless, throughout his account there shine numerous examples of the portrait of Judas as disciple and as apostle, but most notably as friend of Jesus. Matthew was already in touch with traditions that had lost the meaning of Judas's involvement in the process of taking Jesus captive. In his efforts to relate the events of Jesus' life, and especially the ambiguous role Judas played in it to the purposes of God, Matthew used Hebrew scriptures in a way that is unacceptable to us today.[45] Judas did not die, as Jesus may have done, in order to fulfill some divine plan. He died because he was a faithful disciple to the end, after he carried out the wish and command of his master. When things got out of hand and he saw them taking a course from which Jesus was not willing to extricate himself, he did what all the disciples did, he fled. But he never returned and, according to Matthew, sealed his witness with his death. Matthew does not scold him for that; perhaps the very fact that he tells the story means that Matthew did not want us to lose the fate of Judas. He left a memorial for his fellow disciple. Unfortunately, we have misread it for some centuries now. That is not Matthew's fault and we still have an opportunity to consider what we should make of Judas. One also has the feeling that Matthew didn't have the matter entirely sorted out, even by the time he wrote the last draft of his Gospel.

Matthew's most important contribution to our discussion may well be that he provides us with insight into the way the early Christians, as well as the disciples who traveled with Jesus, sought to live with each other. The patterns of rebuke, mutual forgiveness, confronting, and, above all, acceptance and forgiveness of a fellow disciple's sin—up to seventy times seven= infinite—should become the measure by which all statements in the New Testament about Judas are to be tested.

We can assume that the disciples followed some Jewish standards on how to deal with conflict or differences among them. In this they may have followed the community at Qumran, but they also undoubtedly made their own adaptations, depending upon what they were learning from Jesus. We can be sure that they agreed with Jewish teaching and practice that if a community either ignored a sin about to be committed or merely vilified the perpetrator after it was done, the group had seriously violated an essential aspect of community. It is possible that Matthew, and even more likely John, was not in touch with this manner of being in community. It is hard to believe that this loss of true community could already have happened when Jesus was relating to Judas—in short, that there was no connection between their life together and the later instructions Jesus gave Judas. Enigmatic as the sayings are that went between them, there is no rebuke in them. Can we really say that Jesus allowed his fellow Jew to write a passage ticket to hell?

This becomes, then, an additional reason to reject the notion of a betrayal. It would have violated a fundamental rule of Judaism if Jesus had told Judas to go out and deliberately commit a sin. Instead, it is more plausible to assume that he sent Judas forth on a mission and that Judas faithfully carried out that mission for his master.[46]

Regardless, now began a process of vilifying Judas for what he did, representing Judas as an "evil" actor in the drama of divine redemption. At the same time, Matthew does not exaggerate the role that Judas played. The use of dialogue between Judas and others makes him a living person who, along with the others, seeks to affirm his loyalty to the God of the Hebrews while at the same time to follow the greatest teacher of Torah they had encountered. While the influence of Matthew on a historical portrait of Judas is more baleful, his Gospel is not to be blamed for the later perversion of Judas. At least, not his alone.

Excursus
The Kiss of Judas and Jesus

Three Gospels report that when Jesus and Judas met in the garden, they kissed each other. The following variations between Mark, Matthew, and Luke can be noted:

Mark 14:43-46	Matthew 26:48-49	Luke 22:47-48
Now the informer *had previously agreed with them* on a sign saying: "Whomever I kiss, that's the one; bind him *and remove him safely.*" At once when he arrived he said to him: "Master" and kissed him.	And the informer gave them a sign saying: "Whomever I kiss, that's the one, bind him." And when he had come to Jesus he said: "*Greetings*, Master," and he kissed him.	*The one called Judas, one of the Twelve, was leading them and he approached Jesus to kiss him. But Jesus said to him: "Judas, with a kiss you hand over the Son of man?"*

It is significant that Mark portrays Jesus as somewhat more passive, while both Matthew and Luke offer dialogue between Judas and Jesus. Matthew and Mark indicate that the kiss is a sign of identification. All indicate that the kiss is initiated by Judas; only Luke has Jesus recoiling against it when he asks whether Judas will hand over "the Son of man" with the kiss. Luke has Jesus addressing other individuals directly: man (5:20); by name only: Simon the Pharisee (7:40); Martha, Martha (10:41); Zacchaeus (19:5); Simon, Simon [Peter] (22:31); Peter (22:34), and Judas (22:48).

The way in which Luke handles this event and the omission in John provide evidence that the early church was uneasy with the reporting of this kiss. After all, a public kiss is a dramatic act demonstrating the breakdown of barriers (early Christians referred to a "kiss of peace" or "holy kiss"). What function could the kiss possibly serve as a sign between Jesus and the one handing him over to those who were arresting him? Consistent with the significance of the kiss at the time the Gospels were being written, it could only signify a solidarity of purpose, a oneness between Jesus and Judas which the kiss signified when Christians greeted each other.[47]

Tempting as it may be to take this event far beyond its literal meaning, we had best interpret the act in the light of practice at the time. It would seem highly likely that Jesus introduced into his disciple band the practice of kissing each other when the disciples met after an absence from each other. We can presume that he taught them that such a display of warm affection was a holy, nonerotic, kiss. This sense of closeness was reinforced by the common meals.

Eric Bishop, offended by the possibility of a kiss on the mouth, votes instead for a kiss on the hand. Obviously, he has not watched Near Easterners carefully in this respect, even though he seeks to interpret them for Westerners. In recent Middle East politics, much has been made of the refusal to be greeted at airports with a kiss on both cheeks by various leaders of countries and political factions. When Bishop writes: "There is neither rhyme nor reason for the longish embrace of friends parted for some time; quite apart from the fact that the questioning remonstrance of our Lord would have practically ruled out the embrace as impossible," he may be reflecting the values of British ecclesiastical society, but hardly those of Jewish society—then or now.[48] The kiss of Judas, later the kiss of peace, needs to be seen from that perspective.

Mark also preserves a tradition that Jesus taught his disciples to practice the salt of peace: "Have salt among yourselves; and be at peace with one another" (9:50).[49] Michael Lattke joins others who see the salt imagery as part of the tradition of the earliest church. It has its primary point of reference in a group discipline and may well be a rule for disciples.[50] He concludes: "The wise admonition to share the salt of friendship is an appeal for table fellowship and thus to fellowship in general. The call to be at peace with each other and thus to keep human community intact is bound to it as a close parallel."[51]

But there is also a tradition that during this last meal with Jesus, the harmony was destroyed. According to Mark, when Jesus announced that the one who will deliver him is "the one who eats with me" (14:18), the disciples all became very distressed. Although Jesus specifies that it is the one who dips with him in the dish (Mark and Matthew), the Lukan version reads simply: "Behold the hand of the one delivering me is with me on the table" (22:21). The τρυβλίον (Matt 26:23//Mark 14:20) was a common bowl, so all would have been dipping in it. So Luke and John both change the word.

The most drastic change is that of John, for here "it is the man *to whom I give* this piece of bread when I have dipped it in the dish. Then, after dipping it in the dish, he took it out and gave it to Judas, son of Simon Iscariot" (13:26). By doing so, Jesus as host demonstrated his commitment to care for Judas. By taking it, Judas undertook to carry out his host's wishes. According to Jewish custom, they were bound to each other's destiny as long as the taste of salt remained, about three days. By taking something into yourself that belonged to the sphere of the other, you become united with the other. By eating with another, you establish a covenant of peace.

Invitations to a meal are declined if you do not desire to make peace with those attending. Salt is especially important, for the guest is under the protection of the host "as long as the salt is still in the stomach," or "on the tongue, that is, as long as you can still taste it." Having eaten the food of a stranger, you are in a relationship of obligation and rights.

Expressions like those between two people that "there is salt" mean that they have an unbreakable covenant. Such a phrase is similar to saying, "Between them is salt and ashes."

John's version of the division, appearing earlier in his Gospel, is even more graphic. He introduces this theme in 13:18 where Jesus divides his disciples into two groups: those who do and those who don't do what he teaches. "I know whom I have elected. But that the scripture may be fulfilled: 'The one who chews my bread has turned up his heel against me'" (13:18). It could also be translated: "Even my nearest friend, whom I trusted, to the point of eating with him, turned his heel up against me." But the word for eating is not the usual word, nor the one used in the Greek version of the Hebrew Bible. It is τρώγω,[52] the word for chewing out loud, for which John shows particular fondness.

The allusion regarding a friend is to Psalm 41, whose context is: "Blessed be the One who accepts the lowly and the poor" (v. 2). The enemies come to wish the death of the stricken one. Even the friends come, including the most intimate one, "the man of my peace," one's nearest and dearest friend, the one with whom the psalmist has had an unbroken relationship of trust and friendship. As a sign of this relationship there is the common meal. The meal established and confirmed friendship.[53] Yet all these sacrosanct bonds have been torn apart by the friends.

Three of the four Gospels anchor their discussion of Judas's eating with Jesus in a text from the Hebrew Bible. The place of the Hebrew scriptures in the passion narrative has been studied in great detail.[54] It has proven difficult to decide whether Mark 14:18b is an allusion to Ps 41:9. Some consider it possible that both Mark and John are dependent upon an early church tradition in which Psalm 41 was applied to Judas.[55] If so, it is strange that there is no reference to him, not in Mark at least. Psalm 41 was applied to Ahithophel's relations with David by the Jews.[56]

From the perspective of Matthew and John, the emphasis on the breaking of table fellowship, which was regarded as a time of particular trust and intimacy in the ancient world, makes the psalm so appropriate with respect to Judas's behavior. Thus, Jesus' words during the Last Supper are not intended primarily to identify the betrayer but to point out the seriousness of the act about to be committed to a trusted associate. At the time it made no sense to any of them. The written accounts reflect as clearly the biases and hatred toward Judas the "Defector" as they do anything that "really" happened.

What John at least points to, the enigmatic nature of virtually all that happened at that table, may very well be present in the scene of the arrest as well. Judas kisses Jesus because that is what Jesus had taught him to do. But in doing so he also may be confirming that he is carrying out his part of the covenant of peace. Matthew and Mark suggest it was a sign that Judas had previously agreed to provide them with ("whomever I kiss, that's the one, bind him," Matt 26:48; Mark 14:44). Yet, although it certainly could be a kiss of betrayal or treachery, it could also have been an affirmation of covenant faithfulness. Judas was there to do what had been his commission, and he carried it out as agreed. Commentators suggest that "Judas' embrace of Jesus was a tragically clever move to point out Jesus in the darkness of Gethsemane." Possibly. But there may have been more to it than that. Otherwise John's silence is inexplicable. What could he not have done dramatically with a "traitor's kiss."

The tragedy in the act is not in what was being done by the partners in the deed. Each one was simply carrying out his assigned duty and playing out his role. The tragedy came about when good people seeking to do their duty (Caiaphas, Pilate, Jesus, Judas) came into conflict with each other and when their differing perceptions of God's will and kingdom clashed.

When Jesus embraced Judas, it can be argued that he gave him the seal of approval for what he had done. Both Luke and John, however, could not allow that kiss to happen—John simply suppressed it altogether, and Luke depicts the attempt but will not allow it to be completed. Instead, he asks: "Judas, with a kiss you hand over the Son of man?" (22:48). As noted in our treatment of those words we are left here with a statement that is ambiguous and therefore open to more than one interpretation.

In the history of art this scene has laid its spell on the artists. In my opinion no one has done justice to it like the Italian painter Giotto. Historians of art have pointed out that the flowing yellow robe he puts on Judas denotes cowardice. There is, moreover, a complex history behind the painting itself. Nevertheless, a careful review of the painting shows that Giotto has two real people meeting each other, not a spiritual Christ with halo and Judas, a demon. Moreover, their eyes meet even as their lips come together. Judas is also depicted as the one taking the initiative, with his flowing robe fully embracing Jesus as if Judas is enfolding Jesus to protect him from mob action. The bright color of the two main characters, over against the sinister threatening world with its obscene spears and armaments, reveals a genuine human relationship. It is a peerless contribution to human art in which the human kiss reminds us of one of the most basic human relationships, bringing the Judas-Jesus encounter from the mythological to the historical plane.[57] In an hour of overwhelming anxiety, fear, and bewilderment two male colleagues embrace and in that embrace bring strength to each other for the role God has called them to play. In the history of art, more than once has the artist portrayed Judas as a strong and good man in this encounter, and the texts of the Gospels support that.[58]

Notes

1. Maccoby, *Judas*, 40.
2. Senior, *Passion Narrative*, 1.
3. Brown, *Death*, 60–61.
4. Matt 10:1; 11:1; 20:17; 24:20.
5. Matt 10:5; 26:14; 26:47.
6. As observed by Donald Senior in his excursus on this topic, *Passion Narrative*, 14–17. Essentially the same observations are made by many writers after him.
7. Senior, *Passion Narrative*, 15.
8. Matt 14:31; 16:8; 17:20; 21:20; 28:17.
9. Senior, *Passion Narrative*, 21.
10. Brown, *Death*, 61.
11. Vogler, *Judas*, 71.
12. Italics indicates Matthew's additions to the Markan source. The translation of the NRSV and NEB, "betray him to you," is quite impossible from a purely grammatical point of view, except, of course, in the fifteenth-century meaning of "betray" as "hand over." Fortunately, NIV and NJB have it right.
13. Benoit, "The Death of Judas," 197, notes that owing to literary borrowing, the ἔστησαν of Matt 26:15 must be understood to mean "they weighed," that is, they counted out, they paid, rather than "they fixed" a mere promise. Besides, in 27:3, we see that Judas actually had his hands on the money.
14. Senior, *Passion Narrative*, 41–50, provides a good treatment of this section. He indicates that Matthew's presentation of the betrayal of Judas is essentially the same as in Mark (41). An excellent treatment of this pericope is also found in Nepper-Christensen, *Das Matthäusevangelium*, 154–162. In addition to Klauck, 33–69; Vogler, 57–74; and Maccoby, 34–49, I have found Lohmeyer-Schmauch, *Das Evangelium des Matthäus*, and Bruner's commentary on *Matthew* most helpful. Alan Segal's essays, "Matthew's Jewish Voice," is also useful in seeing the context of the Gospel as Galilee rather than Antioch.
15. Lohmeyer-Schmauch, *Das Evangelium des Matthäus*, conclude: "Both literary units (Matt 26:14-16 and 27:3-10) are joined together by the motif of thirty pieces of silver. The true content of the narrative is what happens to them" (375). So also Gärtner, *Iscariot*, 15–21.
16. Billerbeck, *Kommentar*, 1:987.
17. Lapide, *Wer war Schuld an Jesu Tod?* 23–24.
18. Chrysostom, *Homilies on Matthew*, and also his oft-cited Maundy Thursday sermon.

19. Nepper-Christensen, *Das Matthäusevangelium,* 158–159. The term he uses is *Bibelstil,* designating the way in which early Christian writers were imbued with narratives from the Hebrew Bible. This method does not make it incumbent upon us to find only exact parallels.

20. Brown, *Death,* 61. He is quite convinced that the common Synoptic passion narrative material was not created by the OT allusions but that the Matthean special material may have been.

21. Irmscher, "Σὺ λεγέις (Mark 15:2//Matt 27:11//Luke 23:3)," 151–158, provides a history of the interpretation of these words, especially from the Greek fathers and rabbinic sources. Among the Greek fathers, he notes a certain "deliberate ambiguity" (157). He also notes its deviation from Jesus' own teaching, "Let your yes be yes and your no be no" (157). Irmscher himself concludes that both the Hebrew original and the Greek contain an affirmation: "However, this affirmation is not unlimited and unconditional. Rather, the partner in the dialogue is permitted to interpret the saying in the light of its background and implications" (158).

22. Rehkopf, "Matt 26:50," suggests that this addition is not a reflection of Matthew's but arose out of the oral tradition which existed alongside the written tradition and put more emphasis on designating the betrayer (29).

23. Lohmeyer-Schmauch, *Das Evangelium des Matthäus,* 355.

24. Auerbach, *Mimesis,* 40–41.

25. Major contributions were made by Chwolson in three stages from 1892 to 1910: *Das letzte Passamahl Christi und der Tag seines Todes; Beiträge zur Entwicklungsgeschichte des Judentums;* and *Über die Frage ob Jesus gelebt hat.* See the summary in David Catchpole, "The Answer of Jesus to Caiaphas," 213–226.

26. *The Oxford Study Bible* (NRSV), grossly oversimplifying, states that it is a "common form of assent in Palestine" (40 NT).

27. Lohmeyer-Schmauch, *Das Evangelium des Matthäus,* 355. M. Smith, *Tannaitic Parallels to the Gospels,* 27–30, argued for the translation "So you say" and took it as intentionally ambiguous.

28. Catchpole summarizes Chwolson's five arguments counting against it: (1) Matt 26:25. (2) John 18:37. (3) The only rabbinic parallel known to him was certainly not an affirmation. (4) Luke 23:4–5. (5) New evidence from a rabbinic source led him to conclude that the phrase is unambiguously a denial, indeed an indignant denial "that you would have the audacity to attribute something like that to me," "The Answer," 214–216.

29. Catchpole, "The Answer," 215.

30. Catchpole, "The Answer," 216.

31. Blass-Debrunner-Funk, *Greek Grammar* (1961): 221. Schlatter concludes, "Jesus himself did not speak the word which uncovers the guilt of Judas. But after Judas had spoken it, he affirms it." Schlatter provides some excellent examples from rabbinic sources in which bad news or indicting answers are obliquely given, *Matthäus,* 740–741.

32. Catchpole, "The Answer," 217.

33. Catchpole, "The Answer," 217, 226.

34. Rieu, *The Four Gospels.*

35. Schlatter, *Matthäus,* 590, offers a number of examples from Josephus of the use of this word to stress a strong relationship of friendship. Künzel, *Studien zum*

Gemeindeverständnis des Matthäusevangeliums, has noted the "unlimited forgiveness" as a basic rule of Matthew's community existence (18:21ff.), 258.

36. Lohmeyer-Schmauch, *Das Evangelium des Matthäus,* 364.

37. Moffatt: "My man, do your errand."

38. Rehkopf, "Matt 26:50," 109–115, here 115. So also Stählin, "φιλέω," 140.

39. Lohmeyer-Schmauch, *Das Evangelium des Matthäus,* 364.

40. Matthew "points out that Jesus actually encouraged Judas to carry out the betrayal," according to Wilson, *The Execution of Jesus,* 64. Strangely, even though Wilson notes that this is also the case with John, he still refers to the "ignominious character of the betrayal" (104) and says the deed is one of "perfidy" (105). It is puzzling indeed that for a deed that "seems to have so little actual importance for what follows" (104), the execution of Jesus, he can conclude: "It is no wonder that the Church remembered (Judas) with such bitterness" (106).

41. Matt 26:75ff.//Mark 14:72ff.//Luke 22:62.

42. Gerhardsson, "Jesus, ausgeliefert und verlassen," 262–291.

43. Maguire, "The Last Supper," 644.

44. Christian, *Jesus und seine geringsten Brüder,* 35. Friedrich, *Gott im Bruder?* 31–46. Friedrich, in testing the genuineness of this pericope, asks whether word and deed harmonize in Jesus. He concludes that they do and that, therefore, it is genuine. Jesus associated with the lowly and also saw this as the core of the last judgment. The elements of hospitality, love of neighbor and enemy, are all pertinent to our account of Jesus' relation to Judas (293–295).

45. Frank Beare speaks for many commentators, most of whom have not bothered to review the way scriptures were used by Jesus' own colleagues, when he says, after rejecting the story of Judas as of no redeeming value: "This is surely the most extravagant example of Matt's handling of scriptures as proof texts. . . . It must be agreed that he botched it badly" (*Commentary,* 526–527).

46. Kugel, *In Potiphar's House,* 214–243, offers a rich collection of texts on this subject. See also Förkman, *The Limits of the Religious Community,* a study of expulsion from the religious communities of Qumran, Rabbis, and Primitive Christianity.

47. A point that logically follows the observations made by John Suggit, "Poetry's Next-Door Neighbour," 12–14.

48. Bishop, "With Jesus on the Road from Galilee to Calvary," *CBQ* 11 (1949): 440. For a quite different approach, see Klassen, "The Sacred Kiss in the New Testament."

49. ἔχετε ἐν ἑαυτοῖς ἅλα καὶ εἰρηνεύετε ἐν ἀλλήλοις. On this difficult text, see Lattke, "Salz der Freundschaft in Mk 9:50c."

50. Lattke, "Salz," 56.

51. Lattke, "Salz," 58.

52. He uses it five of the six times it appears in the NT. See Goppelt, *KTWBNT,* 8:36–237. It appears only once elsewhere in the NT, in Matt 24:38 in the expression "eating and drinking."

53. Pedersen, *Der Eid bei den Semiten,* 24–25.

54. Moo, *The OT in the Gospel Passion Narratives.* He deals with Ps 41:9 on pp. 235–240.

55. Moo, *The OT,* 238.

56. See Billerbeck, *Kommentar,* 2:588; and Gärtner, *Iscariot,* 9–12.

57. Czarnecki, "The Significance of Judas," has failed to convince me that Giotto, in a different painting, has Judas sitting with the Twelve judging the nations. It would appear that he still hangs on a cross in the left foreground, in white to be sure.

58. Puchner, *Studien,* 76–79. The scene of the capture is very popular in church art and often Judas is depicted as a handsome, unreflective youth. "A psychology of betrayal or conflict is totally subordinated to the soteriological fulfilment of the plan of salvation" (Puchner, 77).

CHAPTER SEVEN

JUDAS ISCARIOT IN
THE WRITINGS OF
LUKE

How could Jesus endure to have a man, of whom he knew that he would be
his betrayer, and that all instruction would be fruitless to him, as his constant
attendant throughout the whole period of his public life?

—D. F. Strauss[1]

The overall theme of Luke's Gospel and its social setting
have received abundant discussion in recent literature.[2] Here we concentrate
on one issue: How does Luke portray Judas? Related to that is the question:
Why does Luke introduce Judas at various points in the narrative and how
has he shaped the narratives to further his purpose? As we address these
questions, we may be brought to a firmer foundation regarding what we
can and cannot say with relative certainty about Judas's involvement in the
story of Jesus.[3]

This chapter will consider Luke's treatment of Judas in the light of his
treatment of the passion of Jesus. Apart from the formulaic presentation of
the name of Judas as part of the Twelve (Luke 6:16), where Luke deviates
from his source by calling Judas the *prodotēs* (προδότης=traitor) (thus providing the only text in the New Testament in which Judas is called a traitor),[4]
he appears only in the passion narrative, where he is referred to as the one
who handed him over. In 6:16 Luke uses the standard term employed by
Greek writers for "betrayal" or a "traitor." Josephus (*Ant* 19.61), like Luke,
uses the term with the verb γίνομαι ("to become a traitor") and parallels
Luke's usage. Words on this stem, *prodidōmi* (προδίδωμι), appear in the New
Testament a total of four times, only once as a verb (once as a variant reading, Mark 14:10), and in Josephus some forty-nine times, especially in connection with his own behavior and the possibility that he betrayed his fellow
Galileans or the laws of his people. The noun προδότης=traitor appears three

times in the New Testament, twice in Luke, here and in Acts 7:52, Stephen's speech (betrayal of the prophets), and in 2 Tim 3:4 in a list of vices.

It is therefore understandable that the role of Judas is viewed by Luke primarily in connection with the death of Jesus. But that role is ill-defined and would appear to converge with the role of the leadership in the Temple. In the early speeches attributed to the apostles in Acts, the "handing over" is vague and connected with the disowning of Jesus before Pilate. No reference is made to Judas. The "handing over" means little more than the rejection of Jesus by the Jews and thus the expression is somewhat bland.[5]

In the Bampton Lectures of 1934, R. H. Lightfoot isolated three ways in which Luke strikes a different path in regard to his portrait of Jesus. In this he is a herald of John. The three dimensions are:

1. His emphasis on the connection of Jesus with the capital of Palestine, Jerusalem.
2. Luke's effort, especially in the passion narrative, to write a connected and consistent story/account.
3. More important, the sentiment with which Luke writes of the passion account and his determination to strip the story of all elements of tragedy.[6]

This third point Lightfoot spells out with reference to the part played by Judas, the Twelve, and by Jesus himself.

When we compare Luke with Mark's account of Judas's role in the "betrayal," we find that Luke shortens it by about a third. Moreover, Mark's woe is much longer, although he does not designate who the "betrayer" is. The length at which Luke writes about the "betrayal" makes it seem of great importance. Luke also offers Jesus' lament after the Last Supper, while Mark leaves the timing of it open. In Mark, the arrest places Judas in a prominent position and is described in greater detail than in Luke, even though the account is shorter than that of Luke. Indeed, Lightfoot concludes that "the action of Judas is viewed almost as darkly in our earliest as it certainly is in our latest Gospel."[7]

Luke depicts Judas's act in a less disastrous light by attributing his act to a power other than his own (i.e., Satan). Lightfoot interprets Luke's writing as designed to explain rather than to heighten the offense of Judas. Conversely, in the Fourth Gospel, where "the character of Judas is painted in blackest colors," the reference to Satan is meant to vilify Judas. This is not the only place in which Luke turns the same basic data around for a different purpose.[8]

Since it is impossible to deal with all the commentaries on Luke, I selected one of the finest recent commentaries, that of biblical scholar Joseph Fitzmyer. He finds that in Luke "it is not primarily the Romans who govern

Jesus' fate, but a Satan-possessed disciple, a Palestinian Jewish follower."[9] Judas is numbered among the Twelve, and while Jesus' victory over satanic evil is implied in his prayer for Peter and in his words to the penitent criminal on the cross, they presumably do not apply to Judas.

What is perhaps most regrettable about Fitzmyer's treatment is that there is no analysis of what Luke tells us Judas did. He seems to be aware that the word παραδίδωμι (*paradidōmi*) is not to be translated "betray," for in some instances he translates it "hand over" (1373, 1409). There is no evidence that he draws in the fundamental study of παραδίδωμι by Wiard Popkes and its contribution to this discussion.[10] The dominant motif, which is repeated often, is "the horror of the early Christian community over the betrayal of Jesus by one of his own."[11] Fitzmyer is at a loss to explain why all the twelve disciples are capable of betrayal and why, above all, Luke would mention this fact if Judas's deed is so singularly "horrifying." Unfortunately, his considerable linguistic skills are not marshaled to help us with either the critical word ἐξομολογέω (*exomologeō*), to report to the authorities,[12] or the word *paradidōmi* (παραδίδωμι). He leaves us, therefore, with the traditional viewpoint.

A difficult problem remains: Did Jesus pray, according to Luke, that God might forgive everyone (except Judas)? Or do we have in Fitzmyer's treatment of Judas a reading of the horrible deed of Judas through the eyes of the later church?[13]

Luke describes two instances of Jesus sending forth his disciples. First it is the "Twelve" who are sent out to "overcome all devils and to cure diseases, . . . to proclaim the kingdom of God and to heal" (9:1-2). Later he sent seventy-two followers to announce the arrival of the kingdom (10:1-12). In between, he recounts both Peter's confession and the transfiguration and announces that Jesus is to die in Jerusalem. After the latter account of their mission, Luke has Jesus rejoicing in the fact that demons submit to the disciples and exults: "I watched how Satan fell, like lightning out of the sky" (10:18-21). There is every reason to assume that Judas was present as one of the apostles/disciples on these missions.

John Wesley, after noting that Judas was one of the persons sent out two by two, asks: "And did our Lord know that 'he had a devil'? St. John expressly tells us he did. Yet he was coupled with another of the apostles and joined them all in the same communion. Neither have we any reason to doubt that God blessed the labor of all his 12 ambassadors."[14] The portrait Luke provides of the disciple group is realistic, for they are presented as most decidedly human, even though they also serve as emissaries of the powerful rule of God.

Furthermore, the prediction of the handing over is much abbreviated in Luke. Luke takes only the central verse from Mark, but by his arrangement of the material, Luke avoids concentrating on the crime that Judas is alleged to have committed. By placing the topic after the supper, Luke opens the door first to the uncertainty of the disciples regarding who might do the handing over and then to a controversy among them as to who is greater. The identity of the informer is never revealed. In the arrest itself the account is kept extremely short; Judas does not kiss Jesus and only one question is asked by Jesus. Most important, Lightfoot sees in Luke's portrayal of Jesus a suffering servant whose gentleness manifests itself even in the way he deals with his disappointment that the disciples do not support him in his hour of need.

Josephine Ford has added another dimension to this portrait of Judas, stressing Luke's interest in love of enemies: what she terms "philoechthrology." It then becomes critically important to see what Luke does with Judas who was, by traditional understanding, an enemy of Jesus—and certainly by the time Luke wrote in the eighties, was beginning to emerge as a "traitor" in the eyes of some early Christians. How does Luke cope with this?

The structure of the material leads Ford to the conclusion that Luke has reordered it in order to portray Jesus as a nonviolent king who shows love for his captors, and for Judas as well.[15] This thesis needs to be tested as we review the Lukan material.

Four separate pieces of tradition dealing with Judas in the Lukan narratives deserve analysis.[16]

A. Luke 22:3-6

But Satan having entered into Judas, the one called Iscariot, being numbered among the twelve, went off and conversed with the chief priests and Temple police on how he might report Jesus to them. And they rejoiced and decided to give him silver. He laid a formal charge and sought for an opportune time to deliver him over without a crowd.

The term "conversed" (*sullaleō*, συλλαλέω) in verse 3 is used of the conversation that Moses and Elijah had with Jesus at the time of the transfiguration (Matt 17:3//Mark 9:4//Luke 9:30) and by Luke alone in connection with the dwellers of Capernaum who conferred with each other about Jesus' ministry (Luke 4:36) and about Festus conferring with his advisers (Acts 25:12). Only Luke uses it here in connection with Judas.

The word "Temple official" in verse 4 (*stratēgos*, στρατηγός) appears in Luke only, 22:4, 52 and eight times in Acts. When used in connection with the Temple, it always means the sagan, the captain of the Temple. "He had supreme charge of order in and around the Temple."[17] In rank he was next to the high priest. There were also numerous sagans of lower rank, who were also heads of Temple police but subordinate to the supreme sagan. As

Luke Johnson observes, Luke, by laying responsibility for the capture of Jesus, and ultimately his death, at the feet of the responsibles, diminishes the role of the populace in the death of Jesus.[18]

The decision to give Judas money is described with the term συντίθεσθαι (v. 5). It is used three times in the New Testament, each time in connection with a decision made by Jewish authorities (John 9:22; Acts 23:20), and does not imply that Judas asked for money. Verse 6 is very difficult. The word used here, *exomologeō* (ἐξομολογέω), which I have translated "laid a formal charge," is always used in the New Testament, in the middle voice, to designate a formal public confession; four of the eight times it involves confession of sins[19] and three times publicly to confess Jesus as Lord.[20] Luke 10:21// Matt 11:25 uses it in the sense of response to God for what has been given to Jesus and could be translated as "Praise" or "Blessed be you, God." The word used here by Luke is unique in this kind of context in the New Testament; indeed, Evans states that the word appears nowhere else in the active voice in secular Greek literature.[21]

While Matthew suggests that Judas acted because of love for money or greed, Luke goes considerably beyond that and attributes it to the entrance of Satan into Judas (Luke 22:3). This fits with Luke's notion that the devil left Jesus for a season (Luke 4:13) and then returns. Satan brings the conflict between God and Satan to a decisive point through Jesus' disciple, one of the Twelve.

Luke has only a slight interest in Satan (he uses the word only seven times; and the "devil" [διάβολος] seven times). Still, only Luke has Satan "falling like lightning from heaven" (10:18); only he has the woman who has been bound by Satan for thirteen years (13:16), who is then freed; and only Luke has Jesus saying to Peter: "Simon, Simon, Satan has been allowed to test you as wheat" (22:31), giving him a mandate for what he is to do after the testing or sifting. In short, Luke sees the demonic or satanic as real but also as a power that can be overcome. The nature of the Gospel is that it "turns people from the dominion of Satan to God" to find again their "place" among the people of God (Acts 26:18). Luke shares with John the belief that it was Satan who influenced Judas to hand Jesus over.

It is noteworthy that the devil's role is "not in contradiction to God's Lordship in the passion; rather, it can be seen as evidence of God's sovereignty over history; for as creator of heaven and earth he is also Lord over all that is in it."[22] For Luke, the conviction is unquestionable: none other than God handed Jesus over to his death. All others were but minor players acting at the direction of the Lord of all.[23]

In a later text, the same author refers to Judas's "wages or reward for evil work" (Acts 1:18) using the term "injustice" (ἀδικία), for which Luke has a distinct liking (see the connection with money and injustice in Luke 16:8,

9).[24] With respect to Judas's fate, Luke has Peter say simply: "He went to his own place" (Acts 1:25), after he had relinquished his ministry and apostleship. The low-key way in which Judas is described here is remarkable. Could it be that Luke, in this instance, has access to some genuine tradition about what Peter, conscious of his own betrayal of Jesus, said about Judas? And did Peter have a special sympathy for Judas? Whatever the answers to these questions, there is a crystal-clear affirmation of Judas's apostleship and his relationship to Jesus as servant (Acts 1:17).

Unlike Mark and Matthew, Luke does not have Jesus rebuke Peter with the words: "Get you behind me, Satan" (Mark 8:33; Matt 16:23). Yet in the Synoptic Gospels, only in Luke does Satan enter Judas. Luke, furthermore, sets Judas on equal footing with the chief priests and officers of the Temple when he goes to negotiate with them. They desire to take Jesus into captivity but cannot because of the crowds (19:47; 20:19).

Luke provides a reason for Judas's deed and also prepares for the act that makes it possible to capture Jesus. As in Acts 5:3, where Ananias is possessed by Satan, so here Satan takes over Judas and sets the execution of Jesus into motion.[25] But Luke also portrays Judas as acting in partnership with the upper levels of authority in Judaism.

The most important clue regarding the action of Judas, which is provided only by Luke, comes in his use of the term *exomologeō* (ἐξομολογέω) in connection with *paradidōmi* (22:6). We need therefore to attempt to determine its meaning here. The term has been described as "the former despair of lexicographers and nightmare of translators, now happily cleared up."[26] The word *exomologeomai,* generally in the middle voice, usually means to confess, as in confessing sins publicly. It can also mean to confess one's faith in Jesus as Lord (see above). In the LXX it appears often; most frequently it refers to affirming publicly God's greatness and love, or to praising God.[27] In Josephus the term generally means to admit, although he uses it only eight times, always in the middle voice. The verb in the active, without the preface *ex,* he uses over 125 times.

It is to the papyri, those tiny fragments found in the Middle East, some dating back earlier than the first century, that we must turn, for none of the traditional meanings of the word make any sense here. Generally, translators render the word ἐξομολογέω (*exomologeō*) "agreed,"[28] but that is redundant, since that has already been said. In the papyri, however, the term appears with the meaning of "rendering a formal complaint" to the authorities; in short, of making a deposition or lodging a charge against someone.[29]

We conclude that it is probable that Luke describes Judas as laying a formal charge, bringing the "informing" action to a head here. After the agreement with the authorities, Judas signs an official complaint against Jesus, which becomes the basis for the charges laid against him by the Temple authorities. Since the word *exomologeō* ("informing") is thus used among the papyri, there is no reason not to accept it as the most logical usage here as well.[30] However, this usage is usually rejected because Judas did not show up to testify against Jesus at his trial.[31] Surely it frequently happens that informers fail to show at trials, although it may in fact be the case that Judas was at the first hearing. Matthew 27:3 suggests that Judas knew what was happening to Jesus and, indeed, that his remorse began as soon as he saw that the case of Jesus was not being dealt with by his fellow countrymen but was being referred to the Roman authorities. That was never his intention.

B. Luke 22:21-23

But after all, the hand of the one who will hand me over is *with mine on the table.* For the Son of man goes *as it is has been appointed;* but alas for that man through whom the Son of man will be taken into captivity. *And they began to argue with each other about who it might be that would possibly do this.*[32]

Rehkopf's literary analysis of verse 21 led him to conclude that both the transition and the prediction or announcement give evidence that Luke is not following Mark here. Indications of the fact that we are in the presence of ancient materials here come from the use of the term "hand" for the informer, the present participle in a futuristic sense, and the semiticized ἰδού ("behold") without a copula.[33]

Moreover, an analysis of verse 23 made Rehkopf believe that Luke was carefully reworking a text that was not Mark 14:19.[34] His preference for indirect discourse over direct discourse points to a more sophisticated writing style.[35] Given the way in which Luke stressed dialogue in the rest of his Gospel, its omission here can only lead us to conclude that the Judas narrative was not one that he wished to highlight. Adolf Schlatter notes the way in which dialogue allows the more affective side to emerge, which he considers more characteristic of Palestinian teachers than of those in other parts of the Roman Empire. He concludes that Luke is working with an independent Palestinian source. At the same time, all sources reveal Jesus, not as a proclaimer of timeless truths, but "everywhere in our Gospels, teaching, διδαχή, is conceived of as a pastoral [*seelsorgerliche*] instruction of the community or the individual. In that process dialogue is indispensable."[36]

The introduction of the subject also points to a reworking of a pre-Lukan source not related to Mark. The fragment provides, according to Johannes Weiss, an unusual opportunity to study the growth of a tradition.[37] Rehkopf sees at work the need to expand this little scene, to make it more lively and vivid. In that way, Luke seeks to motivate the interest of the church to explore some reasons for the "inconceivable betrayal" and to see more clearly Judas's motivations.

It is striking that in Luke's description of the last meal, Judas stays until the very end; indeed, he is not even exposed at this meal. If Matthew and Mark have avoided the problem of having Judas participate in this most intimate meal with Jesus by exposing him at the outset, Luke introduces a different problem: How can the informer, possessed as he is of Satan, participate in the inner circle of the Twelve with Jesus? Luke affirms that even in this intimate circle, an informer, whose activity is directed by Satan, is present, is known to Jesus (22:21-23), but not exposed. Instead, in Luke's narrative, after the meal the disciples launch into a jealous argument (22:24-30) about who among them ranks the highest.

Perhaps it is Luke's way of saying that the act of desertion is not restricted to one person alone. Although Judas's act is singular, there is in this context also a reminder that Peter will deny his Lord three times, in spite of his asseverations that he will not. No mention is made of Judas leaving the circle, and he is present when the kingdom of Jesus is formally handed over to the disciples, because they have "remained faithful to him during his time of trial." He presumably is therefore promised an opportunity to eat with Jesus at table in his kingdom, and a throne along with the other eleven from which to judge Israel (22:29-30). Nevertheless, we find Judas in the garden leading the party that has come to arrest Jesus. All in all, it's a contradictory way for Luke to deal with Judas.

It could be that Josephine Ford is right about what, on the surface, appear to be Luke's inconsistencies in dealing with Judas. Jesus associates with the lowly. Consistent with Luke's view of Jesus, even if Judas is a treacherous betrayer under the control of demonic powers, Jesus loves his enemies and eats with them, just as he ate with Pharisees, tax collectors, and sinners. The hand of the deliverer is on the table. Jesus and the deliverer join in intimate fellowship, whatever the future may bring to them. There is no reason, given Luke's perspective, why the one who taught his disciples to bless those who curse them could not receive a kiss of respect and affection from Judas as a means of delivering him over to those who sought to destroy Jesus. But Luke cannot get himself to portray such a kiss.

C. Luke 22:47-53

While he was speaking, behold a crowd, and *the one called* Judas, one of the Twelve, *was leading them. And he drew near to Jesus and was about* to kiss him. But Jesus said to him: *"Judas, with a kiss you deliver over the Son of man?"* Those *with Jesus, seeing what was about to happen, said:* "Sir, *shall we wade in with the sword?"* And one of them swung away at the official of the high priest, and severed his right ear. *But Jesus answered them and said: "Let them have their way."*

And Jesus touched his earlobe and healed it. But Jesus said to the ones approaching him, the chief priests, the officers of the Temple police,[38] and the elders: "As a thief you have come against me with swords and cudgels? Was I not daily with you in the Temple *and you did not lay your hands on me? But this is your hour and the time for the rule of darkness."*

The words "with . . . Judas . . . at their head" (v. 47) are Luke's own, stressing Judas's leadership role. He does not actually depict Judas kissing Jesus, although it is clear that Judas intends to do so. Only in Luke, Jesus addresses Judas by name with no qualifiers, which signifies an early tradition. Most striking is also the way in which Jesus queries Judas: "With a kiss you turn me in?" (v. 48). The question contains no rebuke,[39] indeed may have been a gentle tease between two friends, despite the seriousness of the occasion. Jesus seems to have been fond of this kind of playful tease. His facial expression is, unfortunately, not recorded.

But Jesus' words may also "breathe the sadness of a deeply wounded love."[40] Whatever they may signify, Luke concludes that "the hour of darkness may now reign" (v. 53), although ultimately Jesus remains in charge. As Grundmann has said: "The One who has come to free those sitting in darkness . . . came under their power himself through those who served it. Their hour will, however, be ended by his hour and the power of darkness will be overcome through his victory."[41] Where one of his own takes a sword, far from "approving of the violence of his followers, he ministers to his enemies. . . . We have the dignity of a surrender to all that is involved in the hour of his enemies and [to] the power of darkness."[42] His words, "Let them have their way" (v. 51b), restore their swords to their proper place, allowing the Temple servant to return to his duties[43] and Jesus to get on with the work assigned to him by his Father—but not until he questions the Temple authorities.

Only in Luke does Jesus address these questions to the Temple authorities: chief priests, Temple police, and the elders (v. 52). In Mark (14:48) and Matthew (26:55), the query is made of the crowds. Luke, showing his respect for those in authority, has Jesus dealing with those responsible for the Temple in which Jesus taught daily. Then, in the Temple, they did not "lay their hands on him" (only in Luke). Now he is being treated like a common thief. Yet he concludes his inquiry by submitting to them with the words: "But this is your hour and that of the power of darkness." It is useless to expect logic or allowances from those intent on doing their duty.

D. Luke 22:34

Jesus said: Father, forgive them, for they do not know what they are doing.

Although this text does not mention Judas, we must weigh whether he is included or whether he belongs in the discussion.

It is well known that many scholars do not treat this prayer as authentic and that, in fact, it does not appear in some of our most ancient manuscripts. Even if the overwhelming majority of manuscripts omitted these words (they do not), we might say, nevertheless, that the whole life of Jesus spoke these words eloquently through his actions. He lived and died for others. This prayer is in harmony with all that he stood for.

There is, however, no blanket absolution, no *absolvo te* here. Jesus is offering a prayer for his murderers and expressing the desire to God that they may find forgiveness in the sight of God. It is important not to distort the nature of forgiveness. It should always be a deliberate and conscious act. At the same time, there is something exceptionally magnanimous in this act of Jesus. While his prayer for forgiveness has a precedent in Socrates, who bore his enemies no malice, that fact neither diminishes its importance nor makes it *eo ipso* suspect from a historical point of view.

Our concern now is with the meaning of Jesus' prayer, and the reasons for excluding or including Judas in the prayer.

Two scholars have made some important contributions to our understanding of this prayer. The first is David Daube, whose concern is fourfold:

1. Was the prayer originally in Luke?
2. On whose behalf was it offered?
3. What kind of ignorance is envisaged?
4. Can a basis for it be discovered in contemporary Jewish thought?

Daube does not answer the first question but lays out the difficulties posed by each traditional response. With regard to the second question, Daube provides two options: The prayer was intended for the Romans or for the Jews. If it was for the Romans, they did not know the gospel and thus lacked essential information. If it was for the Jews, they did not see the implications of the gospel and lacked understanding of it, even though they were not ignorant of it. Daube calls our attention to the Socratic notion that no one ever does wrong except from ignorance of themselves, their place in the world, or the ultimate good. He states generally that Jewish law does not excuse an act on the basis of lack of understanding.

He deals, however, with a remarkable verse, which is an exception:

> And it shall be forgiven all the congregation of the children of Israel and the stranger that sojourns among them, seeing that all the people were in ignorance (Num 15:26).

In the Pentateuch, the verse is confined to ignorance in the sense of lack of information. Eliezer the Great, in the first century of our era, saw in this verse an indication that even a presumptuous sin would be treated by God as, in a deeper sense, unwitting.[44] In a Baraitha, an early Jewish source, Moses intervenes with God, asking that he treat a conscious sin as an unwitting one. No doubt the text in Heb 5:2, which describes the high priest as "compassionate on the ignorant and on them that are off the way [πλανό-μενοι]," has something like that in mind. Daube concludes: "Considering a doctrine like that of Eliezer the Great, and an intercession like that of Moses for his backsliding people (as the Rabbis understand it), it would be unreasonable to deny the possibility of Luke 23:34 being a prayer for the Jews and having a thoroughly Jewish background."[45] Jonah was the usual reading for the Day of Atonement, and the concluding verse of that book—with its reference to "six score thousand who do not know the difference between their right hand and their left"—clearly deals with this issue. In numerous texts in the New Testament,[46] reference is made to ignorance as an extenuating circumstance.[47]

David Flusser has also given the verse detailed attention and provided a history of the interpretation of this saying. Daube and he share one question, although Flusser does not refer to Daube's work.[48] The question is: Does the request include the Jews, or is it meant for the Romans only?

Flusser begins with the chilling reference to the first Crusade, during which thriving Jewish communities in Germany were attacked and destroyed and many Jews killed for their faith. Rabbi Schelomo ben Schimschon, who wrote about the pogroms, ascribes to the leader of the Crusade the following words:

> You Jews have killed and crucified our Lord. And, after all, he [Jesus] said: "The day will come when my sons will come and avenge my blood." And we are his sons and it is our duty for his sake to wreak vengeance on you for you are rebellious and disobedient toward him. Never has your God found gratitude among you when he did good things for you for you have dealt evilly against him. So he has forgotten you and he no longer loves you for you are a stiff-necked people. And he has rejected you and has given us his light and has taken us to be his own.[49]

Flusser is convinced that the Crusader's words attributed to Jesus are a pure fabrication. He quotes Mussner as saying that we should never forget that Jesus prayed for his opponents on the cross and asks: "Would not God have answered the prayer of his Son?"[50] He thinks it is possible that Luke believed that Jesus was praying for the Jews. This is an important motif of hagiography. The martyr prays for those who are killing her or him. Luke 22:37 and its allusion to "being numbered among the lawbreakers" reminds us of Isa 53:12.

More important is the content: Jesus prays for his persecutors. A similar event takes place with Stephen in Acts 7:60. If Jesus on the cross prayed for his enemies, he was simply practicing what he had taught. When the words of Paul and Jesus are similar, they are clearly drawing from the same common Jewish roots.[51]

So Flusser concludes: "They stem from a comprehensive, inclusive command to love an enemy who hates you and to pray for the persecutor. This is open to abuse, to be sure, but psychologically very difficult and not without hindrances."

This step was made possible in certain circles through the influence of the Essenes. Romans 12:8b–13:7 indicates that Paul is indirectly dependent upon a pre-Christian written Essene parenesis, exhortatory writing. Flusser suggests that a new Jewish humanism comes to expression here and forms the foundation of Jesus' teaching.

In those Jewish circles which have formed the periphery of Essenism, the Essene hate-love (*Hass-Liebe*) leads to a breakthrough of love for the sinner to enemy love and then to praying for the persecutor. These Jews freed themselves from the Essenes' theology of hatred by holding on to the rabbinic demand of love for all without differences. Flusser sees the Jewish source to be the *Didache* and the *Testament of the Twelve Patriarchs*.

He shows how Jesus' prayer increasingly came to be seen as directed at the Jews, for they were the ones considered responsible for Jesus' death.[52] Flusser thinks the forgiveness prayer was removed from the text of some Lukan manuscripts by those in the early church who thought that the Jews knew what they were doing to Jesus. In their mind, the verse did not belong.

On the other hand, the saying was a good incentive for Christian mission for the conversion of the Jews. Jerome spoke about the deep love that Jesus had for Jerusalem, so deep that he wept over the city and lamented its rejection of peace. Even when he hung on the cross, he said: "Father, forgive them, for they don't know what they are doing." Jerome claimed that his prayer achieved its goal: Jesus received what he asked for and immediately many thousands of Jews believed and they were given time for repentance until the year 42.

Flusser brings his essay to a close by citing the unpublished "*Historia Passionis Domini*." In it, the Lord Jesus does not think of the wrong being done to him and he graciously prays for his enemies. He does not, however, pray for those who acted against him out of evil intentions: thus, not for the traitor Judas, not for the high priest Caiaphas, and not for Pilate. But he did pray for the whole people of the Jews and the Gentiles, the simple ones who had been misled by the leaders and did not know what they were doing.[53]

Summary

Luke offers few elements of the tradition on Judas that are not found elsewhere in the New Testament. Yet the shape and form that he gives it are
uniquely his own, tailored no doubt to his own community. By now it is
clear that a supranatural element is needed to account for the action of
Judas, and thus Satan is for the first time connected with it. By having Judas
at the Last Supper throughout the evening, Luke shows that Satanic powers
can permeate the very inner circle of believers when they meet with their
Lord. His Judas does not seek repentance. His life ends with an accident or
by natural—or divine—causes (Acts 1),[54] but that does not alter the fact
that "he had this ministry with us" (Acts 1:17). But Luke's understanding of
salvation history also includes the victory of Jesus over Judas; the victory of
good over evil, of light over darkness. Above all, it must be clear that Jesus
did not die to satisfy the claims of Satan. "He will die in order to conquer
death to destroy him who has the power of death. He will die not as a
passive victim, but as a divine invader! . . . The death of Jesus is not a tragic
accident—it is the will of Jesus. Jesus is in charge of the situation, aggressively wading into the final battle that will topple Satan and bring in the
Kingdom of God."[55] Thus the Lord's Supper can be seen as a victory
banquet.

One other factor in Luke's portrait of Satan needs to be considered. In
Jewish sources the identification between Satan and the informer is often
made. And in such circumstances it is not surprising that Satan appears along
with the sons of God before the heavenly throne (Job 1:6) and God hands
him over to Satan for testing (Job 1:12) with clear limits on what he can do.
At the second phase he "delivers him up to the Devil" (Job 2:6). The role
of informer moves toward that of Satan or evil *yezer*.[56]

Most important, perhaps, Luke provides us with fascinating evidence that
Judas publicly either confessed who Jesus was to the Jewish authorities or,
perhaps more likely, filed a formal charge against Jesus, a charge about which
he was prepared to testify in court. Luke, therefore, also forces us to review
the nature of the evidence that one might argue convicts Judas of treason
or, at the very least, of betrayal of his master.

The question remains whether Luke sees any alienation between Jesus
and Judas and whether the act of Judas was meant to further God's rule or
to subvert it. At the time Luke wrote, he could not make a decisive statement on that point, yet it is also clear that he could not explain the action
of Judas. Was he perhaps drawing from an Aramaic source that was in touch
with older traditions, less hostile to Judas?[57] We can only conclude that
anyone who wishes to make of Judas a villain who "betrayed" Jesus in the
usual meaning of that word cannot call on Luke as a witness. One will have
to go elsewhere for that kind of evidence.

Excursus
The Arrest of Jesus and the Role of Judas:
The Ear of the High Priest's Servant

All four Gospels record the cutting off of the ear of the high priest's servant. Mark 14:47 tells about the incident as if filing a police report, crisply and clearly in seventeen words. Matthew 26:51-54 uses twenty-three words but adds a lesson of forty-eight words. Luke 22:49-51 expands the narrative itself to forty-three words and adds a homily of forty-seven words. The Fourth Gospel's account (18:10-12) is fifty words and about half of that is homily.

This story is important for our study of Judas, for it highlights the attitude of Jesus toward his being "handed over," in contrast to that of one other disciple, the one who wields the sword. It may attempt to vindicate the disciples by reporting that when Jesus was being handed over they rushed to his defense, even though Jesus found the act quite unacceptable. "It may also be noteworthy that the sword thrust was not directed *at* Judas."[58]

The fact that all four Gospels record this incident, as they do the action in the Temple, signifies its importance in the passion accounts. John adds important details not found in the other accounts, for example, the name of the wielder of the sword is Peter and the name of the servant is Malchus. John shares with Luke the detail that it is the right ear, and both Mark and John refer to it as the earlobe. It has been argued that the term "earlobe" (*ōtarion,* ὠτάριον) is significant in that it is not the whole ear but merely the lobe that is being clipped. Numerous commentators have noted that the act is a symbolic form of dismembering, thus disqualifying the servant, and the high priest, for service in the Temple.

In the LXX the word that both Mark and John use, ὠτάριον ("earlobe"), does not appear; rather, the term ὤτιον ("ear") is used. But the earlobe is the member of the body that is pierced to mark a slave who has chosen to serve for life (Deut 15:17). The standard formula regarding revelation is that "the Lord revealed to NN's ear" (1 Sam 9:15); or Saul revealing something to his son Jonathan,[59] where it means simply to "tell."

The ear has a religious connotation in 2 Sam 7:27: "reveal to thy servant, David, saying: 'You shall build my house.'" The most frequent references to the ear are in the use of the term οὖς ("ear"), not ὠτάριον ("earlobes") (nearly two hundred times). In comparison, ὀφθάλμος ("eyes") appears about four times as often![60]

For our purposes, the most important usages are those in connection with the priest's ears. Here we find that when Aaron and his sons were consecrated as priests, the lobes of the right ears were anointed with the blood of the bull (Exod 29:20; Lev 8:23). During the guilt offering the priest also places the blood and the oil on the right earlobe of the man seeking cleansing (Lev 14:14). These references show that the *right ear* is of special significance to the priest in performing his services.[61]

M. Rostovzeff[62] was apparently the first to recognize that what is involved in the act of cutting off the ear is an attempt not to kill but to maim. Although Matt 26:52 and John 18:11 seem to have missed this point, it would seem that both Luke and Mark allow for that possibility.

There is then also the intriguing suggestion of Norbert Krieger that the "servant of the high priest" mentioned in John is none other than Judas himself and that the name Malchus, provided only by John, is his free invention to obscure that fact.[63]

But the most important question is the function this narrative plays for each of the Gospels. The best study of that subject with respect to the Synoptic Gospels has been carried out by Alfred Suhl.[64] He concludes that the narrative of the use of the sword by one of the disciples has a clearly recognizable and quite different function in each of the three Gospels and that it contributes to the action as part of the overall purpose of each writer. He also ties it together with the Gethsemane accounts[65] in each Gospel, as well as with the cry of dereliction. For Suhl explores in detail one facet of these narratives, namely, how the prayers of Jesus illuminate the relationship to God expressed in each passion narrative. He concludes that Mark depicts Jesus as caught between being forsaken by God, who remains silent, and by disciples who cannot remain awake. Far from depicting Jesus as the dying of a good man, Mark shows Jesus as being aware of the absence of God at a time when most needed. An important development takes place when the arrest party arrives and Jesus gives voice to his desolation by speaking first to his disciples: "Still sleeping? Enough! The hour has come. The Son of man is handed over to sinful men. Up, let us go forward! The one who hands me over has arrived" (Mark 14:41-42). Even though God is distant, the hour has come and Jesus shows no vacillation now.

As Judas identifies Jesus, greets him with a kiss and addresses him as Rabbi, and gives the order: "Seize him and get him away safely," Jesus is immediately bound. At this, Mark reports that one of the bystanders drew his sword, struck at the high priest's servant, cutting off his ear. This incident illuminates most clearly the disciples' lack of understanding of Jesus' mission. In spite of all that they had experienced with Jesus, above all his repeated statements that he would need to be delivered into the hands of sinful men, they don't seem to get the point.

This action of cutting off the ear, although not ascribed to a disciple in Mark, is attributed to such in the other three Gospels. It is a most critical deed at a most difficult time. It does not evoke a response from Jesus at all in Mark. Instead, Jesus addresses the arresting party and expresses surprise that although he has taught publicly in the Temple, they come for him with swords and sticks. Nevertheless, the time has come and he will not engage in debate about issues of procedure or content. Instead, he yields himself to the fulfillment of God's will. "Let the scriptures be fulfilled," he says, and they are the last words Jesus of Nazareth speaks to his disciples in Mark. And the disciples? "They deserted him and ran away" (Mark 14:50). One, whom they tried to seize, lost his linen cloth and "he ran away naked" (Mark 14:51-52). All in all, the encounter was not a great credit to the disciples.

Suhl has observed that in Matthew the Gethsemane story does not depict Jesus as demanding of God in his prayer as he does in Mark. He notes the difference between "All things are possible to you; take from me this cup" (Mark 14:36) and "If it is possible, let this cup pass me by" (Matt 26:39). The imperative is changed to a "respectful indirect 'let it pass me by.' Accordingly from the beginning the theme of submission becomes more prominent in the petition."[66] Matthew portrays Jesus as moving step by step toward insight into and affirmation of the divine saving will, which will be accomplished through the Son. This reminds us of the commitment to fulfill all righteousness (Matt 3:15), which Jesus himself anchors in the divine necessity to fulfill the scriptures (26:54). It remains for the bedeviled wife of Pilate to give her testimony that Jesus is righteous (*dikaios,* Matt 27:19).

As Jesus comes closer to God and more deeply committed to doing God's will, he removes himself more from his disciples. This is the more remarkable since, in Matthew, Jesus is portrayed as being much closer to them than in Mark. The prayer scene in Gethsemane illustrates this, for it has Jesus asking all the disciples to "Sit here while I go over there to pray" (26:36-37); then, taking only three disciples with him, he says to them, "Stop here, and stay awake with me" (26:38). He himself "went on a little" and prayed alone (26:39). The Greek verbs to describe his departure in verse 42 and finally in verse 44 stress the degrees of separation involved and the profound aloneness Jesus had as his disciples were unable to stay awake.[67] Mark has Jesus moving between two walls of silence, left in the lurch by both God and the disciples. Matthew portrays all the disciples as sleepy; their behavior becomes a foil for the obedience of Jesus. In Mark, Jesus asks that this hour may pass him by (14:35), but in Matthew the hour has come and he asks only that the cup may be taken from him (26:39).

Moreover, while Mark suggested that Jesus will die in Jerusalem, certainty on that point is not reached until Gethsemane. In Matthew, however, after his last speech to the disciples, Jesus himself gives the "start signal" for the events of the Passion.[68] For Jesus says to his disciples: "You know that in two days' time it will be Passover and the Son of man will be handed over to be crucified" (Matt 26:1-2). It is only after that the chief priests confer about how to arrest him.

One remarkable feature of the sword incident in Matthew is that it provides Jesus with an opportunity to teach the crowd: Ἐν ἐκείνῃ τῇ ὥρᾳ εἶπεν ὁ Ἰησοῦς τοῖς ὄχλοις: "In that hour Jesus spoke to the crowds." This formula provides an atmosphere of dignity and sovereignty to the scene. He reminds his listeners that sticks and swords were not his standard equipment. He taught instead in the Temple, where the authorities never bothered him. He took the opportunity to remind them that his arrest and capture were taking place in order that the writings of the prophets might be fulfilled (Matt 26:56). The irony of it is that he was already bound (26:50). Even on this occasion "all of his disciples deserted him" (Matt 26:56). For Matthew, the fulfillment of scriptures is a necessity and applies only to the yielding of the Son of man to the process of being "handed over." It never applies, in any of the Gospels, to the role that Judas plays in the handing over.

Here Matthew uses this opportunity in a way not used by any other writer to drive home the point that violence is not the way of the Son of man. He fulfills scripture precisely by rejecting violence and continues to respond to evil in the arrest scene with what he started in his ministry (Matt 12:14-21). He could have called legions, but he did not. Suhl aptly comments: "He fulfills thereby in an exemplary manner the refusal to meet violence with counterforce. He is consistent with his instructions to the community in the Sermon on the Mount fundamentally to renounce violence, for violence can only be overcome by abstention from violence grounded in love."[69]

The same note is struck in Luke's account. Luke, too, portrays Jesus as being in charge during the arrest. Here his disciples even request permission to use their swords (Luke 22:49). Apparently without waiting for a reply, one of them uses the blade. Jesus not only heals the victim's ear but also sharply rebukes the sword wielder with the words: "Desist. No more!" (Luke 22:51). This is the hour when darkness reigns and it should have its moment to assert itself. For Luke, the arrest, including the sword stroke, provides an opportunity to highlight the difference between the kingdom of light and that of darkness, giving him an opportunity to show how fully Jesus is prepared to live according to the plan of God.

John's account is much briefer, but it illuminates the same point. While more specific in that the sword wielder is identified as Peter, Jesus rebukes Peter with the words: "Sheathe your sword. This is the cup my father has given me; shall I not drink it?" (John 18:10-11). As in the other Gospels, John seeks by means of this story to demonstrate that by the time of the arrest, Jesus had clearly decided that he would drink the cup. He would not allow anyone, for whatever motives, to obstruct him from going through with his fate. Was it Judas, whatever the ambiguities attached to his action, who served as God's instrument in the handing over of the Son of man to evil men? Was he, at this critical hour, the only one of the disciples who contributed to Jesus' fulfillment of the divine plan by assisting Jesus in moving toward the destiny he had chosen?

Notes

1. Strauss, *The Life of Jesus,* 605.
2. See, among others, Fitzmyer's masterful commentary on Luke (*ABC*); Johnson, "Luke-Acts, Book of," *ABD,* 4:403–420; Karris, "Missionary Communities: A New Paradigm for the Study of Luke-Acts"; idem, "Luke 23:47 and the Lukan view of Jesus' Death"; Conzelmann, *The Theology of St. Luke;* idem, "Historie und Theologie in den synoptischen Passionsberichten," in *Zur Bedeutung des Todes Jesu,* 35–54; and F. Rehkopf, *Die lukanische Sonderquelle.*
3. In addition to the literature cited above, the following monographs on Judas: Klauck, 33–69; Vogler, 75–92; Maccoby, 50–60; and the passion narratives have been found useful: Brown, *Death,* 64–75, 86–93, 102–104, and bib. 157–162; 1060–1173; and H. Klein, "Die lukanisch-johanneische Passionstradition," 155–186. Also in Limbeck, ed., *Redaktion,* 366–403; Rese, *Alttestamentliche Motive in der Christologie des Lukas* (StNT 1); Roloff, "Anfänge der soteriologischen Deutung des Todes Jesu (Mk 10:45 und Lk 22:27)," 38–64; and Taylor, *The Passion Narrative of St. Luke* (SNTSMS, 19).
4. See also chapter 3, above.
5. Schütz, *Der leidende Christus,* 34 n. 112.
6. Lightfoot, *History and Interpretation,* 164–171.
7. Lightfoot, *History,* 172.
8. Pagels has not convinced me that "in both Luke and John . . . Jesus himself identifies his Jewish opponents with Satan" (*Origin,* 88). I concur with Leslie Houlden's critique of the book. What may be true of the Fourth Gospel is not necessarily true of the others and "in Luke the business of blaming the Jews is much less clearcut than Ms Pagels makes it seem" (*New York Times Book Review,* June 18, 1995: 10).
9. Fitzmyer, *Luke,* 1367.
10. Although W. Popke is cited on a related topic on 1401.
11. Fitzmyer, *Luke,* 253, 620, 1374, 1409.
12. Fitzmyer, *Luke,* 1375.
13. In a letter to me (October 5, 1992), Fitzmyer states that we have access only

to stage three of the Gospel tradition, which is "the way the evangelists record and react to what took place in stage one." He urges that we forge ahead in analyzing the Jesus of history.

14. Wesley continues: "And why did our Lord send him among them? Undoubtedly for our instruction. For a standing unanswerable proof that 'he sendeth by whom he will send' (Exod 4:13), that he can and doth send salvation to men even by those who will not accept it of [for] themselves" (Wesley, *The Works of John Wesley, Sermons* 3:473).

15. J. Ford, *My Enemy Is My Guest: Jesus and Violence in Luke,* 108–117.

16. Klein, "*Passionstradition,*" 155–186; Linnemann, *Studien zur Passionsgeschichte;* and Rehkopf, *Die lukanische Sonderquelle.* Italics in the text indicate that these are Luke's additions to Mark's text.

17. Schürer, *The History of the Jewish People,* rev. ed. 1979–87, 2:277–279.

18. Johnson, "Luke-Acts, Book of," *ABD,* 4:414.

19. Matt 3:6; Mark 1:5; Acts 19:18; James 5:16.

20. Rom 14:11; 15:9; Phil 2:11.

21. Evans, *Luke,* 776. So also Bauer, *Lexicon,* 276.

22. Schütz, *Der leidende Christus,* 88–89.

23. Schütz, *Der leidende Christus,* 88.

24. The term appears six times in Luke-Acts, never in the Synoptics, and only once in John (7:18). Connected with μισθός ("wages"), it appears in 2 Peter 2:13–15. Karris, "Luke 23:47," has a good treatment of justice as a pervasive motif in Luke-Acts, 70–73.

25. For a good overall treatment of the way the demonic appears in Luke, see Garrett, *The Demise of the Devil: Magic and the Demonic in Luke's Writings.* Unfortunately, she does not deal with Judas. Elaine Pagels, in "The Social History of Satan, Part 2: Satan in the New Testament Gospels," sees Satan, especially in the Fourth Gospel, as working through human instruments of which Judas is one and Luke does not absolve Judas "from bearing his guilt" (37). See also now Pagels, *The Origin of Satan:* "Jesus himself declares that neither Satan's role nor God's preordained plan absolves Judas's guilt: 'The Son of man goes as it has been determined; but woe to that man by whom he is betrayed' (22:22; cf. Mark 14:21)" (93). Woe surely cannot be treated as impugning guilt.

26. Derrett, "The Iscariot," 15.

27. One is tempted to see here an allusion to the meaning of Judas's name: Yehudah=praise. Could it be that in the earliest Aramaic/Hebrew-speaking churches it was known that Judas praised God precisely in the act of handing Jesus over? "One thing they [evangelists] were clear about was that [the name] Judas= confession," Derrett, "The Iscariot," 15. Lapide also expresses strong emotional attachment to the name and its religious significance, *Schuld,* 15–16. Michael Lattke observes that the aspects of praise and thanks are often very clear and they are often synonymous to *homologeomai.*

28. See NEB. Louw and Nida, *Greek-English Lexicon,* 1:420. KJV has "promised" NIV, "consented"; *Gute Nachricht,* "war einverstanden"; *JB,* "accepted"; Rieu, "so he undertook the task"; Brown, *Death,* 1403, is at a loss what to do with this word here and allows the possibility that Judas made a confession to the high priests of his complicity in following Jesus. Michel (*KTWBNT,* 5:213–237) concludes that it has various shades of meaning and settles for "promise."

29. Preisigke, *Wörterbuch der griechischen Papyrusurkunden,* "to report to the au-

thorities," 520. Note also Liddell and Scott's statement that, especially in legal formulae, it means "to acknowledge" or to report a transgression.

30. Marshall, *Commentary on Luke,* ad loc., recognizes the usage as "unparalleled," yet goes on to cite "an excellent parallel in Lysias 12:8f." The word in Lysias is ὁμολογέω and does not apply here.

31. Brown, *Death,* 1400–1401.

32. See the detailed comparison of this pericope with Mark 14:18b-21 in Rehkopf, *Sonderquelle,* 7–30.

33. Rehkopf, *Sonderquelle,* 13.

34. Rehkopf, *Sonderquelle,* 27.

35. On the place of dialogue in Luke, especially in comparison with Mark and Matthew, see Schlatter, *Die beiden Schwerter,* 15–16.

36. Schlatter, *Die beiden Schwerter,* 16.

37. Weiss, "We are not always able to study the growth of a tradition as precisely as we can in this case" (*Die drei älteren Evangelien,* 44, cited by Rehkopf, *Sonderquelle,* 28 n. 2).

38. See note 17 above. Here again Luke alone has "officers" (στρατηγοί) and here he adds: "of the Temple": ἱεροῦ.

39. There is no reason to agree with Klostermann, *Markus,* 1st ed., 128, that the kiss of Judas serves to characterize the traitor as a man who has fallen very far.

40. V. Taylor, *Behind the Third Gospel,* 47, quoted by Rehkopf, *Sonderquelle,* 51, ftnote 2.

41. Grundmann, *Lukas,* ad loc., THKNT (Berlin, 1974).

42. V. Taylor, *Behind the Third Gospel,* 47.

43. See the treatment of this incident on pp. 129–33.

44. Daube, "'For they know not what they do,'" 58–70.

45. Daube, "'For they know not,'" 68.

46. E.g., Acts 3:17; 13:26–28; 17:23; 1 Tim 1:13–15.

47. Daube, "'For they know not,'" 67.

48. Flusser, "'Sie wissen nicht, was sie tun': Geschichte eines Herrnwortes," 393–410.

49. Flusser, 393, quoting from *Das Buch der Judenverfolgungen in Deutschland und Frankreich* (Jerusalem, 1945). Hebrew.

50. Flusser, "'Sie wissen nicht,'" 394.

51. Flusser, "'Sie wissen nicht,'" 397.

52. Flusser, "'Sie wissen nicht,'" 404.

53. Flusser, "'Sie wissen nicht,'" 405.

54. The text from the book of Acts pertaining to the death of Judas is dealt with in the chapter on the death of Judas; see below.

55. Kallas, *Jesus,* 179.

56. S. Schechter, *Aspects of Rabbinic Theology,* 252.

57. So Sydney Temple, "The Two Traditions of the Last Supper," 77–85, esp. 78–79.

58. Schneider, *Die Passion Jesu,* 44.

59. ἀποκαλύπτω and ear, 1 Kings 20:2, 13; 22:8, 17; 2 Kings 22:45.

60. The observation that the Hebrews "experienced the world primarily through listening, the Greeks through seeing," seems not to be supported by these statistics. See Boman, "Hebraic and Greek Thought-Forms in the New Testament," in W. Klassen and G. F. Snyder, eds., *Current Issues in NT Interpretation,* 1.

61. Viviano, "The High Priest's Servant's Ear: Mark 14:47," has explored the significance of this event and sees it as a decommissioning of the high priest's servant. Daube has made the point that the action would also decommission the high priest since his commission is tied to that of his servants. Viviano's case can be strengthened by the addition of the material presented above on the role of the right ear in the ordination of the priest and in the discharge of their duties.

62. "Οὓς δεξιόν ἀποτεμνεῖν," ZNW 33 (1934): 198. See Horst, in KTWBNT, 5:543–58, esp. 558.

63. Krieger, "Der Knecht des Hohenpriesters."

64. Suhl, "Die Funktion des Schwertstreichs."

65. Where he builds in particular on the work of R. Feldmeier, Die Krisis des Gottessohnes.

66. Suhl, "Gefangennahme," 309, quoting Feldmeier, 10.

67. Suhl, "Gefangennahme," 310–311, citing Feldmeier.

68. Suhl, "Gefangennahme," 308, 310, 312.

69. Suhl, "Gefangennahme," 313.

CHAPTER
EIGHT

THE FOURTH GOSPEL

John had his failings. . . . He was anything but the delicate, affectionate disciple of love. . . . That he so often spoke of charity and understood it so deeply is possibly due to the fact that he did not possess it—at least not the charity of kindness. . . . Humanly speaking he must have loathed Judas like poison.
—R. Guardini[1]

As is the case with the three other Gospels, the Fourth Gospel has been the subject of considerable research over the past decades. It is no longer possible simply to accept the picture of Judas presented to us in this Gospel as definitive. It certainly does not have the power to change our perception of what the other Gospels present, although there are still those such as Raymond Brown who are inclined to take the evidence of the Fourth Gospel with utmost seriousness, and in some matters rely on John to make historical judgments about Judas. Brown's two-volume work on John has many references to Judas. Basically, Brown accepts what Judas did as a "betrayal," an evil deed, and suggests that John perhaps picks up an original event in Judas's protest against the money being spent for anointing. He also thinks "this remembrance was lost in the Synoptic tradition, a genuine historical fragment. . . . There is a better chance that the characters of Mary and Judas were originally part of the story and that their names were lost in the Synoptic tradition."[2]

In his most recent work Brown warns us that "so much skepticism" with regard to John's storytelling sense is not warranted even if we cannot be certain. Indeed, he ventures to draw into the Synoptic accounts of the anointing the Johannine observation that Judas complained about its waste: "In confirmation of this (and perhaps as part of a stubborn rejection of Jesus' condoning the waste), Judas, one of the Twelve, goes to the chief priests and helps their plot by offering to give Jesus over, a betrayal for which he is promised silver."[3]

Generally, efforts have been made to find the Fourth Gospel's place in early Christianity rather than to adjudicate the genuineness of his materials.[4]

It is not an easy task to deal with John's portrait of Judas. In so many aspects it is different from Mark and the other Gospels. From a strictly methodological point of view, I cannot attribute the same historical reliability to the Fourth Gospel as to the Synoptics, especially to Mark. In other words, throwing all four Gospels together and thus arriving at a New Testament teaching about Judas, as Karl Barth does, is not an option.[5]

Of course some information that John supplies has the ring of authenticity, maybe even can be considered as historical fact; for example, his statement that Judas carried the purse for the disciples. That is very likely the case. We cannot, however, (12:6; 13:29) accept as historical fact John's interpretations or glosses; for example, his allegation that Judas stole from the communal treasury (12:6). There is simply no other evidence of such a deed. It is the kind of thing, were it known, that would certainly have appeared in one of the other Gospels as well. It seems difficult to believe that a group as intimate as the disciples of Jesus would have carelessly selected its treasurer and not provided him with at least a periodic review. One cannot imagine the disciples tolerating someone who was guilty of embezzlement of the group's limited funds. Such cautious and careful interpreters as C. K. Barrett, while convinced that "psychological reconstructions of the character and motives of Judas are not profitable," recognize that with the accusation of thievery John is already "constructing" a picture of Judas and so conclude that John here "more probably represents the traditional and progressive blackening of Judas' character."[6]

Credulity is also stretched when John affirms that Judas, one of the Twelve, early on in Jesus' ministry was already "a devil" (John 6:70). That is a very harsh accusation and it is not easy to decide what to make of it. The most likely explanation is that John is trying to convince Jews that Jesus truly was the Messiah and therefore knew what Judas was up to. He was trying to counter arguments such as those used later in the attack launched against Christians by Celsus, a Roman philosopher, who wrote just after the martyrdoms of 177. He made much of the fact that Jews, whose writings Celsus used, could not accept Jesus as God. Jews are quoted as saying:

> How could we have accepted as God one who, as was reported, did not carry out any of the works he announced, and when we had evidence against him and denounced him and wanted to punish him he hid himself and tried to escape; who was captured in a disgraceful manner and even was betrayed by one whom he called his disciple? Surely if he was God he would not have needed to flee, or been taken away bound, and least of all to be left in the lurch and deserted by his companions, who shared everything with him personally, considered him their teacher, . . . Saviour, Son and Messenger of the highest God.[7]

What seems evident is that John is a theologian first and has historical interests only secondarily, whereas Mark reverses the two interests. Yet it is incumbent upon us to give John his say. Not only has he the most to say about Judas of all New Testament writers, he is also the most critical. Could it be that he is correct? Certainly we cannot rule out that possibility simply by saying that his story is totally implausible. Possibly Judas was the villain he is depicted to be in John. It is also possible that John (the final editor? the community of the Fourth Gospel?) is guilty of slandering and vilifying a fellow disciple.

John's Gospel is a great spiritual resource for many people, and has been through the ages. His exalted view of Jesus is not under discussion here. Rather, we are concerned with the evaluation he provides of Judas and of the Jewish people, and with the effect of his Gospel upon the way Christians have acted toward Jews and thought about Judas.

There are a total of five references to Judas Iscariot in the Fourth Gospel.

A. John 6:64-71

"But there are some among you who will not believe." For Jesus knew from the beginning there were certain ones who would not believe and the one who would deliver him over. And he said, "Because of this I said to you that no one is able to come to me unless it is given to him by my Father."

After this many of his disciples went away from him and no longer walked after him. Then Jesus said to the Twelve, "Surely you also do not wish to leave, do you?" Simon Peter answered: "Lord, to whom shall we go? Words of eternal life, you have. And we have believed and have known that you are the Holy One of God."

Jesus answered them: "Have I not chosen twelve of you? And of you, one is a devil?" And he said this of Judas son of Simon, son of Iscariot. For that one, one of the Twelve, was about to hand him over.[8]

The introduction of Judas's unbelief so early in the ministry of Jesus is unique. While the Synoptic Gospels have also introduced Judas when naming the Twelve, they have only identified him further with the words "the one who handed him over." John, however, introduces Judas here to show that Jesus is aware that, although he chose twelve, one of them ranks with those who do not believe, which presumably Jesus knew from the start (6:64). More serious still, he adds, "one of you is a devil" (v. 70). Later, of "the Jews," Jesus says that their "father is the devil" (8:44). The same author, 1 John, states clearly that children of the devil are those who do not do right (1 John 1:10), people such as Cain who killed his brother (1 John 3:11); in short, "the one who sins is a child of the devil" (1 John 3:8).

John wishes to affirm that Jesus knew everything: "Jesus knew from the first who those were that did not believe and who would hand him over" (6:64).[9] Where Luke speaks of Satan entering into Judas during the last week of Jesus' life (but before the Last Supper [22:3]), John states flatly: "One of you is a διάβολος (diabolos) (6:70). John's gloss explains that "He meant Judas, son of Simon Iscariot." After he has taken the morsel from the hand of his Master, John says that "Satan entered into him" (John 13:27).

The closest parallel is from a different account in Matthew and Mark. After Jesus has been rebuked by Peter for suggesting that Jesus should reject the path of suffering, Jesus rebukes Peter very sharply by saying: "Get thee behind me, Satan" (Matt 16:23//Mark 8:33). The Greek is striking: καὶ προσλαβόμενος αὐτον ὁ Πέτρος ἤρξατο ἐπιτιμᾶν αὐτῷ λέγων: ἵλεώς σοι, κύριε, οὐ μὴ ἔσται σοι τοῦτο—but he (Jesus) turning to Peter, said: "Get you behind me, Satan. *You are a stumbling block [σκάνδαλον] to me*[10] because you think not the things of God but of man" (Matt 16:21-23).

Mark omits some of the dialogue but retains the sharp word *epitimao* (ἐπιτιμάο, "rebuke"), both for what Peter did and what Jesus did. Also, instead of telling us what Peter said, Mark has, "But he having turned, *and seen his disciples,* rebuked Peter and said: 'Get you behind me, Satan'" (Mark 8:31-33). It is the only place in the New Testament where anyone rebukes Peter so sharply. Is it possible that John, seeking to make Peter look better than the other Gospels, decided to put an anti-Judas spin on this story? Accordingly, words that were originally spoken to Peter are taken by John and applied to Judas. By the time John wrote, around 90 C.E., Judas had been so completely maligned that he took no risk in doing so. Hengstenberg, although showing no favoritism toward Judas, admits that "perfectly analogous" to this incident in John 6:64-71 is the one in which Jesus calls Peter Satan. "There also Peter is a Satanic man, an incarnate Satan."[11] The sharpness of the rebuke and the words used make it almost certain that Mark's is a genuine tradition.

Luke has a similar incident involving Peter. For Jesus, the reality of Satan is such that he does not hesitate to warn Peter that Satan is on the lookout for him and that he will be sifted as wheat (Luke 22:31). No doubt Jesus was aware that satanic forces seek to ensnare and that a given act could be attributed to God or to Satan. But Luke protects Peter even though he joins the three other Gospels in recording Peter's denial (22:55-62).

Satan and the Devil in the Gospels

A brief treatment of the way in which the devil and Satan were viewed by the Gospel writers may help to put the matter in perspective, especially since modern psychiatry shows some interest in using similar language to explain human behavior.[12]

In the Hebrew scriptures David's census of the people was attributed by one chronicler to Satan (1 Chron 21:1) but by another to God (2 Sam 24:1-2). In both cases the deed was seen as a sin for which God punished David. In Revelation to John there is a similar usage (Rev 12:9) when the accuser is thrown out of heaven. We observe that both the Satan (ὁ σατανάς) and the Devil (ὁ διάβολος) consistently appear with the article in all four Gospels. Even where John omits the article it is implicit: "one of you is a *diabolos* (διάβολος)" (6:70). Indeed, the term can be used in the plural in later New Testament writings (2 Tim 3:3; Titus 2:3).

Apparently Jewish thinking about Satan and the demonic had not yet crystallized to the point where the word διάβολος (Satan) meant a personal agent of evil—say, Beelzebub. The term the people of Qumran preferred was Beliar, which appears only once in the New Testament (2 Cor 6:14-15). What is affirmed here is that human beings can allow themselves to be directed by satanic or demonic forces. Indeed, one of the strongest parts of Jesus' work was to cleanse people of unclean spirits or of demons that possessed them. Demonic possession was always treated in the Gospels as a force that had to yield to the sovereignty of Christ. Far from such a state being hopeless, the power of Christ was made available to just such people.

Critical to our understanding of the way in which the term is applied to Judas by Luke and John is that it has at this early stage no connotation of being "the" devil or being possessed of the devil. It, rather, has that broader meaning so prevalent in the Hebrew scriptures, where the accuser can appear among the sons of God (in Job 1) and put God's servant to the test. Both Peter and Judas, as indeed all the disciples, were vulnerable to being human instruments turned to purposes not in accord with the will of God. John judges Judas's act by its immediate consequences. Then his perspectiveallows him no other alternative but to ascribe it to the devil, just as he ascribes what the "Judeans" do to their father the devil (8:44). But he also lumps Judas with the Jews or Judeans as not having faith (6:64).[13]

Had John followed the practice of Hebrew scriptures, he could have had Jesus saying that Judas was inspired by both God and the devil, as they had inspired David.[14] In that context, he would not have viewed Judas as totally evil and beyond redemption. It may very well be that John has taken a statement Jesus made in a lighter vein, using *diabolos* not to mean "the devil," for later in 13:2, 27 he clearly differentiates Judas from the devil who influences Judas and enters him. So it is likely that Jesus means that Judas is an adversary in the legal courtly sense and that he will be at Jesus' right hand presenting the evidence, just as the *diabolos* did in Job 1 and in Zech 3:1. Then the role of the *diabolos* is defined as it is in Ps 108:6 (LXX): "Let his adversary stand on his right hand." In Zechariah he stands as an opponent. But in both cases the scene is a courtroom and Jesus is predicting that Judas will stand "in the position of greatest trust, that is at the right hand of the defendant."[15] That, of course, is precisely where John has him standing in the arrest, only he is standing with *them*. At the same time, if these are the enemies of Jesus, Judas may have understood the teachings of Jesus in that vein. Solidarity with Jesus does not mean hating or killing enemies.

With this reading of the Johannine adversary statement the conclusion of the arrest passage in John makes some sense: "Again Jesus asked them, Whom do you seek? And they said, 'Jesus of Nazareth.' Jesus answered, I have told you that I am he. Since therefore you seek me, release these others so that the words which he said may be fulfilled: 'Of those whom you have given me, I have not lost one.'" Is Judas included in his group? If not, John is more careless in his editing than he is in chapter 17:12. Is it possible that once again the fate of Judas is not as firmly sealed as John would have it be? The better solution is to see John as a literary artist doing with the character of Judas whatever he needs to make it a good drama. In John 6 the disciples are depicted as witnesses to the faith that Jesus is the Holy One of God.

John depicts the responses of the people to Jesus very vividly. There are those who are open to the light that Jesus represents (such as the Samaritan woman), and there are those who are opposed, usually called the "Judeans." There also are those who are undecided, such as Nicodemus. The disciples are also somewhat in this gray area, and certainly the Twelve "have no authority in the eyes of the Evangelist."[16] For John, however, Judas emerges as "the most blatant and blackest example of disloyalty."[17] There is no dualism of decision here, for in John's view Judas is chosen by Jesus to be the traitor and he becomes the "son of perdition" "through the determination of God, before whom the hearts of men are like rivulets."[18]

The Gospel writers increasingly saw the relations between Jesus and the leaders of his people as a classic conflict. As they did so, the role of Judas was seen in the Fourth Gospel as one who had changed sides and gone over to the other side. He fought then under the leadership of Satan, and the authors are particularly adept in developing new motives for his actions. Soon those same motives were imputed to all who defected or became heretics.[19]

There are other ways of approaching what happened. From Judas's perspective we can visualize it as something like this: In his wrestling with the picture of the kingdom of God which was emerging, and especially in regard to the increasing alienation between Jesus and the Jewish leadership (which had come to a climax with Jesus' action in the Temple), Judas may have felt a strong need to get Jesus and the Jewish authorities together.

He knew the passion that Jesus had for his own people, for the Temple, and for the role that God had assigned to Israel to be the light to the Gentiles. Jesus had zeal for the Temple, the Lord's house where he taught, and had demonstrated his devotion on many occasions. In the Fourth Gospel, in Jesus' discussions with the high priest, he is questioned about his disciples and his teaching. He replies that he has "spoken openly to all the world, beginning in the synagogue and the Temple" (John 18:19-23). He has not spoken in secret and he encourages the high priests to inquire from his listeners what he has said.

During his arrest when Peter moved in with his sword to decommission the high priest's deputy so that he could not serve again in the Temple, Jesus rebuked him by saying: "Sheathe your sword. This is the cup the Father has given me; shall I not drink it?" (18:10-11). Jesus may have expressed reservations about the Temple and, indeed, acted decisively against some of the abuses in its administration, but he was not about to use violence to lead his disciples to occupy the Temple or to seek an end to the ministry of those who served there. His agenda is different. Neither Judas nor Peter, both (?) as instruments of Satan, can deflect him from it. His capture, which Judas has facilitated, is the cup the Father has given him and he is prepared to drink it (John 18:11).

Peter's impetuosity once again reflects more of the way of the devil. Jesus rejects it and follows the path that Judas has made possible. It is of one cloth when, in the Fourth Gospel, this same Peter a few hours later denies Jesus and shows no remorse until after the resurrection. Nevertheless, John does not criticize Peter, beyond describing his threefold denial of his relationship to Jesus (18:12-28), and repentance, which he does obliquely in the last chapter of the book.[20]

On the other hand, Judas is unsparingly criticized. With singular harshness the author of the Fourth Gospel consigns Judas to the realm of the demonic.[21] Commentators have had a field day suggesting that, from Capernaum days, Judas had been disaffected with, if not disaffiliated from, Jesus.[22] We can only attribute to John's own biases this harsh verdict rendered against Judas. There is certainly no evidence outside the Fourth Gospel that Jesus treated Judas as someone who was a Satan or even possessed of Satan. Luke, consistent with his own editorial approach, attributes Judas's deed to Satanic influences near the end of Christ's life (22:3), but that is a very different matter. For it would have been wholly inconsistent with the mission of Jesus for him to drive demons out of other people's lives and free them from the bondage to Satan while allowing his own disciple, Judas, to be possessed of Satan. He rebuked Peter in love to save him from such a fate. Is there any reason to believe he would not have done the same if that possibility existed for Judas?

Jesus' whole mission was a struggle with the satanic. It was during the mission of the seventy that Luke reports, upon their return, they discovered that "demons" were subject to them "in his name" (Luke 10:17) and that Jesus saw Satan falling like lightning from heaven (Luke 10:18). He was exuberant upon their return (Luke 10:21) because he saw now that the kingdom would come through the work of his disciples who had shown that they, too, could carry out the mission that Jesus had begun. Judas was most likely a part of that entourage. Now, however, Judas had a different role, one that would be subject to severe misunderstanding on the part of all his fellow disciples.

The satanic element may be analyzed in the light of an account from the Hebrew Bible. The high priest Joshua was standing before the angel of the Lord with the Satan standing at his right hand to accuse him. The Lord said to the Satan, "The Lord rebuke you, Satan, the Lord rebuke you for venting your spite on Jerusalem" (Zech 3:1-10). Satan's concern would appear to be for the integrity of the high-priestly service. For Joshua, the high priest, "was wearing filthy clothes" (v. 3). It was the Satan's role to protect the integrity of divine service. In this case, perhaps as always, the Satan was unable to invoke the mercy and compassion of God and lived only as a result of God's holiness and justice, which he also sought to promote.[23] If it is satanic to become fixated on one dimension of the divine, for example, God's wrath over against divine love and compassion, then both Peter and Judas can equally and accurately be described as acting on Satan's directives.

Perhaps this, too, was Judas's dilemma. Devoted as he was to both Jesus and his kingdom, as well as to the Jewish people and the Temple leadership, he could not understand where Jesus was going. In that, he was not alone. Neither did any of the other disciples, and all deserted, except for such women as Mary his mother, her sister, Mary the mother of Clopas, Mary of Magdala (John 19:25), and "Salome and several others . . . who had followed him from Galilee" (Mark 15:40-41). So Judas, following the orders of Jesus, had decided that the time had arrived for someone to play the role of the informer (מסר). When Jesus handed him the bread, Judas knew he had been selected.

Judas therefore went to the priests and told them that the direction of Jesus' ministry could well lead to the destruction of the Temple—in other words to the destruction of the form of worship and service known to the Jews at that time. The role of the Temple in the arrest of Jesus deserves some discussion.

The Temple and the Mission of Jesus

Recent interest in the Temple has to be attributed to more than merely the interest generated by the discovery and publication of the Temple Scroll from Qumran. In the early Christian writings themselves, there is an "implicit though clear threat of destruction in Mark 11.15b-17," and warnings about the demise of the Temple are frequent in the tradition. Marcus Borg cites explicit references: in Q: Luke 13:34-35//Matt 23:37-39; Mark 13:2; 14:58; 15:29; L: Luke 19:42-44; 21:20-24; Acts 6:14; and John 2:19. In addition to Jesus speaking about it, his opponents did as well (Mark 14:58; 15:29; Acts 6:14), accusing Jesus of threatening its destruction.[24]

Paul and Hebrews, although recognizing the historical role the Temple had played in divine history, seem to think beyond it. Although in the Hebrew Bible, Ezekiel's vision culminates with a magnificent temple, the prophet John, in what he describes as the revelation of Jesus Christ, clearly envisions a future without a temple: "For a temple, I did not see in it (the Holy City, new Jerusalem) for the Lord God, the All-powerful one and the Lamb is her temple" (Rev 21:22).[25]

To be accused of threatening the destruction of the Temple was a serious matter. No doubt the authorities needed to base any action on some specific word that Jesus had said, in addition to using his action in the Temple. The closest they could come to a specific saying was some vague reference to "destroy this temple and in three days I will raise it up"—one of those enigmatic sayings so common on the lips of Jesus.[26] But the authorities had, in fact, already announced that they were looking for someone to inform on Jesus. The call had gone out that they welcomed an informer to come and lay a legal charge against him (11:56-57): "Now the chief priests and the Pharisees had given orders that anyone who knew where Jesus was should let them know so that they might arrest him."[27]

B. John 12:1-8

Now therefore six days before the Passover Jesus entered into Bethany where Lazarus was, whom Jesus had raised from the dead. Therefore they made a supper for him and Mary served but Lazarus was one of those reclining with him. Then Mary took a vial of aromatic ointment and anointed Jesus' feet with it and wiped his feet with her hair. The house was filled with its pleasant aroma.

But Judas the Iscariot, one of his disciples, the one who was about to deliver him over, said: "Why was this myrrh not sold for thirty denarii and given to the poor?" But he said this, not because he cared for the poor but because he was a thief and having the purse used to steal from it.

But Jesus said: "Leave her alone. She has kept me until the day of my burial, but the poor you have always with you, but me you do not always have."

John's editing of the anointing story builds on certain traditional materials; only here does John refer to Judas as "Iscariot" and only here (and 6:8) does he use the expression εἰς τῶν μαθητῶν αὐτοῦ, "one of his disciples." He prefers the term ἐκ τῶν μαθητῶν ("from among the disciples," 18:25), and only here does he use the traditional formula "the one who will hand him over." What is new in this story is:

- that Judas alone complains about the waste,
- that he does so because he wants the money for himself,
- that Judas served as treasurer,
- that Judas was a thief who pilfered the money put into the common purse.

Even scholars who lean in the direction of seeing Judas as originally part of this story, his name having been lost in the Synoptic tradition,[28] cannot escape the fact that "John's portrait of Judas in xii 4-6 is even more hostile than that of Matthew, for John here presents Judas as a thief."[29] Some scholars consider it a possibility that this identification "was part of the popular tendency to present Judas in a hostile light."

If indeed we have here a case of John's tendency to identify unknown characters with known characters and the confused transferral of details can best be explained as reflecting the oral stage of tradition, we have no choice but to see a process of vilification at work. For this either the oral reporters or the final redactor of John must carry responsibility. Furthermore, it has to be called what it is: bearing false witness, slander, and calumny. In view of the severe condemnation this sin carries and the destruction it can bring to people's reputations, indeed the harm it has done to the person of Judas in history, it may be time to come to terms with it and bury once and for all the belief that Judas was a thief or was motivated by demonic forces. Not for a moment does it seem credible that the Johannine portrait of Judas could be authentic. Even Brown asserts that what Judas did was "wicked" and detects "malice" in what, in fact, Jesus urges him to do. "Indeed having recognized the irrevocability of Judas' malice, Jesus hastens him on." This seems totally incredible given Jewish views on how love for one's fellow human being is expressed; clearly it contradicts love as we have learned to know it from Jesus. If we wish to affirm the Jewishness of Jesus and retain some shred of his love teaching, we will have to find a better way out of the dilemma.[30]

Obviously Judas is demonized here for a very specific purpose: he assists the church in neglecting the poor and invest in expensive projects to honor Jesus instead. Rainer Storch concludes:

> No matter how highly one values John's Gospel, . . . as far as the anointing story goes, his form of the story offers the highest degree of bias away from the point toward pure fiction. Here the development in the wrong direction has reached its worst end. . . . The massive nature of the polemic, in which "the actual point was lost"[31] (Bultmann) can hardly be explained in any other way. Here actual divisions about an expensive veneration of Christ were being strengthened.
>
> John applies with a high degree of precision a means often used and well

attested which one would just as soon have missed here: When the factual arguments are difficult to marshall, then you merely need to discredit or demonize the one who advances them. Judas fits it perfectly. So it is not only "some" who object to this unnecessary expenditure, and certainly not the disciples, but the one who later betrayed him. Whoever is not persuaded by this objection, well, for that one there is no additional reason. Add to that, Judas has to be made into a thief.[32]

That should suffice to silence those who use similar arguments to oppose an expensive cult and prefer to give their money to the poor. Did they really want to stand at the head of the line with Judas, the thief and betrayer? (Bultmann notes that according to Acts 4:37 it is assumed that the early church raised and distributed funds for the poor.)[33]

It is hard to resist the temptation to posit a development in the story to the effect that in Mark's account a certain group of those who stood around watching objected to the waste. With Matthew, it is the Twelve; and with John, it is only Judas. By the time of John, the protest against the act had been muted and therefore it served his purposes best to present the Twelve in a better light. On the other hand, the only tradition available to him may well have been the Judas tradition. Scholars are divided on whether John or the Synoptics draw from the older level of tradition. The reader is left to decide the issue, for no firm verdict can be rendered. Surely we would agree that natural justice demands more than one witness; John alone cannot be allowed to have his say in this matter. We must accord the other Gospel writers their say as well. In this writer's opinion, the other Gospel writers, especially Mark, are closer to a description of what happened; the truth of the event itself is another matter in that each writer exercises his own craft.

John shares with the other Gospels a desire to contrast the event with the later deed of the disciples: Judas, Peter, and the rest. Like the contrast between Nicodemus and the Samaritan woman (John 3 and 4), so, here, the male leaders with their more "practical" concern for the poor miss the point. However, the contrast should not be pushed as far as Hengstenberg takes it, stating that "This house was disinfected by the savour of Mary's ointment from the pestilential vapours with which Judas had previously filled it."[34]

C. John 13:1-30

Jesus knew that his hour had come and that he must leave this world and go to the Father. He had always loved his own who were in the world, and now he was to show the full extent of his love.

The devil had already put it into the mind of Judas, son of Simon Iscariot to deliver him. During supper Jesus . . . rose from the table, laid aside his garments, and taking a towel, tied it around him. Then he poured water into a basin, and began to wash his disciples' feet and to wipe them with a towel. . . .

Jesus said, "A person who has bathed needs no further washing; that one is altogether clean; and you are clean, though not every one of you." [He added the words, "not every one of you" because he knew who was going to inform on him.] . . . I am not speaking about all of you; I know whom I have chosen. But there is a text of scripture to be fulfilled: "The one who eats bread with me has turned against me" (literally "has lifted up his heel at me"). I tell you this before the event so that when it happens you may believe that I am who I say I am. . . .

After saying this, Jesus exclaimed in deep anguish of spirit, "I solemnly affirm that one of you is going to inform on me." The disciples looked at one another in bewilderment: whom could he be speaking of? One of them, the disciple whom Jesus loved, was reclining close beside Jesus. So Simon Peter nodded to him and said, "Ask who it is he means." That disciple, as he reclined, leaned back close to Jesus and asked, "Lord, who is it?"

Jesus replied, "It is the man to whom I give this piece of bread after I have dipped it in the dish."

Then, after dipping it in the dish, he took it out and gave it to Judas, son of Simon Iscariot. As soon as Judas had received it Satan entered him. Jesus said to him, "Do quickly what you have to do."

No one at the table understood what he meant by this. Some supposed that, as Judas was in charge of the common purse, Jesus was telling him to buy what was needed for the festival, or to make some gift to the poor. As soon as Judas had received the bread he went out. It was night.

The context of these accounts is the footwashing and the Last Supper.[35] Judas serves as the backdrop of the footwashing, for, having spoken of his willingness to demonstrate the love Jesus had for his own, the narrative abruptly jars us with: "The devil had already put it into the mind of Judas . . . to hand him over."[36] The meaning of this phrase, literally, "having cast it in his heart," has been debated. The phrase allows for the possibility that so far only the devil, not Judas, had made the decision, thus, "And during the meal as the Devil had decided in his heart that Judas, Simon Iscarioth's son might hand him over." The classical expression *ballein eis tēn kardian* (βαλλεῖν εἰς τὴν καρδίαν) means to "lay" or "take to heart," "plan," or "consider." Hein concludes: "John 13:2 certainly says no more than that Judas is of a mind to betray Jesus."[37]

We are led to believe that Judas participates in the washing of the feet without objection. The gloss that John adds in verse 10 informs us that Jesus was aware of who would hand him over. He also knows whom he has chosen, but one of them has excluded himself from this choice, "the one who eats bread with me has lifted his heel against me." Jesus is then described as being in "deep agitation of spirit" (v. 21) because of the insult visited on him by a friend who has just eaten with him.

The scene has some similarities to that of the Synoptics: the disciples ask who it is, and finally, with Jesus dipping bread in the dish and giving it to Judas, the secret is revealed. The text, however, stresses the painful insult created by the deed. Some background information may help to illuminate it.

Anyone who has ever visited among rural Palestinians knows that you do not cross your legs in public or show your heel. That is very discourteous and insulting. The sole of the foot is not to point to others. The lifting up of the heel is not merely a sign of impoliteness or discourtesy. "It goes deeper—a revelation of contempt, treachery, even animosity."[38] The LXX text reads: καὶ γὰρ ὁ ἄνθρωπος τῆς εἰρήνης μου, ἐφ᾽ ὃν ἤλπισα, ὁ ἐσθίων ἄρτους μου, ἐμεγάλυνεν ἐπ᾽ ἐμέ πτερνισμόν, literally translated: "The man of my peace, the one on whom I placed my hope, he who eats my bread has raised his heel against me." The idea of exalting himself is in the text but most likely it is to be seen as a play on the words "washing someone's feet" and "raising one's heel." In both cases, the heel is lifted and extended to the one serving.

"The NT phrase means 'acted treacherously' and applies to deeds. But the emphasis would seem to be that one, with whom one was bound by a covenant of peace, who partook of one's bread, had violated the laws of hospitality, and had turned on his host."[39]

In his related article "Hospitality," Kooy notes that Bedouins considered hospitality a sacred duty, "more heartily and stringently observed than many a written law. . . . The guest enjoyed protection, even if he were an enemy, for three days and thirty-six hours after eating with the host (the time sustained by his food). Hospitality was to the Bedouin what almsgiving was to the later Jews—an expression of righteousness (Judg 19:15-21; Gen 19:1-3)."[40]

"As soon as Judas had received it, Satan entered him." When Jesus tells him, "Do quickly what you have to do," no one at the table understood what he meant. The perplexity of the disciples also indicates that Judas was not an "outsider." Even John lets slip that none of the disciples suspected Judas at the time. Rather, the reference to Satan entering him after he ate the bread indicates that Judas was a believer like the other disciples. He fully participated in their common life with Jesus. Twice John says that he received the bread (vv. 27, 30). But for John, light and darkness are essential parts of moral reality. When Judas departs, he takes leave of the light and goes out into the darkness. "Jesus knows what is about to happen and dispatches Judas."[41]

What is remarkable here is that prior to this occurring, Judas fully participates in the communal act of footwashing and allows Jesus to teach him about servitude. As Sandra Schneiders has observed, what is at stake here is a lesson that Jesus introduces on the new model of servant relationships. "Peter's refusal of Jesus' act of service was equivalent . . . to a rejection of the death of Jesus, understood as the laying down of his life for those he loved, and implying a radically new order of human relationships."[42] Judas, by contrast, does not reject this act of service.

How radically the act of Jesus violated contemporary standards has been documented by Duncan Derrett.[43] He reminds us that the washing of feet was reserved for slaves; in the Hebrew tradition Abraham delicately suggested that his heavenly visitors could wash their own feet (Gen 18:4). Even the high priest washed his own feet on the Day of Atonement. Jesus, Derrett suggests, was forcing the Twelve, including Judas, to make acquisition of his bodily services, of himself, as their joint bondsman, in short, to acquire him as slave. Thus, they become co-owners of each other—partners.[44]

Derrett then describes the Jewish laws of partnership in order to illuminate what transaction had taken place. He observes that while partnership protects a person from being forced to redeem a partner if he is captured or taken hostage, it was open for the new partner on entering a partnership to offer to give his life, that is, to substitute himself, let alone his goods, to redeem any partner.

In John, he believes the disciples are not bewildered by the announcement that someone will hand him over. They take it in stride. He insists that when Judas acted, he acted for everyone, except that he himself was later excluded by the group. Why? Because at the time that Jesus washed Judas's feet, the devil had already entered him. The Twelve had acquiesced in the event and John may have come upon the partnership concept by thinking about the fate of Judas.[45] To form a partnership in Jewish circles meant "that mutual service was the means to make each other fruitful. This purely Jewish idea had no life outside of Jewish practice."[46]

This pericope has received the most thorough attention from Georg Richter, first by providing us a detailed history of the interpretation of this incident and then by seeking to find its place in the overall Johannine document.[47] He notes that one of the dominant themes here is introduced in verse 1: Christ's love for his disciples. He observes that in only one other place in the Fourth Gospel (John 15:13) is reference made to Jesus loving his disciples and giving his life for them. In addition, Jesus proposes such love as a model for the way disciples are to treat each other.[48] Richter calls for detailed literary critical study of John 13 that is based on its place in the whole of the Gospel. Such a study alone might help to solve some of the very complex issues found in it.[49]

For our interest in Judas there are a number of themes that have critical importance. In spite of the negative portrait given of Judas in the book as a whole, he does not object to Jesus washing his feet. Given the stress here on the love of Jesus for his disciples, this account can only mean that Judas is an object of Jesus' love even though, as John must insist, Jesus is not being tricked. He knows what Judas is planning. This is John's way of expressing his awareness of the fact that what Judas did, he did at the request of Jesus. It is, from John's perspective, one of the strongest cases of Jesus loving his enemy by extending to that "enemy" a menial service. Loving service is not rendered first or given only to one's closest friends and associates. If Peter resists allowing Jesus to wash his feet, perhaps Jesus also has some resistance to washing Judas's feet. That resistance is overcome and there is not a hint that Judas lies outside the pale of Jesus' love. Indeed, John portrays Judas as being in the inner circle.

Nevertheless, one topic that John returns to several times is the "uncleanness" of Judas. The topic is introduced with Jesus' response to Peter's request that all of him be washed: "The one who has been washed (i.e., Peter) does not have need except to wash his feet, but all [ὅλος] of him is clean [κάθαρος], and you yourselves are clean [κάθαροι], but not all. (For he already knew the one who would hand him over, for that reason he said, 'You are not all κάθαροι.')" The theme of purity is important here as it is throughout the ministry of Jesus. It is not a concept that appears in the Fourth Gospel often. In fact, only in one other place does it refer to a state of the disciples when, in the farewell discourse, Jesus refers to the purging that has been done to make a vine more fruitful. He then adds: "Already you are pure [κάθαροι] through the word which I have spoken to you" (15:3).

Purity is an important theme throughout the Bible. Yet only in Mark 7 and 1 Corinthians do we have such a forceful overthrow of all previous categories of what purity is and what it is meant to be within a community. Here Judas the informer (who, as John would have us believe, is alienated already from Jesus and is prepared to report him to the authorities) is a full participant in the proceedings—the footwashing, the meal, the whole celebration of the Passover, despite his lack of purity. The uniqueness of this concept of purity may become clearer if we compare it with Qumran, where the basis for community apparently was the fulfillment of Torah leading to cultic purity. Here washings were of critical importance, particularly before meals.[50]

According to Josephus, entrants into the Essene community took an oath to "keep their hands pure [κάθαρος] from theft and the soul from unjust gain and to stay away from robbery" [λῃστεία] (*JW* 2.141, 142). They could not eat with the community until that oath had been taken (2.139) and they vowed not to eat with the ἑτερόδοξοι (*JW* 2.129, 137). They were bound by oath never to accept food from an outsider (*JW* 2.143). The similarities to the Qumran sect are striking, while the differences with the Jesus community are chasmal.

Had John perhaps access to this Qumranic tradition? Did John prefer to portray Judas in contrast to the generous Mary and her self-giving ministration to the feet of Jesus (12:3) as thief (κλέπτης, 12:6)? The Essenes defined purity broadly as including financial matters as well as ritual purity. John, too, views purity in broad terms. But for him, or at least for his Master, the "impure" disciple needs the washing as much as Peter, the "pure" one. What's more, Judas receives Jesus' act of purification without apparent complaint.[51] If it is John's desire to paint Judas with an evil brush, he leaves many streaks where a different picture of Judas shines through.

D. John 17:12

Not one of them was lost, except the one who must be lost, for scripture has to be fulfilled. (NEB)

Even in the great prayer of Jesus recorded in John 17, the discordant note of Judas is sounded, although he is not named. The standard translations say: "except the son of perdition who must be lost, for scripture has to be fulfilled." It is not clear what scripture is here alluded to. The divine will is applied here to Judas and he is called something similar to the son of iniquity (2 Thess 2:3); that is, someone born from and destined for iniquity. The term "son of perdition" should not be translated as a genitive of purpose (son destined for destruction) or as an adjectival genitive ("destroying son") but rather as a genitive of origin.[52] The Greek word ἀπωλεία (apōleia) probably stands for the Hebrew Abaddon, a term that can stand in general for hell (Prov 15:11; 27:20; 1QH 3:16, 19, 32) or more particularly for the devil or hell personified (Job 28:22; Rev 9:11). The reference to Judas as son of hell/the devil is in keeping with the use of the term "child of hell" and similar phrases as a common form of early Christian invective.[53]

Compared to this treatment of Judas, we find in First John a somewhat similar usage applied to the defectors. In the first reference to them it is simply said:

"They went out from our company, but never really belonged to us; if they had, they would have stayed with us. They went out, so that it might be clear that not all in our company truly belong to it" (1 John 2:19). In line with the strictest division between those who love and those who hate, the former are described as acting out of their relationship with God—being born of God they act in accordance with their patrilineage: a child of God does not commit sin, because the divine seed remains in that one; the relationship to God does not empower sin. This is the distinction between the children of God and the children of the devil; no one who does not do right is God's child, nor is anyone who does not love others. Cain was a child of the evil one and he hated and murdered his brother. To be without love is to be in the realm of death, and everyone who hates his fellow is a murderer (3:13-17).

The "son of perdition" refers to a peculiar figure known from apocalyptic writings, and the point of the allusion to scripture is to explain the loss of one disciple. The term does not occur in the Hebrew Bible although a similar expression appears in Isa 57:4, τέκνα ἀπωλείας in the LXX. In a similar manner the Qumran group referred to "Sons of the Pit" (CD 6.15) and "men of the pit" (1QS 9:16, 22), and while Jesus mentioned the "children of peace" (Luke 10:6), Matthew refers to the "children of Gehenna" (23:15).[54]

But it would seem to refer to an eschatological figure, someone who will bring about a decisive change in the relations between humans and God. Daniel 11:36 may be in view, but if it is, then John has escalated beyond any recognizability of what Judas did.[55] Judas appears more like an automaton than a free, willing person. It is a view hard to reconcile with other parts of the Fourth Gospel and certainly is at odds with the invitation Jesus offers to all who labor (Matt 11:28-30). It has led to the idea that Judas is Satan incarnate and that 2 Thess 2:3 contains a reference to Satan having already appeared in the person of Judas.[56]

W. Sproston surveys the way Satan appears in the Fourth Gospel and concludes that Judas is described in this Gospel as a symbol of evil rather than a common betrayer. She agrees with Bultmann that John portrays not a man acting here, but Satan himself, the antagonist of God and the Revealer, Jesus Christ.

E. John 18:1-11

After speaking, Jesus went out with his disciples and crossed the brook Kedron where there was a garden into which he and his disciples entered. Already Judas, the informer, was at the place because Jesus had often been there with his disciples. Then Judas, having taken a detachment of soldiers[57] and officers provided by the high priests and the Pharisees, came there with lanterns, torches, and arms. Jesus, seeing them all coming toward him, went out to meet them, and said: "Whom do you seek?"

They answered: "Jesus of Nazareth."

He said to them: "I am he."

And Judas, the informer, was standing there with them. Then as he said to them, "I am he," they retreated and fell to the ground.

Then Jesus again asked them: "Whom do you seek?" And they said: "Jesus of Nazareth." Jesus answered, "I have told you that I am he. If then you seek me, let these go away so that the word may be fulfilled which says: 'Of those whom you gave me, I have not lost one.'"[58]

Then Simon Peter drew his sword and waded in on the high priest's servant and cut off his right earlobe. His name was Malchus. But Jesus said to

Peter, "Put your sword back into the sheath. The Father has given me this cup, shall I not drink it?"

And the commander with his troops and the Jewish officials arrested Jesus and bound him.

Torrey suggests that according to the narrative of John 18:6, Judas was more a timid soul than a hardened malefactor; for when at Gethsemane Jesus said to the soldiers, "I am he," and the deed of treachery was accomplished, Judas and the soldiers stumbled backward and fell to the ground.[59] "This narrator, at least, who was free to form his own picture of Judas, did not think of him as a ruffian."[60] Indeed, in this segment (which John not only created but revised), Judas is merely a walk-on. He is barely a member of the supporting cast.[61]

Judas's virtual withdrawal catches our eyes. Described only as "Judas, the one handing over," he appears as the leader of a huge contingent of soldiers and police provided by the chief priests and the Pharisees, who were equipped with torches, weapons, and lanterns. After Jesus had come forward to ask them whom they were seeking and Jesus said, "I am he," John confines himself to saying "and there stood Judas the informer with them."

Throughout his Gospel, John describes only scant interaction between Jesus and Judas, who represents only the darkness of evil. In the final scene in Gethsemane, John maintains that Jesus says nothing to Judas. Luke leaves open the question whether Judas kissed Jesus in the garden, but John portrays no interaction at all between the two. For him the realm of darkness cannot touch the Lord of Light.

Frank Kermode refers to the way John "thickens the narrative" and describes him as the "bolder and more resourceful writer" and a skillful writer who can "manipulate narrative with a measure of assurance."[62]

Others may suggest that we have here an excellent example of myth formation.[63] Myths are not spun out of thin air; rather, they develop from a historical actuality, a kernel, if you will. That kernel in this case was the involvement of Judas in the arrest of Jesus. Since John did not know precisely what Judas had done, and since it was well known that all the disciples had left Jesus in the lurch, it became necessary for one of them to be the scapegoat. That person became Judas, and no one more fully loaded the sin of desertion on Judas than did John. His condemnation of Judas may also have been connected to John's response to the Jewish rejection of Christians, which began to occur shortly after the year 70 C.E.

This evaluation of the way scholars have dealt with John chooses two representative modern scholars: Raymond Brown and Hans-Josef Klauck. Raymond Brown's treatment of Judas in the Fourth Gospel may serve as an illustration of what happens all too easily. He recognizes that the word παραδίδωμι (paradidōmi) "does not necessarily have a connotation of treachery or betrayal"[64] and he is aware that "literally" the word means "handing over." At the same time, the noun he uses to describe the one committing the act is "betrayer" and the act "betrayal."[65] Even when the verb is "literally" translated as "hand over," Brown does not hesitate to provide the traditional designation of the act as "betray."[66]

Nor is Brown in any doubt about the act itself. Judas does wrong by accepting the morsel that Jesus offers him at the Last Supper because he did not "change his wicked plan to betray Jesus." This means that he has chosen for Satan rather than for Jesus. How Brown can visualize a Jesus who loves his disciples yet who "hastens [Judas] on" to his destruction is not clear.[67] The evidence showing "malice" on the part of Judas is not offered. John provides Judas as a solemn warning to those who would be disciples of Jesus.

Another scholar, from the same faith community as Brown, takes a very different route. Hans-Josef Klauck concludes that John's Gospel began the "unredemptive anti-Judaistic evaluation of the figure of Judas." What happens to Judas in John "makes the limits of Johannine theology painfully visible." He cites the relatively harmless and indeed amusing observation of J. B. Bauer that Judas must have been unmarried, otherwise he would have returned home after a year when he discovered Jesus was going to suffer.[68] He provides other more harmful attempts to psychologize Judas, which the Fourth Gospel more or less invites. The critical question whether the Fourth Gospel has any parenetical value he answers aptly and without equivocation: "The Judas of the Fourth Gospel can teach the Christian nothing anymore. Fundamentally all that remains is only a bogey: just don't become like he was, just don't lose your faith, be seduced by Satan, and lose your salvation forever."[69]

He also offers a critique of this use of Judas as a moral example, as in the case of Wieser, who states his purpose: "I have only one objective and only one wish: to awaken in you such a revulsion for the man and Apostle Judas that once and for all you make the holy resolve to kill in yourselves every Judas spirit, destroy every similarity with the Judas mentality, to hate the soul of Judas."[70] Wieser's goal may be honorable enough; unfortunately he wasn't told, you can't get there that way!

Klauck correctly warns that we cannot shy away from a correction of the Johannine theology or be satisfied with the paradoxes that Barth dishes up for us in his attempt to solve the matter through Calvinistic doctrines of predestination. We can and must go beyond that. C. H. Dodd offered the opinion that although the Fourth Gospel stands farthest from the "original tradition of the teaching," it offers "the most penetrating exposition of its central meaning."[71] That verdict cannot be taken for granted any longer.

Possibly, John, from his perspective, was no longer able to enter into the Jewish world of both Judas and Jesus with the sympathy and understanding needed if we are to understand the historical Jesus and Judas. The issue may then be that Jesus kept the Jewish law according to his understanding of it but that the Jewish leadership did not think he did. So the Fourth Gospel reports them as saying: "We have a law, and by our law he ought to die, because he made himself the Son of God" (19:7). He was also considered a *mesith* (מסיח), an enticer trying to persuade other Jews to live as he did. As such he was subject to being denounced or informed on, especially after the Jewish leaders had issued the call inviting people to do so (John 11:57).[72]

Before we turn our attention to some theological attempts to come to terms with the person and role of Judas, we must give special attention to the two accounts of the death of Judas found in the early Christian writings.

Notes

1. Guardini, *The Lord,* 349–351. For this chapter, I am indebted to Vogler, 93–118; Klauck, 70–91; Maccoby, 61–78; Gärtner, 25–29; Dorn, 60–63; and Brownson, "Neutralising the Intimate Enemy: The Portrayal of Judas in the Fourth Gospel," SBL Papers 1992. Elaine Pagels, *The Origin of Satan,* deals with the Fourth Gospel in chapter 4, 89–111.

2. Brown, *The Gospel according to John,* 1:453.

3. Brown, *Death of the Messiah,* 119–121.

4. D. M. Smith, "Johannine Christianity," 222–248. For our topic, Dauer, *Die Passionsgeschichte im Johannesevangelium,* whose conclusion that the Johannine passion narrative shows some influence from the Synoptics but is nevertheless independent has found wide acceptance.

5. Indeed, it seems that whenever he has a choice, Barth prefers the Fourth Gospel. Unfortunately Barth, with his keen appreciation of Schleiermacher, did not learn from him the fundamental rule: each writer of each biblical book has to be interpreted on the basis of the document attributed to that author. See below, chapter 10, for my appraisal of Barth's work on Judas.

6. Barrett, *The Gospel according to John,* 308, 413.

7. See Richter, "Gefangennahme," 77, quoting from Origen, *Contra Celsus* II, 9.

8. Most of the material in the Fourth Gospel shows no direct relationship to the other Gospels and therefore we do not highlight special Johannine materials.

9. Brown notes (*John,* 1:297) that παραδιδόναι "does not necessarily have a connotation of treachery or betrayal."

10. The words in italics are added to Mark's text by Matthew.

11. Hengstenberg, *Commentary,* ad loc., 366.

12. Menninger records his opinion: "Evil goes in many guises and is called by many names. Perhaps the best name for it is the old-fashioned personification, the Devil" (*The Vital Balance,* 378). Also chapters 1 and 5 on possession of the devil and exorcism in the best-seller by Peck, *People of the Lie.* Jung already thought he had learned "where and how the devil can be laid by the heels" through his affair with Spielrein (Bettelheim, *Freud's Vienna,* 61).

13. Some still believe that John is not critical of Jews but only of those who

banned Christians from their synagogues. So Reim states, "When the Evangelist speaks negatively about 'the Jews' he never means the whole Jewish people but the group which, by using the excommunication decree, joins itself to Cain and the devil's murderous intentions and thus make themselves the children of Cain and of the devil" (Reim, "John 8:44," 624 n. 7). See also P. S. Kaufman, *The Beloved Disciple.*

14. "That Satan carries out God's judgment is in accordance with Jewish faith," Büchsel, *KTWBNT,* 2:172.

15. A. E. Harvey, *Jesus on Trial,* 36–39, spells this out.

16. Haenchen, *John* (1984): 307.

17. Schnackenburg, *The Gospel according to John,* ad loc.

18. Haenchen, "Historie und Geschichte," 55–79. These quotations are from his *John,* 1:308.

19. See especially Forsyth, *The Old Enemy: Satan and the Combat Myth,* 16, 315–317. See also Russell, *The Devil.* Now the best treatment of this subject is Elaine Pagels, *The Origin of Satan;* for John, esp. 89–111.

20. Sanders describes Judas as "a masculine Martha gone wrong" (41). He considers him the fourth member of Simon's family. His intervention in John 12:5 "betrays the typical accent of the uncomprehending elder brother" (ibid.). Sanders believes that John is not dependent upon the other Gospels here.

21. Renan, *Life of Jesus,* speaks of the "peculiar hatred toward Judas to be remarked (=noticed) in the gospel attributed to John" and continues, "We still believe that the curses heaped upon [Judas] are somewhat unjust. In his action there was perhaps more awkwardness than perversity" (241).

22. Again there have been exceptions, e.g., Hengstenberg says that Jesus knew about Judas, but the earlier exposure of Judas in the Fourth Gospel was not public. Judas is given every chance to share in Christ's salvation, at the same time Christ cannot be harboring a "serpent in his bosom" without knowing about it (*Commentary,* ad loc., 368).

23. See the perceptive chapter in Caird's *Principalities and Powers: A Study in Pauline Theology* entitled "The Great Accuser"; also see von Rad's and Foerster's excellent articles in *KTWBNT,* 2:69–80. These significant contributions to the history of Satan are unfortunately missing in Elaine Pagels's treatment in *The Origin of Satan.*

24. Borg, *Conflict, Holiness and Politics in the Teachings of Jesus,* 177–178. The section on Jesus and the Temple, 163–199, is a very insightful discussion of this matter.

25. The convergence of focus on the Temple by scholars such as E. P. Sanders, Charlesworth, Borg, McKelvey, Gärtner, and Schwier is significant. David Flusser has shown that Judaism too had a vision of no temple, for he cites a midrash on Isaiah 60 and a psalm and suggests that both draw from the same idea: the Messiah is the lamp (Ps 132:17 and Exod 25:3–5), so no temple is needed, "No Temple in the City," in *Judaism and the Origins of Christianity,* 454–465.

26. Mark reports that certain false witnesses arose and said: "We heard him say, 'I will destroy this temple made with human hands, and after three days build up another not made with human hands'" (Mark 14:57–58//Matt 26:61; cf. John 2:19).

27. The technical word μηνύω for "informing on someone" is used here (John 11:57; cf. Acts 23:30; 1 Cor 10:28).

28. Brown, *John,* 1:453.

29. Ibid.

30. Brown, *John*, 1:453; 2:578.

31. Bultmann, *Johannesevangelium*, 317–318.

32. This verse constructed by the evangelist, says Bultmann (*Johannesevangelium*, 318 n. 1), and many scholars agree with him.

33. Storch, "'Was soll diese Verschwendung?' Bemerkungen zur Auslegungsgeschichte von Mk 14:4f.," 250–251.

34. Brown, *John*, 1:20.

35. Schneiders, "The Footwashing." Also Derrett, "The Footwashing in John 13 and the Alienation of Judas Iscariot."

36. Hein, "Judas Iscariot: Key to the Last Supper Narratives?"

37. Deut. 11:18 and Luke 2:19 and many illustrations Hein provides in his footnote (228).

38. Bishop, *ET* 70 (1959): "'He that eateth bread with me . . . ,'" 332. See also the careful treatment of this allusion to Ps 40:10 in Reim, *Studien zum alttestamentlichen Hintergrund des Johannesevangeliums*, 39–42.

39. V. H. Kooy, "Heel, Lifted," *IDB*, 2 (1962): 577; and Bishop, *ET* 70: 331–333.

40. Kooy, "Hospitality," *IDB*, 2:654.

41. Perkins, NJBC, 974.

42. Schneiders, "The Footwashing," 87.

43. Derrett, "The Footwashing."

44. Derrett, "The Footwashing," 9.

45. Derrett, "The Footwashing," 17–18.

46. Overall, the article is a bit obtuse. It is not clear what point is made and how it relates to the action of Judas. In that respect, Schneiders's work is more useful in illuminating the model of service Jesus is instituting.

47. Richter, in his masterful study of the history of interpretation, *Die Fusswaschung im Johannesevangelium: Geschichte ihrer Deutung*, and also his essay, first published in *MThZ* 16 (1962): 13–26, "Die Fusswaschung, John 13:1–20," and reprinted in *Studien zum Johannesevangelium*, same series as above, 42–57. The most thorough study of the structure of the text itself is M.-E. Boismard, "Le lavement des pieds (Jn 13:1–17)," *RB* 71 (1964): 5–24.

48. Richter, *Fusswaschung*, 316–317.

49. Apparently Richter did not believe Boismard went far enough.

50. Paschen, *Rein und Unrein*, has made a detailed study of the Hebrew scriptures, including Qumran on this topic. Of interest to us is the difference in the way a community is constituted, 106–109.

51. Unfortunately Paschen does not treat John 13 at all.

52. See Brownson, "Neutralising," 49–60; here 52.

53. So Matt 23:15, son of gehenna; Acts 13:10, son of the devil; 2 Thess 2:3, "son of perdition"; Eph 2:3, child of wrath; 2 Peter 2:14, child of curse; 1 John 3:8, 10, child of the devil; *Apocalypse of Peter* 1:2, son of perdition. Cf. John 8:44, "You are of your father the devil." These references are from Brownson, "Neutralising," 52 n. 7.

54. Klauck, *Judas*, 87, n. 216; and Reim, *Studien*, 45–46.

55. Reim, *Studien*, 45–47.

56. Billings, "Judas Iscariot"; Sproston, "Satan in the Fourth Gospel," 309. See

also Klauck, *Judas,* 70–92, esp. 75–76, on the way Judas is demonized in this Gospel and the boundaries of Johannine theology, which become painfully obvious, 76.

57. σπεῖραν designates a detachment of six hundred men in the Roman army.

58. Perkins affirms that all were saved "except Judas, who has been lost to the circle of disciples since Jesus commanded him to depart" (NJBC, 979).

59. Certainly the original text, reading ἀπῆλθαν and ἔπεσαν, leaves that impression. Compare the similar case in Matt 28:7, where from the parallels in Mark and Luke it is evident that the present reading originated in a scribal error, some early copyist having made the extremely common mistake of writing εἶπον ("I said") instead of εἶπεν ("he said"). C. C. Torrey, *The Four Gospels,* 327–328.

60. Torrey, "'Iscariot,'" 57–58.

61. So Dauer summarizes it: "In this presentation the traitor does not play the slightest part, he is merely a walk-on," *Passionsgeschichte,* 29.

62. Kermode, *Genesis,* 92–93.

63. "Myth is a deceptive word shaped in the image of truth" (μῦθος ἐστὶ λογὸς ψευδῆς εἰκονίζων ἀλήθειαν), a saying coined (?) by Plato (*Politeia* 377A) and found in slightly different form in Plutarch, *De gloriae Athenae* 4, 348D, and in Theon, *Progymn* 3. Plato argued that the politician especially found myth formation useful, but so did teachers of morality.

64. Brown, *John,* 297.

65. Brown, *John,* 807; cf. 552 and 299.

66. Brown, *John;* cf. 573 and 807.

67. Brown, *John,* 578.

68. Klauck, *Judas,* 75–76.

69. Klauck, *Judas,* 91.

70. In his sharp critique of S. Wieser's book *Der Kreuzweg des Verräters,* 1922: Klauck, *Judas,* 91 n. 231.

71. Dodd, *The Apostolic Preaching,* 75. Affirmed also by D. Moody Smith, "Johannine Christianity . . . Theology," 169.

72. Reban, *Inquest on Jesus Christ,* 22–28, esp. "Jesus Christ and the Law," and his summary of the Jewish laws on heresy (24–28) taken from Stauffer, *Jerusalem und Rom im Zeitalter Jesu Christi.*

CHAPTER
NINE

THE DEATH OF JUDAS

The Death of Judas[1]

The dead lose all rights from the very first second of death. No law protects them any longer from slander, their privacy has ceased to be private; not even the letters written to them by their loved ones, not even the family album left to them by their mothers, nothing, nothing belongs to them any longer.
—Milan Kundera[2]

It is not easy to write about the death of a close associate, especially when that death takes place "prematurely." It is even more difficult if that death is in some way related to the death of the founder of a movement to which the writer belongs. Most important, it is extraordinarily difficult to write about a death when it is a suicide of a close friend and associate, one who was numbered among us but has deserted us. If one has been closely linked in a major project or work, the suicide of a colleague states rather unequivocally that we are not as close as it seemed and that the abrupt end which the associate brought to the relationship cannot begin to be adequately grieved. Apart from the moral evaluation one may have of the act itself, there remains the element of judgment of oneself and of the deceased, and many unanswered questions.

This point has been painfully illustrated by the suicide in 1963 of Sylvia Plath, whose life and death called forth a considerable amount of research and reflection during the last three decades and brought home the ambiguity of biographical writing, especially when many close friends and family members are still alive.[3]

The earliest Gospel writers faced a similar dilemma. They had in the first instance a desire to write about Jesus, his life and death. Writing about his death was made somewhat easier because Jesus had tried to prepare them for it. They believed that in some way his death fit into a divine plan, a perception helped by their belief that God had raised Jesus from the dead.

The resurrection made the death of Jesus easier to accept; it exonerated him of whatever role he played in bringing about his own demise.

Each writer, moreover, had materials about Judas which they wove into the literary fabric of Jesus' passion. We have already noted that Mark has little interest in Judas and says very little about his role in the passion of Jesus and nothing about the death of Judas. John reveals considerable interest in Judas but not in his death. Luke decides to incorporate the death report into his narrative of the early church but makes it part of the opening of the book of Acts (1:12-26).

Max Wilcox detects in Acts 1 an Aramaic tradition (which may have reached Luke already in Greek form) that links the Judas tradition to the Aramaic Targum of Gen 44:18. There Judah intercedes in protecting Benjamin from being "handed over" to Joseph. He concludes that Judas as one of the Twelve played a "special role" and that the Acts account deals with that rather than primarily with the election of Matthias.[4] Let us begin with a review of the text in Matthew.

A. Matt 27:1-10

Morning having come, all the chief priests and elders of the people took counsel against Jesus in order to put him to death. And having bound him, they took him away and handed him to Pilate, the governor.

Then Judas, the one who handed him over to them, seeing that Jesus had been condemned, was deeply moved with remorse. He returned the thirty pieces of silver to the chief priests and elders, saying: "I have sinned in delivering over to you an innocent person." But they said: "What business is that of ours? You see to that."

Having thrown the silver down in the Temple, he went away. He went and hanged himself. Then the high priests, having received the money, said: "It is not lawful to put this into the Temple fund, for it is blood money." Having taken counsel, they bought a potter's field to be used to bury strangers. Therefore, that field was called "field of blood" until this day. Thus was fulfilled the word which came through Jeremiah the prophet: "They took the thirty pieces of silver, for that was the value set on a man's head among the sons of Israel, and gave the pieces of silver for the potter's field, just as the Lord had ordered me."

Only Matthew makes the report of Judas's death a part of his Gospel; indeed, he gives a fairly detailed account in a segment that is tied to the passion narrative but also has its own agenda. He places it in between the trial of Jesus and his crucifixion, and he describes the death of Judas as suicide.

Matthew reports that Judas changed when he saw that Jesus was being handed over to Pilate. The implication is clear: this is not what he had intended. To be sure, Judas had handed Jesus over to the high priest, but with the change of venue to Pilate, a very different scenario develops. Jewish sources have much to say about when and under what circumstances Jews are in a position to hand over fellow Jews to pagan authorities (see above, chapter 4). No doubt Judas was familiar with such a problem and, indeed, may have had assurances from the high priest that this would not happen to Jesus. As A. E. Harvey aptly observes, "The implications of such a handing over (to a pagan ruler) have not received the attention they deserve."[5]

According to Derrett, putting a Jew, whether righteous or sinful, into the power of a Gentile ruler, benevolent or oppressive, for a purpose that might involve death was one of the most serious crimes known to Jewish law.[6] Little wonder that Judas is caught in a difficult personal circumstance. According to Matthew he does three things:

- He changes his mind about what he did.[7]
- He returns the money.
- He goes out and hangs himself.

1. The Meaning of "Changing His Mind" (27:3)

Although most translations render the verb *metamelomai* (μεταμέλομαι) as "repent," the usual word for "repent," *metanoeo*, does not appear here. Instead, we have the word *metamelomai*. Second Cor 7:8-10 is often cited to illustrate the difference, for there Paul uses both terms. According to Paul, genuine sorrow leads to repentance, *metanoia* (2 Cor 7:9), but it is not manifest that Pauline usage should be used to clarify Matthew's text. At any rate, Matthew uses the term *metamelomai* in 21:30 and 32 in connection with a story told only by Matthew about the two sons who receive orders from their father to go work in the vineyard, who have second thoughts about their response.

Here in verse 3 the word means that Judas changed his mind, although it does not have the religious overtones attached to the usual word for repentance. The Greek text (τότε) explicitly says that this change of mind occurred as a result of something that just transpired: *tote,* then, (contra van Unnik) does not mean "on the spur of the moment." It draws attention to the fact that something has changed and that Judas reacts to it forthwith. The element of regret at this change of Jesus' state is highlighted. It leads to Judas's startling and agonizing insight: "I have sinned in that I have handed over innocent blood" (27:4).

The element of regret and remorse is transparent here, and the confession of sin stands front and center. Judas acknowledges that he has misjudged the entire situation, thereby committing a grievous sin. One should not overlook the high tribute Matthew pays Judas here. For the greatest achievement is not to be flawless, which is impossible for humans. It is, rather, to have the courage to acknowledge when a sin has been committed. Judas saw that Jesus had no way of escape, that he could not hope to extricate himself from Pilate's power. Whatever Judas's precise role in the whole affair, the words that Matthew puts on his lips, "I have sinned," open up the doors to the love of God and to the gospel that Jesus had proclaimed.

Judas makes an admission of his own sin, but he also offers an affirmation about Jesus. This statement about Jesus is found only on the lips of one disciple, those of Judas: "I have handed over an innocent man to his death." He takes responsibility for his action.

The expression "innocent blood," as van Unnik has shown, is not widely used. Yet to hand over someone of "innocent blood" is generally thought to be one of the most serious transgressions in Hebrew life. Nor should one find here a veiled reference to the sins of the Jewish leaders, for Judas confesses his own sin, not anyone else's. For Matthew, the term "innocent blood" designates a member of the people of Israel who has committed no crime.

Jeremiah the prophet warned that if he as a true messenger of God were killed, "you bring innocent blood on yourselves and on this city and on its inhabitants" (26:15). Manasseh's greatest crime was to shed innocent blood; he "filled Jerusalem with innocent blood" (2 Kings 21:16). Even Israel itself is accused of pursuing idolatry and the offering of children; "they shed innocent blood" (Ps 106:38), polluting the land with it. Such an act invites God's curse and makes one unfit to dwell in the land. To kill without reason is to sin against innocent blood, and a special blessing is reserved for the "one who does not take a bribe against an innocent person" (Ps 15:5). The only possible atonement under Jewish law when innocent blood is shed or handed over is for someone to die.

The leaders of the Temple, however, brush aside Judas's attempt to rectify matters with the words: "See to it yourself," thereby indicating that the whole business of sin is Judas's concern, not theirs. They do not receive his confession. Judas has no other alternative but to execute the sentence of Deut 21:23: "Cursed by God is everyone who is hanged." By taking upon himself the curse, it is removed from the people and from the land.[8] Judas is the only one of the disciples who speaks those courageous words, "I have sinned." Even more important, he proclaims the innocence of his Master, Jesus. More people than Judas were responsible for bringing this innocent man to his death. But Judas does more than confess, he returns the money to give credibility to his change of mind, and then goes to his death.

2. The Significance of Returning the Money[9]

The historicity of this incident has been questioned because only Matthew has it and because it may have originated in the words of Zech 11:13: "'Throw it into the treasury'—this lordly price at which I was valued by them." Against these objections Joachim Jeremias enters four arguments:

a. Matthew's account of Judas's returning the money is based on the Jewish practice of the day and could be historical. Jeremias cites evidence from the Mishna, which likely would have been in effect already at the time of Jesus, that in certain instances where the original owner of money refuses to take the money back, the other party could return the money to the Temple to signify that his mind had changed and he wanted nothing to do with the deal. In the case of property, the one who changes his mind has up to twelve months, during which time the money could be left at the Temple to be picked up. Jeremias concludes that Judas returned the money in order to invalidate the deal. The Temple is not mentioned in the quote from Jeremiah in Matt 27:9-10, and so Jeremiah may not be the source of the story.

b. Jeremias also finds other instances in which money that had not been claimed was used to further the common good through the Temple treasury.

c. Moreover, Jeremias cites other land purchases and concludes that the average price for a piece of land would have been about 120 denarii (thirty pieces of silver).

d. Finally, the name of the potter's field bought by the high priests is not called forth by the text from Zechariah. Therefore its reference with respect to Judas is possible from a historical point of view. At the very least, Jeremias is not convinced that there are historical grounds here for considering the return of the silver unhistorical.

Most attention has been given to the usage of the biblical texts in Matthew, especially the ones he attributes to Jeremiah (actually a text from Zech 11:13), which he touched up and interpreted with the help of two passages from Jer 18:2-4 and 19:1-3, on the one hand, and 32(39):6-15 on the other. That Matthew draws on Zechariah, which he translates directly and freely from the Hebrew to suit the application he wants to make, is not in doubt.[10] Not only has he done so before, taking from the same context of the Shepherd[11] (Zech 13:7: "Strike the shepherd, that the sheep may be scattered") a saying that he puts on the lips of Jesus as he goes to Gethsemane (Matt 26:31), but he has also narrated the paying of Judas (26:15) in the same terms that the prophet used to describe the derisory wages paid by the rebellious flock (Zech 11:12).

In the gesture by which Judas throws the silver pieces down in the Temple (Matt 27:5), he emulates that of the Shepherd who rejected his miserable wages in the same way. Since this description of Judas's gesture is based on biblical precedent, Benoit says,

> this perhaps dispenses us from trying to imagine it in concrete fact and to decide whether the traitor could really have penetrated to the sanctuary reserved for the priests which is hardly likely, or whether the word ναός (inner Temple) is not to be taken in the sense of ἱερόν (Temple precincts) here which implies an improper, if possible, use of the word. The way to a solution is to explain these varying descriptions by reference to Biblical precedents which describe the terrible deaths of notorious sinners.[12]

For Matthew's narrative[13] the pieces of silver form a very important role, and their mention forms a "red thread" which goes throughout the whole and keeps the narrative together.[14] According to Lohmeyer-Schmauch, "The main motif is that of the thirty pieces of silver which is elevated to the eschatological earmark of the 'Shepherd'; it began the betrayal and sealed it, around it the repentance is expressed and the demise of the Traitor, the guilt and the sin of the high priests and the providential purchase of the Potters' Field. In all of these individual events these pieces of silver manifest how God's announced purpose is fulfilled for his 'Shepherd' through all human darkness and enmity."[15]

3. He Goes Out and Hangs Himself

Matthew's account that Judas made an end to his life or committed suicide has created many problems for interpreters. It is of critical importance to remember that suicide in and of itself was not considered a crime or sin in Judaism of that period,[16] and in the larger society of the Greco-Roman world it was considered by many people a noble exit from life.

Anton J. L. van Hooff provides a vast amount of material on this subject and analyzes the data on the basis both of myth and "realistic sources." His tables are most instructive. He lists 125 cases of mythical suicide, 164 for the Late Republic, and the largest number of all, 255, for our period, Early Empire (27 B.C.E.–192 C.E.). The number of individuals actually known to have committed suicide is 6,624, by far the highest number for any period.[17]

The role that the suicide of Judas has played in subsequent discussions, however, illustrates the truth of Albert Camus's observation that "there is but one truly serious philosophical problem, and that is suicide."[18] The accounts of Judas's end in Luke and Matthew are profoundly sad. Neither author makes his act appear as a triumphant, noble death. We need to view their assessments in their context, however, as we review the interpretations open to us.

In connection with the Matthean account of Judas's suicide, new ground has been plowed by C. F. Whelan in her analysis of this section of Matthew's

Gospel. Building on recent research into suicide in the ancient world, she seeks to find the reason why Matthew includes the account in his work. She notes that suicide in ancient society was viewed not so much as a personal or an "individual loss, as a threat to the unity and structure of the group as a whole."[19]

We have already noted that Matthew has a keen interest in community. His interpretation of Judas's suicide would fit our conclusions. Of the various motives for committing suicide, Judas's may come closest to that of a Roman soldier: "shamed by false accusations, the soldier's [suicide] was an attempt to restore honour to himself by proving his worth to his comrades."[20]

Whelan suggests that we have been unable to view the suicide of Judas through Matthew's eyes because of our bias against it since the days of Augustine. She is inclined to see his suicide as "closest to the suicides of women for misconduct in that it serves as an act of atonement and an attempt to restore one's honour."[21] She is convinced that the story of Judas's suicide serves to transfer the guilt for the death of Jesus from Judas to those ultimately responsible: the chief priests and the elders.

Although it has been aggressively argued (by van Hooff, Droge, and Whelan in addition to Daube) that there were no Jewish or Christian taboos on suicide prior to Augustine, there is a "reservoir into which the undercurrents of ancient disapproval of suicide come together"[22] in Josephus's speech against suicide at Yodefat. On occasion, obviously, a case was made against suicide on Jewish moral grounds.[23] At best, Josephus is inconsistent on this matter. There is, moreover, an important text from the book of Tobit (3:10, Sinaiticus) in which Sarah, contemplating suicide when her servants mock her because her seven husbands have successively died in the marriage bed, decides she does not wish to bring disgrace upon her father. "It is better for me not to hang myself, but to pray the Lord that I may die and no longer hear insults in my life."[24] What lies behind this sentiment is surely the idea that it is better to die at the hand of the Lord than by one's own hand.

From the Christian side there is also the ancient novel in which Peter persuades a despondent Christian woman not to commit suicide by raising the question: "Will not the souls of those who die that way be punished with a worse penalty because of the self-killing?"[25] Augustine may have made the case for canon law in the fourth century, but most likely there were deep Christian and Jewish aversions to suicide prior to his time. At the same time, however, there was no blanket condemnation of suicide.

There are only two death accounts of central New Testament personalities: Jesus and Judas. In addition, only the deaths of Ananias and Sapphira (Acts 5:1-11) and the martyrdom of Stephen are recounted. No wonder there is so much interest in the demise of Judas. Much curiosity, after all, is aroused about a person's life after that person dies. The manner of death and the circumstances around it are not unimportant. Clearly, the disciples would have had much reason to discuss the death of Judas, the only one of the Twelve whose tragic death is widely known.

The fate of Judas is assumed by many people to be a closed case: it was a matter of suicide arising from an act of greed and deception which, when foiled, led to despair. When they are reminded that the book of Acts has a quite different account of Judas's death (see below), they brush off the differences by stating that the two accounts can be easily harmonized.

Although biblical accounts of the death of Judas have been extensively studied, some scholars have concluded that Judas did not die at the time indicated in our early Christian texts, Matthew and Acts. They argue that accounts of his death are meant, rather, to highlight the fact that he was "a bad man" who had to pay the price for his evil ways.

Our options would appear to be the following:

1. To accept the account of Matthew and see Judas's death as a self-inflicted act open to various interpretations. We can, for example, follow Wrede, who sees in the account of Matthew a "certain gripping psychological truth," to Judas's credit. One should sympathize with the man whose "deed is indeed irrevocable, but whose soul is still capable of a nobler impulse."[26] Most scholars find that Judas did something wrong, for which he should atone. Some even suggest that his confession should have been proffered either to Jesus himself (it is rather difficult to imagine how) or to the disciples.[27]

2. To accept Luke's version in Acts (see pp. 168–74 below) as correct, in which case Judas's death was an accident or a matter of divine intervention. In either case, we are free to question the author's intent in writing about this event and ask how the account fits into the overall presentation/theme of the writer.

3. Since the two biblical accounts contradict each other, it is possible that neither is reliable and that Judas may have lived out his life outside the Christian movement. If that was the case, we know nothing at all about his death.

Although it has been suggested by Klauck that Judas survived beyond the time of Jesus' crucifixion, this seems highly unlikely. Surely some trace of such an existence would have remained. Our hypothesis, deduced from two accounts of his demise, is that he died about the time that Jesus did but that we have to make our choices in arriving at some plausible conjectures about why and how he died.

Even if we were to agree that Judas committed suicide, we have still to ask whether his death at his own hand was motivated by his own sense of guilt and remorse or by his love for Jesus, in which case it could be described as a "noble death,"[28] a term that was used when loyal followers died in solidarity with the king. Arthur J. Droge and James M. Tabor conclude that "Judas' act of self-killing is not condemned," nor is any such act in Hebrew and Christian sources before the time of Augustine.[29] This observation must have a profound effect on the way we view the death of Judas. "It is to Augustine more than anyone else that Christianity and the West owe their condemnation of suicide," they argue, and the example of Judas was very important to Augustine.[30] By ignoring the plain contents of Matthew and building instead on Plato's arguments against suicide, Augustine set the tone for the ensuing years. At present it is especially those deeply influenced by Augustine who sharply condemn suicide and Judas for having committed that act. So, for example, G. K. Chesterton:

> Not only is suicide a sin, it is *the* sin. It is the ultimate and absolute evil, the refusal to take an interest in existence; the refusal to take the oath of loyalty to life. The man who kills a man kills a man. The man who kills himself, kills all men; as far as he is concerned he wipes out the world.[31]

Recent studies of Judas (Klauck, Vogler, Maccoby) reject the idea of suicide. Rather, they assume that the stories about his end are meant to indicate that those who leave the Christian community or the circle of disciples invariably come to a bitter end. They are supported by Luke, who portrays a death by accident or divine intervention or natural causes.

B. Acts 1:16–20

Peter is speaking to a crowd of about 120:

> Fellow Christians. Already the scripture which the Holy Spirit spoke through David was fulfilled concerning Judas who had acted as guide to those who arrested Jesus. For he was one of our number and had his place in this ministry. This one, having bought a field with the reward of his unjust deed, fell forward, his middle burst open, and his entrails spilled out. And this was known to all who dwell in Jerusalem so that they called that field in their own dialect, Akeldamah, that is, field of blood.

The words written in the book of Psalms:

> Let his home place become a desert
> Let there be none to dwell in it.
> And let someone else of a different kind take his assignment.

Verses 24–25: A prayer spoken by "them."

> . . . which of these two thou hast chosen to take the place of this service and apostleship from which Judas strayed[32] and went to his own place.

At the center of this narrative stands Peter, acting as an interpreter of the act of Judas. Missing is any reference to Satan; instead, Peter through Luke's redaction speaks of the way in which scripture was fulfilled through the deeds of Judas. Nothing is said of a betrayal; rather, his deed is described as "acting as a guide to those who arrested Jesus" (Acts 1:16).

To be sure, as Lüthi[33] has noted, while Matthew attributes an immoral dimension to Judas's financial negotiations, here it is explicitly described as "the price of his villainy" or unrighteousness. Luke sees ἀδικία ("villainy") as related to μαμωνᾶς ("mammon," 16:8) and while his account of the death of Judas is clearly secondary to that of Matthew, neither one necessarily reflects historical reality. Luke tied it to two texts from the Old Testament: Psalm 69:26 and Psalm 109:8.

For the Acts account, one literary precedent that best explains πρηνὴς γενόμενος ("falling forward") is Wisd 4:19, which describes the death of the godless:

> In death their bodies will be dishonored, and among the dead they will be an object of contempt for ever; for he shall strike them speechless (ῥήξει αὐτοὺς ἀφώνους), fling them headlong (πρηνεῖς), shake them from their foundations, and make a desert of them; they shall be full of anguish, and all memory of them shall perish.

There is also the mysterious link of the memory of Judas to the field of blood. In Matthew the word "blood" appears three times in this account: innocent blood, v. 4; blood money, v. 6; and field of blood, v. 8.[34] According to Acts, the field was Judas's property which he had bought with the money he got from the betrayal. It also seems that it was his blood that poured on the field at the time of his miserable death and gave the land its name. Matthew attributes the buying of the field to the high priests and explains the name given to it by the blood of Jesus, since it had been acquired with the price of the blood of Jesus.[35]

A Comparison

The two accounts of the death of Judas in the New Testament (Matt 27:3-10 and Acts 1:15-20) have several features in common:

- They draw on popular traditions.
- Both agree that Judas died an unusual death.
- Both are fond of bringing out the application of Old Testament prophecies and both close with Old Testament quotations.
- Both say that land was purchased with the money Judas received.
- They are linked to concrete details of the topography of Jerusalem.
- The name of the land purchased is virtually identical in both accounts.[36]

The differences are also worth noting and we can list a number:

- The manner of death is different. In Matthew he hangs himself, in Luke he falls to his death.
- The time of death is different. Matthew places the death before Jesus himself dies, in Luke there is no indication of time.
- The purchase of the field is brought about by different circumstances and by different people.
- The location of the field is well known as being near Jerusalem, according to Luke, while in Matthew no such indication is offered.
- Matthew records remorse on the part of Judas, but Luke mentions nothing about it.

In comparing them, we are especially interested in knowing what prompted the early church to record the death of this disciple when we do not have an account of the death of any other apostle. According to Pierre Benoit, when we study these two accounts: "We are entitled to find the echo of actual recollections in them, which have been kept alive by their relation to well-known places in Jerusalem."[37] Hence an important clue to the presence of these materials is the light they shed on certain place-names in Jerusalem.

Matthew's account of Judas's suicide is an especially important text in which to study the creative role of the editor in the Gospel's final formation; for, as Donald Senior has noted, it is the most extensive addition interjected by Matthew into the Markan passion narrative.[38] As such, the close parallel established between Mark and Matthew's passion narratives and the "placid harmony" in their literary relationship is broken by this segment of Judas's death. Some consider it probable that we owe the Matthean account to the Greek editor of the first Gospel.[39] What is its function in this narrative? Many suggestions have been made, but no unanimous agreement has emerged. Senior suggests that Matthew must describe the fate of Judas to fill the lacuna left by Mark. A recent commentary on the book suggests that Matthew is describing the "trial" of Judas.[40]

The Matthew text has been related to Ahithophel's death described in 2 Sam 17:23. But a comparison between these two is less than convincing.[41] In the Ahithophel narrative there is no betrayal. He commits suicide because he has forfeited his right to be the trusted counselor of the king and he cannot bear to live with that shame. The parallel seen in their hanging is not too significant, since it was the standard method of suicide among ordinary people. We need not assume that Matthew is copying this method from the 2 Samuel 17 story.

The later church, building on the vilification of Judas, saw the story of his demise in the genre of death stories of other evil men and how they died. Thus Papias tells the story of Antiochus Epiphanes (2 Macc 9:7-12); Josephus tells the story of Herod the Great (*Ant* 17.6, 5, para 169); and Luke himself of Herod Agrippa (Acts 12:23).

In choosing between the biblical accounts, scholars are prone to give the nod to Matthew's account, finding it "a more precise detail that death was by suicide, by hanging."[42]

These accounts represent traditions that were handed down orally to both Luke and Matthew and belong to the category of "aetiological legends," meaning legends that seek to explain causes. The word "legend" does not have a pejorative meaning in our usage, for we have been taught to look for its deeper intention: in this case "the intention is to assert the link between the 'field of blood' which everyone knows and the tragic end of Judas."[43]

Attempts to harmonize the accounts cannot succeed. We will need, therefore, to ask what point the narrators were trying to make by telling the story of Judas's demise. The manner of death is important to answering that question.

The text of Acts does not mention hanging. It is not even apparent that the text envisions a fall. Moreover, it is not certain that Luke is thinking of suicide, for the language indicates that he is thinking of death through accident or by natural (or supernatural) causes.

There is a mysterious link between the memory of Judas and the field of blood, viewed differently by Matthew and Luke.

> When we view the appearance of Ps 65:25 in Acts we are struck by this passage of a psalm in which they found so many other prophetic allusions to the Passion. The first Christians saw it as an announcement of the divine malediction on the traitor: his land was to remain deserted, uninhabited. This was so clearly verified in the unlucky place that it was pointed out as the field of Judas! It could be that he only died there, or was buried there. But popular story-telling added on its own account the details that it was *his* field, that he had acquired it with the money of his crime; and in doing this it expressed the basic truth, the only important aspect, collected by St. Luke, that the ill-gotten gains of the avaricious apostle did not profit him.[44]

Another aspect of this story should be noted: the relation of extirpation and excommunication to death. It is possible that the main point of these stories for the writers of Matthew and Luke was the indication that Judas no longer was a member of the Jesus community. He removed himself from them. There could possibly be a link, then, between the way in which Second Temple Judaism dealt with the defector, the way Qumran in particular extirpated or excommunicated someone, and the way the early church told stories about Judas's death. Judas could not live on among the disciples, for his role in the death of Jesus was too complicated. Thus, for some sectors of Second Temple Judaism, the acts of banning, expulsion, and premature death were connected. Being "cut off" from the people could take the form of excommunication or premature death.[45]

Repentance before Death

One of the finest treatments of the death of Judas, and of his life and deeds, is that of a nineteenth-century Congregational preacher, Joseph Parker, who never studied formal theology.[46] Influenced perhaps by de Quincey, Parker insists that we treat Judas as a human being with the same capacities for error and mischief that we all have. The mystery of why Jesus chose Judas is no more profound than why he chooses any one of us.[47] That Judas should have slain himself by his own hand Parker takes to be "wholly in his favour . . . the proper completion of his insufferable self-reproach."[48] And yet it is most important to note that Judas Iscariot uttered "the most effective and precious eulogium ever pronounced upon the character of Jesus Christ. How brief, how simple, how complete—'innocent blood.'"[49] This, coming from someone who knew Jesus very well, who had lived with him for three years, and who had struggled to understand the direction that Jesus' ministry was taking, provided a strong—and, for Judas, an agonizing—witness to the integrity of Jesus' mission. "Judas died not with a lie in his right hand, but with the word of truth upon his lips, and the name of Christ was thus saved from what might have been its deepest wound."[50]

In Acts 1:25, Peter refers to "this ministry and apostleship from which Judas turned aside to go to his own place." Parker takes this comment as an "instance of exquisite delicacy on the part of Peter: no judgment is pronounced; the fall is spoken of only as official and as involving official results, and the sinner himself is left in the hands of God."[51]

The accounts of the death of Judas have two distinct purposes. In Acts, they would appear to stress the role of Peter in forming the Twelve as an unbroken unit. But no severe criticism is made of Judas and no mention is made of a breach of trust or deed of infamy. Judas died not by his own hand, although his death could be seen as being in line with the death of other "evil" persons.

In Matthew, it cannot be overlooked that by all canons of traditional repentance, Judas met the three fundamental conditions. He showed contrition and "changed his mind"; he confessed, admitting that he had sinned; and he tried to make restitution by returning the money. Whether there is more than an "outside chance that Matthew is describing a true repentance"[52] the reader will have to decide. Certainly some in the Catholic tradition have been convinced there was hope for Judas.

Vinzenz Ferrer (1350–1419), an influential Dominican preacher cited earlier in this book, said in a sermon in 1391 that Judas having betrayed and sold the Master after the crucifixion was overwhelmed by a genuine and saving sense of remorse. He tried with all his might to draw close to Christ in order to apologize for his betrayal. But since Jesus was accompanied by such a large crowd of people on the way to the mount of Calvary, it was impossible for Judas to come to him and so he said to himself: since I cannot get to the feet of the master, I will approach him in my spirit and humbly ask him for forgiveness. He actually did that and as he took the rope and hanged himself his soul rushed to Christ on Calvary's mount, asked for forgiveness and received it fully from Christ, went up to heaven with him, and so his soul enjoys salvation along with all elect.[53]

He could well be indebted in part to Theophylact (seventh century), who also has an interesting account of what happened in the case of Judas. Theophylact believed that Judas was Jesus' favored disciple, the one whom Jesus had especially honored by making him treasurer:

> Some say that Judas, being covetous, supposed that he would make money by betraying Christ, and that Christ would not be killed but would escape from the Jews as many a time he had escaped. But when he saw him condemned, actually already condemned to death, he repented since the affair had turned out so differently from what he had expected. And so he hanged himself to get to Hades before Jesus and thus to implore and gain salvation. Know well, however, that he put his neck into the halter and hanged himself on a certain tree, but the tree bent down and he continued to live, since it was God's will that he either be preserved for repentance or for public disgrace and shame. For they say that due to dropsy he could not pass where a wagon passed with ease; then he fell on his face and burst asunder, that is, was rent apart, as Luke says in the Acts.[54]

What then can be said about the historical kernel in these narratives about the death of Judas? Or are the stories purely fictional accounts?[55]

After a careful study of all canonical and extracanonical accounts of the death of Judas, Klauck concludes that "from a historical point of view we know nothing about the fate of Judas, especially about his death. I cannot see how, on the basis of the texts, we can come to a different conclusion. . . . Even the church which tells these stories knows nothing about him."[56] He speculates that Judas left Jerusalem and lived as a Jew among his people until his undramatic death. Brown ventures the possibility that in the case of Matthew's account of the manner of Judas's death, "the OT background may have actually generated the stories."[57]

Summary

Few topics are as emotionally laden as the topic of suicide, and the issues around it are still vigorously debated.[58] It is perhaps most important to respect the courage—and be sensitive to the pain—of those who have taken their own lives, and to refrain from speculation about the reasons that lie behind such a drastic, irreversible move. Above all, we should refrain from making judgments about their fate. Here, in the presence of what is surely the most deeply personal choice ever made by a human being, we had best stay within the shadows of uncertainty and live with the riddle of the deed.

For a community, such an act often weighs heavily as an indictment that its members were not listening to the cries of help coming from the distressed soul who takes his or her own life. But neither breast-beating to alleviate one's guilt nor accusations directed to others or the deceased do much to help us to deal with suicide adequately.

Even in speaking of suicide, as Matthew does, we need not use it as a judgment against Judas. We could say that Judas was the first and the strongest witness to Jesus' innocence, making his confession to the highest authorities in the land. He could well have been the first to die with Jesus. Thus, in solidarity with Jesus, he would have died for what he believed: that Jesus was a good man, innocent of death, deserving no evil.

Notes

1. On this topic, see Klauck, 92–123; Vogler, 65–71, 85–89; and Benoit, "The Death of Judas."

2. Malcolm, "Annals of Biography: The Silent Woman," *New Yorker,* Aug. 23 and 30 1993: 104.

3. Malcolm, "The Silent Woman," 84–159, grippingly deals with this. When anger is not resolved or openly dealt with or when the desire to understand loses out and people become intent on fixing blame, the deceased's legacy becomes a seriously flawed one, as seen in Hammer, *By Her Own Hand: Memoirs of a Suicide's Daughter.* Le Anne Schreiber says, "The agenda of 'By Her Own Hand' it turns out, is not resurrection but damnation" (*New York Times Book Review,* July 7, 1991: 8). Much more healing is the approach of Sue Chance, a psychiatrist, whose son committed suicide (*Stronger than Death*). On the subject in general with a chapter on Plath (19–56), see A. Alvarez, *The Savage God.* For our consideration Peter Boyer's "Life after Vince" [Foster] (*New Yorker,* Sept. 11, 1995: 54–67) is especially evocative.

4. Wilcox, "The Judas-Tradition in Acts i.15–26," 438–452.

5. Harvey, *Jesus and the Constraints of History,* 25.

6. Derrett, "The Iscariot," 4.

7. Van Unnik, "The Death of Judas in Saint Matthew's Gospel," 44–57; and Schwarz, "Die Doppelbedeutung des Judastodes," 227–233. (I owe this reference to Whelan, "Suicide," 522 n. 92.)

8. Van Unnik, "The Death," 55–57.

9. Jeremias, *Jerusalem zur Zeit Jesu,* 2:55–57. The excursus is called "Die Geschichtlichkeit von Mth. 27.7."

10. Note Benoit's careful analysis of this point, followed by many others.

11. Many exegetes think that Zech 13:7–9 originally followed 11:4–17.

12. Benoit, "The Death," 193.

13. Klauck, *Judas,* 93; and Dorn, "Judas," 52–54.

14. Klauck, *Judas,* 93. They are mentioned in verses 3, 5, 6, 7, 9, 10.

15. Lohmeyer-Schmauch, *Matthäus,* 379–380.

16. The work of Daube is most helpful in this regard; e.g., "The Linguistics of Suicide," "Death as Release in the Bible," but above all his essay "Black Hole."

17. Van Hooff, *From Autothanasia to Suicide,* 198–250.

18. Camus, in *The Myth of Sisyphus,* opening lines.

19. Whelan, "Suicide in the Ancient World," 515.

20. Whelan, "Suicide," 519, quoting Suetonius, *Otho 10.*

21. Whelan, "Suicide," 521. The case of Judas shares something else with the suicides of many women: the misconduct was not of their doing.

22. Van Hooff, *Autothanasia,* 181.

23. *JW* 3.8.5.

24. Van Unnik, "The Death," 49, who notes that this reading is found only in Codex Sinaiticus and that Vaticanus and Alexandrinus are quite different.

25. Van Hooff, *Autothanasia,* 183–84, citing *Clementina Homilia* 12,13/14 (*PG* 2, 312 b and c). He provides no name for the novel.

26. Wrede, "Judas Iscarioth in der urchristlichen Überlieferung," *Vorträge und Studien,* 141.

27. Van Unnik, "The Death," cites Lagrange, Schlatter, Floyd Filson, and G. A. Buttrick, 45–46.

28. Seeley, *The Noble Death . . . and Paul's Concept of Salvation,* 87–99. See also Droge's article "Suicide," *ABD,* 6:225–231, who indicates that J. Bels in 1975 first showed this change toward seeing suicide as a sin to have occurred with Augustine.

29. Droge and Tabor, *A Noble Death: Suicide and Martyrdom among Christians and Jews in Antiquity.*

30. Droge and Tabor, *A Noble Death,* 113, 125, 167, 173.

31. Michael Coren, "An Unorthodox Conference," *Globe and Mail,* Sept. 12, 1994: C5.

32. The Greek verb is παραβαίνω, which can mean to wander off the pathway. It is used in the LXX to describe Israel's deviation from the will of God but is a relatively gentle term to be used for what some take to be a classic case of betrayal.

33. Lüthi, "Das Problem des Judas Iskariot—neu untersucht," here 100. He has also written the article on Judas for the *TRE,* 2:296–305.

34. Bruner, *Matthew,* 1021. Y. Yadin, *The Temple Scroll* (New York: Random House, 1985), makes a connection between the strictness of the Temple Scroll and this field of blood. See pp. 134ff. This reference was kindly supplied by Peter Richardson.

35. Benoit, "The Death," 196.

36. Benoit, "The Death," 189. See also Dorn, "Judas," 73–84, for a very succinct and helpful description of the differences and similarities of the two accounts.

37. Benoit, "The Death," 189.

38. Senior, "A Case Study," 23–36, and idem, "The Fate of the Betrayer," 3–10; for this point, see 373.

39. Benoit, "The Death," 190.

40. Bruner, *Matthew.*

41. Whelan, "Suicide," 2–3.

42. Benoit, "The Death," 195.

43. Benoit, "The Death," 192.

44. Benoit, "The Death," 197. See also Haugg, *Judas*, 181.

45. Horbury, "Extirpation and Excommunication," esp. 30–32.

46. Parker, *The Inner Life of Christ*, 3:335–352.

47. Parker, *The Inner Life*, 3:337.

48. Parker, *The Inner Life*, 3:347.

49. Parker, *The Inner Life*, 3:347.

50. Parker, *The Inner Life*, 3:348.

51. Parker, *The Inner Life*, 3:349.

52. Bruner, *Matthew*, 1021, who unfortunately retreats into "historical pastoral wisdom" and warns against "the peril involved in speaking too kindly of Judas' suicide" (1021). Surely we can find other ways to discourage suicide!

53. Dieckmann, *Judas*, 139–140, who accuses later historians of seeking to brush this under the rug.

54. *In Matt.* 27, Migne, *PG*, 123, p. 460 (Enslin's translation, 130).

55. Beare concludes, "The whole story is obviously fictional" (*St. Matthew*, 525). See Klauck, *Judas*, 101.

56. Klauck, *Judas*, 121–123.

57. Brown, *The Death*, 61.

58. Ben Viviano graciously provided me with a copy of *Listening: Journal of Religion and Culture*, which is dedicated to this topic. The essay by Robert L. Barry addresses the topic of suicide in the Bible and puts the suicides of Zimri, Ahithophel, and Judas into the same class: "All suicides of men whose sin and disobedience of God was so profound that they were hopelessly alienated from God," 68. He concludes that the "Christian tradition has held that [Judas] is the only person certainly excluded from the kingdom because he did not repent of his suicide," citing John 6:71 and 13:27.

CHAPTER
TEN

THEOLOGIANS AND
JUDAS ISCARIOT

The more . . . we attempt to formulate the sin and guilt of Judas . . . the more nearly his will and deed approach what God willed and did in this matter. . . .

In one sense Judas is the most important figure in the New Testament apart from Jesus. For he, and he alone of the Apostles, was actively at work in this decisive situation, in the accomplishment of what was God's will and what became the content of the gospel.

—Karl Barth[1]

Theologians have been as much preoccupied with the personality of Judas and the implications of his involvement in the death of Jesus as biblical scholars have been. That is especially true of those theologians, Catholic and Protestant, who have tried to develop a theology based on the Bible. We shall look at several modern representatives, including Harald Wagner,[2] Helmut Gollwitzer,[3] and Bernhard Dieckmann,[4] whose theology had a keen ethical dimension. Major attention will be paid to Karl Barth, who gave a detailed and extensive treatment of Judas in his multivolumed *Church Dogmatics*. Barth is probably the most influential theologian of the twentieth century. Because he took the Bible so seriously, he is important to our quest. As a dialectical theologian he is also perhaps the most difficult to comprehend in this regard. Some of my theological colleagues, admirers of Barth, have been reticent to encourage me to pursue this line of inquiry. But it surely behooves us as scholars to engage in some dialogue with each other on such important matters. I therefore present my reading of Barth's view of Judas (and Judaism) and encourage response and correction.[5] Since Barth's position is again on the table for discussion, it may not be impertinent to allow this contribution to the understanding of Judas found in the New Testament to be heard.

Furthermore, Bernard Dieckmann, a historical theologian whose recently published treatment of Judas from a historical-theological point of view seeks to deal with Judas as scapegoat,[6] deserves treatment because he writes not only about the theological significance of Judas but also of his influence in art and literature. Because only Barth is available in English and because Barth's extensive essay is difficult to follow, it has been thought best to summarize the work of the theologians and to use their own words more extensively and frequently than otherwise would be done. The selections are representative and not intended to be complete. For the history of the interpretation of Judas since the Reformation, the work by K. Lüthi is recommended, for it has not been superseded.[7]

Harald Wagner

Wagner's perspective involves the relation of the divine and the human in the drama of salvation history. Within that broader topic, he is specifically concerned with the issue of sin, its universality and mystery. He sees Judas as the one who initiated a chain of events that brought Jesus to the cross. This means that out of the deed of Judas arose an event that, according to Christian belief, gave birth to the redemption of humanity. Yet the deed of Judas, and even more the personality of Judas, has been assailed relentlessly and painted in darkest colors. Wagner cites Cyril of Syria's homily on the Passion written in the fourth century.

> At eventide Judas left the dining hall and the disciples, who had been depressed, remained behind in deepest peace. The vessel of wrath left his master and the devious one separated himself from his associates. The dining chamber rejoiced that the darkness had lifted from the Twelve and the goat had fled; now the wheat had been purged of weeds and the vines of the vineyard of wild grapes. The owl, which praised darkness, left the doves alone and flew out squawking. The house became bright with light in which the hidden sun remained with its beams; it rejoiced because the cursed viper, who had destroyed himself, had departed. As that one left his head was heavy, his face was glowing red, his countenance distorted, his heart was racing, his whole being disturbed, his teeth chattered, his knees shaking. His mind had left him, his powers of deliberation gone from him.[8]

Wagner's interest stems from his agreement with Guardini that Judas has a way of revealing who we are. All humans are sinners; therefore, all are existentially involved in the deed of Judas. His goal is to inquire about the meaning of Judas within the Christ event.

But the New Testament is remarkably reluctant to name Judas's sin. Wagner concludes that the sin of greed, since early times considered a serious transgression of Judas, may in fact be the key, for this sin means that God is removed from the center of one's life and one acts out a refusal to be dependent upon God as provider. He also recognizes that Judas's sin represents a failure of the church, the inner circle of disciples with whom Judas lived, which was unable to bear his pain and to protect him. He cites Augustine, who saw in the election of Judas by Jesus an attempt to teach the disciples how to bear sinners and not divide the body of Christ.[9]

The main questions Wagner deals with are the predestination of Judas and his free will. Again, he quotes from the church fathers to support both free will and the choice of God. He seeks to solve the riddle of how the act of Judas, which he sees as "negative" (22), can turn out in such a positive manner. Where in all this, he wonders, is the free will of Judas or the fore-knowledge of God?

Wagner rejects process theology and seems equally dissatisfied with the traditional theories of predestination. Judas therefore becomes important because he does not provide answers to the traditional questions but forces us to continue to ask these questions in a new way, a way in which we must review our definitions of human freedom, but also what it means that God is above all and in all (1 Cor 15:28). The strength of Wagner's approach is that he asks these questions in dialogue with his Jewish colleagues. Their search is presented in the same volume.

Helmut Gollwitzer

Helmut Gollwitzer dealt with Judas under the title "Good News for Judas Iscariot" and ascribed central importance to Judas precisely because his deed did not separate him absolutely from the other disciples but joined them in his faithfulness. "All of them sat on the same bench."[10] Gollwitzer does not seek to absolve Judas; rather, he treats him as a sinner, along with all others. Like every other human being, Judas failed in some unspecified way, and the debt of that failure cannot be undone. "The New Testament is the book of great concern about Judas Iscariot because it deals with his plight, the plight of us all," says Gollwitzer, citing "Judas, Eichmann, Stalin, Hitler, U.S. president L. B. Johnson and [military leaders] Ludendorff and West-moreland and all their subordinate blood-stained officers who flew napalm-laden planes (in Vietnam), and all the unnumbered thousands who have shed innocent blood."[11] Regrettably, Gollwitzer misses the mark from our perspective because he begins with a false reading of the New Testament data on the nature of Judas's deed. At the same time, he poses the right question.

The overriding question Gollwitzer wishes to address is: What would Jesus say to Judas if he had met him on the way to hanging himself? Would he have given him another chance?

To this, Gollwitzer replies that the only new words Jesus might have spoken would have dealt with the resurrection. Certainly Jesus, as one who preached love for one's enemies, would have forgiven Judas, but that is too general and does not advance the discussion. So Gollwitzer composes some words that Jesus might have spoken to Judas. They are worth quoting in full:

> When I called you to be one of the Twelve I already knew you as the one who you are today. You did not destroy the hopes I had misplaced in you. Nor were you merely a pawn in a higher plan, "to fulfill Scripture" in order now to be cast away. I accepted you as the one who you have now proved to be, you are the one I love, you are the one I wanted by my side in order to be for you. For a long time it was apparent that not only you but that all of you [my disciples] would bring me death according to who you are and who I am. Why did I not protect you from your guilt by protecting myself from you? The servant is not above his Lord, so I said to you, and I am not above the One who sent me, who wishes to be there for you through me. He whom we together, since the time of our ancestors, call the God of Israel does not seek to preserve himself. Together with me you have handed him [God] over, now you know that, that is why you no longer can tolerate yourself or the world. Together with me that One allowed himself to be surrendered. In that manner it became apparent how matters stand; and more. So he allowed himself to be done away with together with me, in the same way as you now wish to do away with yourself. But because of my call, long ago he accepted you who will put him away. As the unbearable one, he accepted you in order to bear you. Both of us, he and I, died on your account. Therein you also died. For to be with me was your life; you knew that, now you know it even better. Therefore my death was your death as well. You don't need now to seek it, it has already happened. I bound you to me so closely that my death was yours as well. Therefore you can no longer be freed from me. When upon my election of you, you elected me and became my disciple, you recognized your life in me. You were not disappointed, as you now think, when you think that precisely that choice brought you and me our death. We both, he and I, remain life for those who cast us into death—not only as long as they do not do it, but especially when they do it. We have joined ourselves to you, the one bringing us death, for the sake of your life, not for the sake of your death. I am so much for you and he is with me for you so much that we have made your death ours by our own death. To advance your life against yourself, that was the issue, when we surrendered ourselves to you. Now your death has already taken place but our life remains for you. For your sake I too was in death, the death which you brought me; for you, now also take my life for yourself! That is why I am now talking with you. The death into which you cast us was not the last, as you now think, as you cast yourself into it. I was for you the word of life; I still am, even from then on I was, in order that I could be even more now. For you I allowed myself to be killed by you in order that the death might be past and that now only the word of life might affirm itself to you. In me, the One who sent me chose for himself death; but for you, his murderer, he chose life. Long ago I accepted you just as you are, therefore accept yourself now

in hope of what you can become through me! Your right to life you have squandered. I am your new right to life.[12]

Gollwitzer indicates that this is not a pure imaginative fabrication. Rather, it is an attempt to translate "the word of reconciliation" which is at the center of the New Testament. He insists that Judas belongs along with the other disciples under the message of resurrection and life which is so central to the gospel. Judas must be told the word of resurrection so that he may share in the life that allowed itself to be killed—and through that death became life for the murderer. "Only boundless forgiveness is actual divine forgiveness" (282).

Gollwitzer sees the New Testament as the book that concerns itself with the murder of Jesus, of which Judas is the extreme representative. Not even the Gospel writers can bring themselves to put in a good word for him. Nevertheless, the New Testament offers good news for Judas (282–283) as well as for the rest of humanity.

Gollwitzer's presentation of the Judas figure and his attempt to relate it to the core of the gospel is arresting. Indeed, if you accept the classical doctrine of betrayal, it is an important corrective to the mass of materials that have been written about Judas's evil deed and the ultimate destiny of Judas. It is an attempt that sees squarely the open and liberating word Jesus spoke to many.

Above all, Gollwitzer does two things. He binds into an inextricable unity the life and death of Judas, Jesus, and God. The solidarity of the death of God on Calvary in the form of God's son Jesus with the disciple Judas is decisively affirmed. Moreover, Jesus affirms Judas just as he is. His love for Judas is irrevocable and in no way dependent upon whatever good or bad Judas may do. Here Gollwitzer keeps in faithful touch with the gospel.

Bernhard Dieckmann

As we have tried to demonstrate in the exegetical section of this book, there is no clear indication of betrayal anywhere once we translate the word παραδίδωμι correctly. There is even without that no evidence that Judas used treachery. Rather, every indication is that the element of surprise was missing and that Jesus knew perfectly well what Judas was doing and indeed that Jesus, according to John, ordered Judas to do it. Under such circumstances we will have to let go of the drama and the tragic element and content ourselves with a less dramatic picture than tradition offers. It is possible that Judas betrayed—but whom? or what? and why? To accuse him of treachery and unfaithfulness and greed—all of this may be justified, but there certainly is no convincing evidence in the text.

In the light of these imponderables, other theologians have taken the scapegoat theory seriously and it has been much discussed.

The fruits of such mutual efforts have been demonstrated most clearly by Bernhard Dieckmann, whose book *Judas as Scapegoat* incorporates theological reflection about Judas with literary history and the history of art. He considers questions raised by writers and artists as an asset to theology because they force us to address issues we would rather avoid. The many interpretations of Judas they provide force exegetes and theological writers to deal with the *man* Judas, not as theological cliché or caricature.[13]

On the theological side, he examines the question of how so much good has come from the "betrayal" of Judas, and therefore the possibility of a "saving" betrayal. There is no doubt that one can speak of such in connection with Joseph's betrayal by his brothers. But it is not clear how the action of Judas fits into this situation. If the death of Christ was necessary, how can the action of Judas (who made it possible) or the deed of Judas be considered a "betrayal," and the most reprehensible sin of history?[14]

Dieckmann concludes that the "interpretation of Judas" is the incomplete task and urgent desideratum of theology. He therefore calls for an analysis of the accounts in the New Testament about the sequence and nature of the events.

The main issue for Dieckmann, however, is the scapegoat dimension of the Judas story. Dieckmann's strongest contribution is to treat the scapegoat theory seriously and explore it at length. This has been missing in most treatments of Judas. Moreover, he listens to the questions that artists are asking of exegetes and theologians: "The exegetes are being asked whether the biblical affirmations about Judas are really so uniformly negative as the tradition presupposes, the theologians are being asked how the usual picture of Judas squares with the Christian view of God, and finally the churches are being asked whether this picture of Judas may not be a symptom that they missed the spirit of love and still do." Judas becomes thus a key figure for the understanding of Christianity and the church.

Karl Barth

The first theologian in our century to raise his voice on behalf of Judas, and the one who did so most extensively—although he also, paradoxically, condemned him—was Karl Barth. In Barth's 1957 volume, *Church Dogmatics,* Judas receives nearly fifty pages of fine print. A summary of his position and a brief critique from a theological layperson's point of view may help us to understand Judas. It is important to see this as part of Barth's narrative exegesis. His treatment of the story of Judas comes at the end of a series that tries to show that God responds with a blessing even to those who are rejected. He uses Leviticus 14 and 16, the narratives of David and Saul, and 1 Kings 13, before coming to the culmination of his essay, where Judas is the central theme. Here Barth's "typological exegesis reaches its greatest concentration."[15]

Some Theological Reflections: Judas's Apostolate

The rubric under which Karl Barth deals with Judas is the election of the individual; the title of this section is "The Determination of the Rejected."[16] For Barth, it is important that the problem of the rejected is concentrated and developed in Judas. The rejected one, counterpart of the elected one, is not an opponent from outside who opposes the kingdom of God but rather exists in sinister proximity to Jesus Christ and the apostles. This closeness of the rejected one to Jesus also reveals the relativity of rejection. It can express itself only under the direct supervision and control of the overruling power and effectiveness of the Lord himself, only in the work of a disciple and apostle.

For Barth, Judas was both a disciple and an apostle. As much as Peter, as much as John, "more so rather than less so, to the extent that he alone among the twelve belongs like Jesus to the tribe of Judah, the seed of David" (459). Accordingly, he deems it important that Judas played a full part, active and passive, in all Jesus did with his disciples and apostles, that he received what Jesus gave at the Last Supper. "Strictly speaking, however, not a single stone is thrown at Judas."[17]

But the treatment of Judas does not proceed from any interest in Judas as an individual. Three stand in solidarity and are joined in identity at what he calls this "paltry" act: Judas, a disciple and apostle, together with the church which is formed by this group, and, second, Israel, which rejected its Messiah, and, third, the heathen world, which allied itself with this Israel. To speak of "treachery," even technically, raises for Barth ideas far too complicated to account for the Judas transaction.

Nevertheless, the act of Judas was both paltry and yet had tremendous consequences. The apostle Judas Iscariot is the special agent and exponent of Jesus' handing over, as it was decreed necessary in the counsel of God. Furthermore, although the New Testament displays an "extraordinary calm," Barth is convinced that "the New Testament unquestionably regarded and judged the action of this man as sin and guilt of the most atrocious character. . . . Judas is *the* great sinner of the NT."[18]

Unfortunately, this serious charge overlooks the relatively small amount of space given to Judas in the New Testament and grossly exaggerates the negative light in which his deed is seen. Most disturbing, the statement lacks historical perspective. How, for example, does Judas's action relate to the verdict Paul passed on himself that he (Paul) was "chief [πρῶτος] of sinners"

(1 Tim 1:15)? Or, indeed, the sharp words Jesus addressed to Peter: "Get you behind me, Satan"? It is highly doubtful that any comparisons between sin would have been meaningful to members of the early Christian community. They certainly came not from their master, who had a habit of telling stories about people who thought themselves to be quite good, only to find out that the very people they despised were in God's sight "justified rather than the other" (Luke 18:14)—and that tax gatherers and prostitutes were at the head of the line of those being admitted to the kingdom (Matt 21:31).

Not once in this discussion does Barth refer to Jesus' sharp rebuke to Peter in addressing him as "Satan." It is Judas who represents the unclean feet of the disciples; he "is in a special sense the bearer and representative of this remaining uncleanness of theirs" (462).

And what is the sin that Judas committed, or what is that uncleanness of which John speaks? Barth finds the clue in the Johannine version of the anointing story (John 12:1–8). The contrast between Mary and Judas is that Mary was prodigal in her show of affection toward Jesus, while Judas was niggardly. She is extravagantly affectionate toward Jesus' feet, yet Judas cannot and will not accept such prodigality. He wants, instead, that a good and profitable work may be carried out through the strength of this devotion. He "wants to exploit it." This view, this attitude, makes Judas unclean. "It was because of this that Judas 'handed Jesus over,'" Barth contends (462).

Still, Barth does not define why this event played such a role in Judas's thinking and what the link is between this event and his "handing over." Surely the most serious weakness of this point of view is that Judas is criticized for showing some concern for the poor. Given that Jesus persistently showed care for the poor and in what he says about the poor, Judas was simply drawing a logical conclusion from what Jesus had taught him. Even if on this occasion Judas was not in tune with the thinking of Jesus, I cannot imagine that Jesus would have condemned Judas.

Barth argues, however, that by going to the authorities, Judas in effect was rejecting the claims of Jesus. He reserved for himself the right to decide what apostolic discipleship really involves. The claim of Jesus to total faith, absolute humility, and increasing prodigality stood between him and his enemies. Judas's position could only hand Jesus over to be crucified, "for Judas Jesus was for sale" (463). Judas had to maintain his freedom. Having turned to Jesus, he had not bound himself to him. How does Barth arrive at this conclusion? It is clearly based on the Fourth Gospel augmented by a healthy dose of Barthian imagination. Is it possible that historical critical exegesis has given way here to typology? Is common sense displaced by sentimentality? Barth seems to arrive at motivations on the basis of the way the Gospels have arranged the material, choosing the least reliable Gospel from which to draw a historical conclusion.

Barth's connections between certain acts and events are made possible only by the way in which the Fourth Gospel arranges the available material. Putting together various pieces of the puzzle of Judas, as Barth does, leaves us not with four portraits of Judas, or a synthesis of the four, but only one: "The Judas that emerges is thus the Judas of the canonical gospel, not, or not only, the Judas of any individual Gospel."[19] Such a position is totally unacceptable. Theologians, especially biblical theologians, must also concern themselves with historical probabilities. They must be able to sort out superior sources from inferior ones. They must also be able to see the difference between characters being depicted and historical personalities.

Barth defines the act of Judas as bartering Jesus for a reward: Judas's sin is that, with all Israel, he wants this evil reward. For him, Jesus can be bartered.

But what does Barth make of Judas's reported repentance? He notes that Judas had wanted only the first small step, not the final outcome. He was not for Jesus in the way that we must be if we are not to be against him. When things went differently (Barth does not say what Judas may have had in mind), he repented. Barth sees "no reason not to take seriously this repentance, this confession, this attempt of Judas to make restitution" (466).

Moreover, he describes that attempt as "in its way more complete than that of Peter" (466). The deed of Judas is to lead the officers of the high priest to the spot where they could arrest Jesus without disturbance. In comparison to Peter's sin, is this really worse?

Barth also has to come to terms with the effect upon Judas of the Last Supper and the footwashing. His solidarity with the other apostles makes it necessary to see all the apostles together.

> On the one hand, according to all the Evangelists he is still an elect and called Apostle of Jesus Christ and all the Evangelists concede that he took part in the Lord's Supper or in the feet-washing. And it would be an unspeakably hard affirmation (to say) that there was no forgiveness of sins for Judas, that what was symbolised in those actions had no positive meaning for him, that Jesus died in vain for him. After all, his act only revealed what was concealed in Peter as well and all the Apostles (475). . . .
>
> Does then the prayer of Luke 23:34, "Father, forgive them, for they know not what they do," exclude Judas or is it ineffective in his case? (476).

Putting the question in this form, it would be hasty and illegitimate to give a final answer one way or the other. For it is clear that Jesus is for Judas even when Judas is against him. Yet Barth warns us that we can find nothing to support either final damnation for Judas or his forgiveness.

On the one hand, the New Testament places no limits to the grace of Jesus Christ, even with regard to Judas. It sets Judas against the brightest radiance of this grace. At the same time, it offers not a word indicating that Judas is an example of the restoration of all things.

The critical point is that Judas is the apostle who put his hand to the lever. It was in *his* act that Israel finally demonstrated itself to be the people of God who, because they would not wholly serve their God, would not serve God at all. By his act, Barth contends, the tribe of Judah rejected the promised Messiah; and the apostolic group itself became guilty of this rejection (466). Because the act could not be reversed, no repentance by Judas, no matter how sincere, could in any way alter the verdict of woe Jesus spoke against him. He could not make restitution for his deed. He carried the fault of providing "the first link in the chain, the smallest, but one which involves and controls all those which follow" (460), and his repentance remains an open question which is not heard or answered by a promise of grace.

What Barth calls the "unreality" of Judas's repentance (467) is demonstrated in his refusal to accept Jesus unreservedly as his Lord, wholly surrendering himself to the glorification of Jesus' death. "According to the NT view, no promise of grace could be held out for Judas, and no genuine penitence was possible" (467). The time had passed, as indeed had the time of the Temple of Jerusalem, for "the special worship in this city" and the "existence of Israel as a special people of God" (468). By disposing of Judas's reward as they did, the high priests and elders sign the death sentence on Judas, as well as their own sentence of rejection and a sentence on Israel itself (469).

The Meaning of παραδίδωμι: The Act of Judas

Critical to Barth's case is the meaning of παραδίδωμι (*paradidōmi*) of which he also makes an extensive study.[20] He concludes: "It has a decidedly negative and only negative character as applied to the act of Judas" (480). McGlasson concludes, "No other expositor, ancient or modern, has used this word and concept to make the exegetical points that Barth makes. . . . Barth's reading is a technically brilliant achievement."[21]

Barth derives the meaning of Judas's act from a series of New Testament texts in which the word appears which deal with arrests.[22] He maintains that Judas treats Jesus exactly as described there, for "in all these contexts 'delivery' is the handing over or transfer of a free or relatively free person to the confining power of those who wish him harm, and from whom he must expect harm. And it is the sin of Judas that he delivered Jesus in this way" (481).

Judas has taken it upon his conscience to bring Jesus into a situation where, apart from God, no one can help him; to place into the hands of men a power over Jesus which renders him utterly powerless and finally kills him, and from which he can only call upon the power of God.

Barth notes that in Luke 22:3; John 6:70; and 13:2, 27 Judas's act is described as that of one possessed of Satan. On the one hand, Barth says that Judas disowned his apostolic office by doing what he did, yet he recognizes that the act had another meaning. This he bases on the positive meaning of the word "deliver," even though he said earlier that with reference to Judas the word has only a negative meaning. He misses the mark here; although, given his method of rejecting historical–critical methods when it suits him, this is not surprising.

Barth contends that the deed of Judas cannot be weakened or transformed into a positive definition. His disobedience was certainly not obedience. On the contrary, he affirms, it was total disobedience. What he did was a rejection, an evasion and nullifying of the Word of God (483).

The savage and sinful handing over of Jesus by Judas, in itself absolutely without justification, corresponds objectively to the handing over of Jesus into the hands of men, which is the meaning and content of the apostolic ministry by which the church on earth is established and maintained. The latter handing over rectifies the mischief done by the former (488). The activity of Paul, himself once a deliverer like Judas, shows that an active participation in the positive task of the apostolate cannot be denied even to the apostle Judas and his handing over (488).

God's Act of Handing Over

Karl Barth's theocentric theology affirms itself in his treatment of the Judas story as well. Beyond the human delivery of Jesus to his death stands God: "Before Judas had handed over Jesus, God had handed Him over, and Jesus had handed over Himself" (489). "It is not permissible to understand any other delivery except with reference to this one" (ibid.).

The freedom of Jesus that was robbed by Judas is "clearly only a pale reflection of the divine freedom of which God robbed Him, of which He robbed Himself" (490).

In this context it would have been helpful if Barth could have explained the relationship between the covenant that God had with Judas and his act. Was Judas not being faithful to God's covenant in handing Jesus over?

The Centrality of Christ

Barth's theology and hence his approach to Judas is centered in Christ. What Jesus Christ suffered innocently was undoubtedly the punishment of the man handed over by the wrath of God, the judgment that humans bring on themselves, and, like Judas, must execute upon themselves in their freedom to continue doing evil.

Does this mean that Judas was himself evil? Barth answers, "Of course

not!" (495). Jesus alone drinks the cup; not Peter, not Judas, not those who
are delivered up by the wrath of God; none of us who also deserve to be
delivered up in this way.

To be sure, evil must be taken seriously. To be a Pharaoh, whose heart
was hardened by God, a Saul whose spirit left him, a Judas, an Alexander
and Hymenaeus, whom Paul consigned to Satan (1 Tim 1:20), is a serious
matter. It is, Barth declares, a life-and-death matter to be threatened by hell,
sentenced to hell, worthy of hell, and already on the road to hell. We must
stress the fact that we actually know of only one certain triumph—the
handing over of Jesus—and that victory over hell took place in order that
hell would never again be able to triumph over anyone. What Jesus did
takes absolute precedence over everything else that has been done or can be
done, whether good or evil, actively or passively (496).

Our faith in Jesus Christ does not allow us to consider any of those who
are handed over by God as lost. We know of none whom God has wholly
and exclusively abandoned. We know only of One who was abandoned in
this way, only of One who was lost: Jesus Christ. And he was lost (and
found again) in order that none should be lost apart from him.

Is There Hope for Judas?

This leads Barth to pose the question whether Judas may indeed be numbered among the saved. Barth responds that scripture speaks of countless
men, as it does of Judas, in such a way that we must assume that they have
lived and died without even the possibility, let alone the fulfillment, of any
saving repentance. If there is light and hope for them, it can only be because
and if there is an eschaton, a final judgment, which confronts the status and
fate of the rejected. For them, the absolutely new factor is the handing over
of Jesus and all that it involved—their cleansing from sin. Jesus is our pledge
of hope. The rejected also stand in this light (497).

But what is the specific relationship of Judas to the decisive act of handing Jesus over? (501). Just as early on Judas is said to have dislodged the first
stone, so here Barth accuses Judas of everything which others apart from
and after Judas inflicted upon Jesus, up to and including the act of his final
murder. Everything followed from that which Judas did, just as the insignificant seed already contains and represents the entire growth that emerges
from it (501).

But did it flow *inexorably*? we ask. Is it not possible for Judas to have acted
in obedience to the command of Jesus and then events to have turned out
in such a way as to lead him to experience remorse?

In the dialectical thinking of Barth, he concludes that the more profoundly and comprehensively we attempt to formulate the sin and guilt of
Judas, the more nearly we see that neither his will nor his deed approached

what he himself willed; and the more nearly his will and deed approached what God willed and did. The divine handing over worked to cleanse sinners from the sin against God of which they are guilty. It is Judas who, now at the head of all sinners, incurs the guilt (501). "Consider the sin of Judas in its ultimate most terrible meaning. The Adam who, listening to the suggestion of the serpent, only wished to be like God, a divine man alongside God, unlimited and undisturbed by his mere creatureliness in its distinction from God, has now gone on to an open assault upon God" (501). In these lines one hears clear echoes of Daub, cited in our first chapter.

At the same time, Barth affirms that Paul is right, especially in regard to Judas, when he says that where sin abounded, grace even more abounded.

> The act of Judas cannot, therefore, be considered an unfortunate episode, much less as a manifestation of a dark realm beyond the will and work of God, but in every respect (and at a particularly conspicuous place) as one element of the divine will and work. In what he himself wills and carries out, Judas does what God wills to be done. He and not Pilate is the executor of the new last will and testament (*executor Novi Testamenti*). But with his vile betrayal of Jesus to His enemies he is also the executor of the surrender which God has resolved to make. (502)

Again the fine-tuned dialectic leads Barth to conclude that for all its insincerity, the treacherous kiss by which Judas distinguishes Jesus from the surrounding disciples at the arrest is the sign of gratitude of lost humankind for the existence of the God who now wills to intervene on behalf of humans (502). And yet "the clear command with which Jesus, as it were, takes from [Judas's] hand that which he is planning, Himself deciding that what Judas intends to do with Him shall actually be done. . . . In one sense (and only in that sense), Judas is the most important figure in the New Testament, apart from Jesus" (502).

Was it not Judas, the sinner without equal, who offered himself at the decisive moment to carry out the will of God? There is nothing here to venerate, nor is there anything to despise. "Veneration is just as misplaced as contempt," says Barth (502). There is place only for the recognition and adoration and magnifying of God. Judas is so clearly abandoned that no defense is possible and all praise would be folly. But censure and condemnation are also folly, Barth says, because what was done here by the One who was so very differently abandoned—namely, God—makes them superfluous and irrelevant. For when God abandoned Godself, it pleased God so to confront Judas, who was also abandoned, that he of all people became God's direct servant in his blatant rejection, as not even Paul and Peter were God's servants. That is, Barth says, he became the servant of the work of reconciliation itself, in which these others shared only later and as witnesses.

Because the divine handing over is the content and subject of the apostolic tradition, it would not exist apart from Judas and his act. Barth contends there can be no doubt that fundamentally Judas cooperated positively, although against his will, in the task of the apostolate and the church, grounded on the election of Jesus Christ (503). It is puzzling that Barth can say with such authority that Judas did this "against his will and deserts" when there is no such evidence.

McGlasson may be right in his appraisal of Barth's contribution to the use of the word *paradidōmi*. As for Barth's conclusion, "we can only say that even technically the use of the word 'treachery' raises ideas far too complicated to account for the transaction in question" (460). One wonders what might have happened had he disciplined himself, as he did in so many other cases, to take the meaning of the word seriously. He has been accused of "biblicism," a kind of slavish adherence to the meaning of the biblical text and a concern about the author's intention. In this case it can only be said that at least slightly less scorn for the historical-critical method—if not a deeper commitment to historical-critical exegesis in addition to his narrative exegesis and even typological exegesis—might have served him well.[23] But there is worse to come.

Barth's View of Israel

The most serious side of Barth's position is not what he says about Judas but what he says about Israel. Judas acts not only on his own behalf and on behalf of the disciples; for Barth, Judas "represents the Jews" (464). What he does is "merely that which Israel has always done in relation to Yahweh" (ibid.). Israel itself delivers up Jesus to be slaughtered. And what does Israel gain from this? Here Barth's incipient and disturbing anti-Semitism shines forth most clearly: "The thirty pieces of silver and the modicum of religion with which it tried to buy off its God, [made] a good enough contribution towards repairing over and over again the dilapidated Temple!" (464–465). All that Judas got out of his betrayal was thirty pieces of silver—"Judas and all Israel, Judas and in and with him the Jews as such" (465).

Both Acts and Matthew's account of what happened to the reward of Judas "confirm the fact that both Judas and Judah—Judas as the embodiment of Judah, and Judah as embodied in Judas—have, in fact, no future as such and in and for themselves" (469).

According to Barth, "Israel's right to existence is extinguished, and therefore its existence can only be extinguished. . . . It has fulfilled and vindicated the meaning of its existence by giving rise to Jesus Christ" (505).

After what Israel has done to Jesus Christ, Barth declares that Israel is always a past and rejected people to the extent that it has not arisen to new life in the church. It is, however, says Barth, still true that with its evil human "tradition" Israel was the instrument by which the church of Jesus

Christ was built. For this writer and many others, Barth's comments sound dangerously close to saying that Israel's only reason for existence was the founding of the church and that it no longer has any reason for existence.

The designation of Israel's "tradition" as evil and human is, of course, a play on the word "hand over." Still, it is especially insensitive, if not insulting, to observant Jews—to say nothing of Israeli citizens—as it probably would have been to both Jesus and Paul. This type of statement has to be rejected as flying in the face of the fundamental message of the New Testament. It only enflames the fires of anti-Semitism and is an insult to all Jews and increasingly more Christians as well.

Barth's own candor in facing the question of anti-Semitism comes out in his letter to Marquardt. Here he acknowledges his aversion to Jews and his inability to deal with an adequate Jewish-Christian theology. His sons, he says, are better equipped to do this than he is. At least he acknowledges that there is work to be done.[24] As an interjection here, it is important to consider the writings of Pinchas Lapide, who has provided some provocative and stimulating ideas for the discussion both of Jesus and, more recently, of Judas as well.

Lapide is concerned about the "oldest and most murderous weapon of the arsenal in presumably 'Christian' anti-Judaism, the so-called betrayal of Judas and the accusation lumped together with it: the murder of Christ at the hands of the Jews."[25] Lapide traces the way in which Judas has been treated in art, especially the altar drawings of Western churches, and shows how few are the exceptions to a demonic picture of Judas. He observes:

> Iscariot serves either as a scapegoat or as a whipping boy for the passion of Christ or as a cipher for all conceivable horrors which have been laid on his shoulders in word or picture.[26]

He concludes further that "Had Iscariot been named Jacob, David, or Jonathan instead of Judas, a name which too easily could become universalized to become a symbolic figure for all Jews, who knows how many could have been spared a martyr's death?"[27]

Summary

Whatever we say about Barth's treatment of the Judas figure, he does demonstrate once more how drawn we are to the figure of Judas and how important it is to utilize all the tools of biblical research to isolate the options available to us in our interpretation of the historical Judas. To be sure, Barth did not say the last word about Judas—and, thankfully, not about the fate of the Jewish people or the role of Israel in history. It appears obvious that a joint effort between theologians and exegetes can bring forward the discussion. Barth's malicious treatment of Jews in this discussion, bordering as it does on pure theological anti-Semitism, should remind us that discussions on this topic should be done in partnership with Jewish colleagues. Taken together with David Hartman's stress on tolerance for people of other faiths, and his insistence that the living covenant provides for innovative adaptations to the culture in which we live, Barth's desire to let the strength of Christian uniqueness stand out can be honored. We might then learn that Barth's fixation on election cannot be countered by a stress on Jews as God's chosen people, valid and integral as that idea is to all covenantal religions, but rather by the recognition that God has only chosen peoples.[28]

On the basis of what we have seen in our investigation it is surely not in order for us to justify the need for a "Judas figure" as is sometimes done. For example, R. P. Scharlemann[29] suggests that "the actuality of Jesus as the Christ involves a triadic structure constituted by the relations of Peter and Judas to each other and to Jesus. . . . From the thesis, it seems to me to follow that Christianity, even at its most exclusive, requires that there be others, not Christians, *just as Jesus' living reality required that there be two, equally true responses to his appearance, those of Peter and of Judas.*"[30] "Judas does not represent the reprobate," and when we compare Peter's denial of Jesus, made in a moment of weakness and contradicting his earlier confession, we find it to be of a different order than Judas's *paradidonai* (handing over). He understands Judas as saying by his actions that Jesus is not the Christ.

Scharlemann seeks to reap some benefits from this analysis for interfaith discussion, but I find it less than helpful. In any case, whatever theologians want to make of Judas we will need first to try to see what happened in the earliest years of the Christian movement to this person who began as did the other disciples. Is it too much to suggest that it was not disobedience but rather obedience which brought that about and that there are indeed two parallel lines between Judas and Jesus. The inability of the church to give him a fair hearing may have had historical roots in her relationship with her sister faith, Judaism. The way back to a new reading of the personality of Judas must take us also on a road of interfaith dialogue with our Jewish colleagues. It is difficult to see how Scharlemann's schema can help us on that way.

Notes

1. Barth, *Church Dogmatics,* II, 501–502. For secondary studies of Barth's hermeneutics using the Judas excursus, see McGlasson, *Jesus and Judas: Biblical Exegesis in Barth,* 135–147; and D. Ford, *Barth and God's Story,* 84–93.

2. Wagner, "Judas."

3. Gollwitzer, "Gute Botschaft für Judas Ischarioth, in idem, *Krummes Holz-aufrechter Gang: Zur Frage nach dem Sinn des Lebens,* 271–296.

4. Dieckmann, *Judas als Sündenbock*.

5. In addition to the works cited, in the last phases of this book's gestation I came across Katherine Sonderegger's *That Jesus Christ Was Born a Jew: Karl Barth's "Doctrine of Israel.*" It made it clear that this topic deserves discussion here.

6. Dieckmann, *Judas als Sündenbock*.

7. Lüthi, *Geschichte*; idem, "Das Problem des Judas Iskariot," 296–304. Ray Anderson's attempt in *The Gospel according to Judas* to go beyond the accusatory stage and absolve Judas for his betrayal is commendable and a good counterbalance to the stream of accusations made against him. Using an imaginary dialogue between Jesus and Judas, he vividly paints the doctrine of forgiveness as applied to Judas. It is more in the realm of pastoral theology than either biblical or systematic theology.

8. Wagner, "Judas," 11–12. The quotation is from his first homily on the passion of Christ in *Bibliothek der Kirchenväter*, vol. 6 (Syrian Poets) (Kempten and Munich, 1912). My translation from the German.

9. Wagner, "Judas," 17.

10. Gollwitzer, *Krummes Holz-aufrechter Gang*, 271–296, here 272.

11. Gollwitzer, *Krummes Holz-aufrechter Gang*, 276.

12. My translation used by permission of Chr. Kaiser Verlag, Munich. Copyright © Chr. Kaiser Verlag, München. Taken from *Krummes Holz-aufrechter Gang: Zur Frage nach dem Sinn des Lebens*, 279–280.

13. Dieckmann, *Judas*, 227–228.

14. Dieckmann, *Judas*, 228.

15. Ford, *Barth*, 85.

16. Barth, *Church Dogmatics*, II, 458–506.

17. Barth, *Church Dogmatics*, II, 460.

18. Barth, *Church Dogmatics*, II, 461. With respect to the question whether Judas can be treated as anything but evil, Benoit refers to him as Judas the Traitor, "the Sinner above all others," in "The Death of Judas," 194.

19. McGlasson, *Jesus and Judas*, 136.

20. McGlasson rightly observes the uniqueness of Barth's treatment of παραδίδωμι (143) and how it extends and deepens his portrayal of Judas.

21. McGlasson, *Jesus and Judas*, 143. The praise heaped on Barth is justified, although he might have mentioned Popkes's subsequent work.

22. Matt 4:12; 5:25; 18:34; Mark 1:14.

23. McGlasson, *Jesus and Judas*, 116.

24. *Karl Barth Letters* (1961/68), 261–263. I am indebted to Lloyd Gaston, who first called this to my attention.

25. Lapide, *Schuld*, 9.

26. Lapide, *Schuld*, 15.

27. Lapide, *Schuld*, 15.

28. So Walbert Bühlmann, a Roman Catholic missiologist, rightly entitled his book. For Hartman, see *A Living Covenant: The Innovative Spirit in Traditional Judaism*. In addition, the historian Akenson has analyzed the effects of a narrow view of "chosenness" and election when applied to "land" (*God's Peoples: Covenant and Land in South Africa, Israel and Ulster*).

29. Scharlemann, "Why Christianity Needs Other Religions," in *Christianity and the Wider Ecumenism*, ed. Peter Phan (1990): 35–46.

30. Scharlemann, "Why Christianity," 37.

CHAPTER
ELEVEN

JUDAS AS SEEN BY
JEWISH INTERPRETERS

<hr>

The need to exorcize the Judas Iscariot image, and to restore the name "Judas" to honour, is part of a confrontation with the imaginative, mythic basis of antisemitism. Such a confrontation . . . is far more important than rationalistic discourse on the causes or evil of antisemitism.

　　　　　　　　　　　　　　　　　　　　—Hyam Maccoby[1]

Although there have been Jewish interpreters of the New Testament prior to the rise of Zionism and the formation of the Jewish state in 1948, with the founding of the Israeli state Jewish scholars have felt a greater freedom to deal with Jesus and the history of the early church. We have, therefore, been the beneficiaries of some superb studies of Jesus by first-rate scholars, among them Josef Klausner,[2] David Flusser,[3] and Geza Vermes.[4] We are, moreover, fortunate that in North America we have a number of superb New Testament professors in seminaries and university departments of religion who are practicing Jews teaching early Christian literature. I have found my teaching of the New Testament enriched by having Jewish students in my classes and cannot imagine participation in biblical research symposia without such colleagues. Perhaps the reader will understand why I feel the need to draw them into this discussion as well.

Throughout this book we have indicated our debt to David Daube, whose various articles on suicide and other related topics have informed and, indeed, formed much of what is written here. His knowledge of history and law, his scintillating presentations, and his gracious responses to my inquiries add to the considerable debt I owe him.

David Flusser, although he has presented us with a wealth of materials in relation to early Christianity—and has been particularly keen on noting a relationship between early Christianity and the Qumran community—has not given much attention to the figure of Judas. Indirectly, however, he has made an important contribution to the discussion by his stress on the love command and especially the Lukan text, "Father, forgive them, for they know not what they do." (See above, chapter 7.) Only those who have had the opportunity to work with him directly can understand his passionate concern for doing serious historical research on Jesus and first-century Judaism. His passion for a correct understanding of Jesus comes from a deep conviction that Jesus is to be taken seriously as a teacher and spiritual leader. Flusser, has, in my judgment, written the best book on Jesus our century has produced.

Geza Vermes found his way back to Judaism, the religion of his birth, after having spent some time as a scholar in a Catholic order. His study of the Qumran sources and his attraction to Judaism also drew him to the study of Jesus. He has, however, been more interested in messianic questions than in the historical question of Judas and has not addressed the question of the historical Judas to any extent.

Gösta Lindeskog noted that the passion story and the mysterious figure of Judas have a special interest for Jewish researchers.[5] The report he published is fundamental to this topic. Jewish researchers have concluded that Judas either is an invention of the Christian tradition or is unrecognizable in the Gospels; in either case, he came to represent the Jewish people as betrayer of the Christian savior. Most have treated Judas only in connection with Jesus.[6]

In the *Toledoth Jeshua*,[7] Judas is called "Rabi Jehudah isch Bartota." Credited with learning the connection between Jesus and the divine name, Judas is seen as having defiled Jesus, partly because he expected Jesus to wage the wars of God against both the godless and the people of God (*TJ* 16:27-38). The legends arose in an attempt by second-century Judaism to hold its own against Christianity. The Jews from the second century onward glorified Judas as the one triumphant cohort of Jesus who revealed the resurrection to be a fraud.

Klausner was the first to give detailed historical attention to Judas in connection with his study of Jesus. He also drew attention to the section in *Aboth* on the disciples of Balaam, the profligate, which condemns those disciples to inheriting the punishment of the Valley of Gehinnom, where they will fall headlong into a deep ravine, just as Judas is reported to have done.

> And you, God, will cast them headlong into a deep ravine, men lusty for blood and falsehood. They will not attain unto half of their days (Ps 55:24. cf. *Aboth* 5.19).[8]

Klausner's keenest interest lies, however, in trying to place Judas during the time of Jesus' arrest and trial. He considers him the only one of the Twelve from Judea.[9] Judas is perceived as a competent and loyal disciple at the beginning who later began to lose his enthusiasm once he started to look at his master with a critical eye.

Judas became aware that Jesus did not always heal people successfully, that he was afraid of his enemies and persecutors, and indeed hid himself from them. He also noticed the many contradictions in Jesus' teachings. At one time, Jesus insisted that the smallest details of the Torah must be observed, sacrifices had to be brought, appearances had to be made before the high priest. He interpreted scripture verses like a genuine Pharisee; yet at another time he allowed forbidden foods, concerned himself as little about Sabbath observance as he did about washing his hands and made allusions to putting new wine into new containers, as if Jewish laws were no longer adequate.[10]

Judas was also concerned about the ability of Jesus as Messiah to rescue his people. After all, Jesus made statements about the destruction of the Temple, regarded by fellow Jews as the holiest place in all the world, saying that he would rebuild it. Little by little, says Klausner, Judas became convinced that he had a false messiah on his hands, that Jesus was mistaken and leading others into error. He considered him a false prophet, whom the Torah commanded should be killed; one who should not receive pity or compassion and who certainly should not be spared or forgiven.[11]

Yet, until the momentous announcement at Caesarea when Jesus admitted that he was the Messiah of God, Judas had expected nothing more from Jesus than he did of a regular rabbi. But now, Judas expected that he would move into the holy city, the religious and national center of the Jewish people, to carry out great miracles. He would destroy the Romans, force the Pharisees and the Sadducees to recognize him as Messiah, and, in his greatness and glory, be recognized by the whole people as the "last Redeemer." But Judas saw nothing of this, and only Matthew reports that Jesus did some miracles in the Temple (21:14).

Furthermore, the mighty Messiah retreated in fear every evening from Jerusalem to Bethany. Apart from angry words against the elders, Jesus did not announce a clear plan. Judas was an educated person from Judea, with a clear and keen intellect and a cold and calculating heart.[12] He was accustomed to criticizing and scrutinizing people, but these same gifts blinded him to the many virtues of Jesus. Klausner sees the other disciples as all uneducated Galileans, at the time considered dull of intellect and basically unsophisticated country folks. They could not bring the two parties together. Without the betrayal, Jesus' enemies could not have found him.[13]

For Klausner, it is inconceivable that Jesus did not know that Judas would betray him: "Jesus knew of the treachery from the beginning, indicated Judas as the Traitor, and actually referred to him as such by name."[14] Judas was simply obeying the Jewish law when he handed Jesus over. Is it not one's religious duty to report such a deceiver to the ruling authorities in order to fulfill the Law: "Thou shalt destroy the wicked one among you"? (Deut 13:2-12).

Throughout an energetic publication program, Pinchas Lapide has provided some provocative and stimulating ideas for the discussion both of Jesus and more recently of Judas as well.[15] He gives most attention to Judas in the book in which he seeks to determine who was responsible for Jesus' death.[16] His more recent "letter to Judas" notes that he has long been concerned about Judas.[17] He expresses the conviction that Judas was a member of the Zealot party whose loyalty to Jesus never wavered but who, like Peter, could not understand the course of Jesus' ministry and therefore offered a helping hand by turning him over to the Jewish leaders. Over against the myth of Judas, Lapide invites us to consider the possibility that he was a freedom fighter or Zealot. Lapide follows Oscar Cullmann and to a lesser extent Martin Hengel in the importance he attaches to the Zealots of that time.[18]

Lapide also deals with some difficult passages that are quoted from the Hebrew Bible in the early Christian writings and concludes that the two most noteworthy suicides reported in the Bible are those of Ahithophel and Judas.

In dealing with the financial agreement between Judas and the high priests, Lapide notes that the four Gospels really present us with four different portraits of Judas. He also is convinced that we are dealing with at least two anachronisms. Silver coins were no longer in currency, had not been for some three hundred years, and the weighing of silver as money was no longer done either, for coins needed merely to be counted once they had been minted.[19]

What captured Lapide's attention most forcefully, however, was the repeated use of the term παραδιδοῦναι. Six times this key word is repeated and it means not "betray" but "handed over." Taking various references to the word in the New Testament sources he concludes:

> Starting with Rom 8:32 the whole Passion is made into a chain of sevenfold handings over:
>   Judas hands over Jesus to the High Council,
>   which gives him over to Pilate,
>   who in turn hands him over to Herod,
>   who hands him back to Pilate,
>   who hands him over to the Legions,
>   who nail him to the Cross,
>   where Jesus hands over his soul to the Creator. (Luke 23:46)[20]

Hyam Maccoby has also been interested in the Judas figure, and his treatment of Judas is of critical importance.[21] He considers the story of Judas as "almost entirely fictitious," but he sees the disentanglement of the historical from the fictitional elements of great interest.[22]

> Indeed since a myth is to be tested by its social effects and antisemitism can only be dealt with on the mythic level, it is necessary to exorcize the Judas Iscariot image, and restore the name "Judas" to honour, as part of a confrontation with the imaginative, mythic basis of antisemitism.[23]

As part of this process, Maccoby carries out a detailed study of the image of Judas in each of the Gospels. A whole chapter is devoted to the question, "Who was Judas Iscariot?" followed by a reconstruction of the Prince Judas. He affirms that "to some extent the historical Judas Iscariot can be recovered."[24]

That person, he says, was a biological brother of Jesus of Nazareth,[25] possibly the author of the book of Jude[26] and a prince in the house of David. "Judas Iscariot the Betrayer of Jesus never existed" (153). He also takes the word Iscariot to mean that Judas was a Zealot (153–154).

A fundamental weakness of Maccoby's treatment is his ambivalence about whether one can isolate any historically reliable features in the Judas story. Furthermore, his important reconstruction of how the figure of Judas attained mythic proportions is curtailed by the historical straitjacket he places on the early Christian story. There is, however, a good deal of material, freshly written and worthy of serious consideration, in his book. The stimulating hypotheses he presents are an invitation to critical dialogue.

It is remarkable that virtually every Jewish interpreter of Jesus concludes that Judas was a Zealot or had leanings in that direction. As one example we can cite Irving Zeitlin.[27] Zeitlin argues that if there is a single general concept that can effectively guide our analysis of Jesus, it is the concept of charisma. Although he bases his view of charisma on Weber, he goes beyond it. Pure charisma is by its very nature the opposite of all "institutional" social structures and independent of them.

An essential element of charismatic leadership is the challenge it presents to traditional authority. In regard to Jesus, "the question of Jesus' relationship to the Zealot movement is crucial for a clarification of his self-understanding; and no less crucial for a clarification of how he was perceived by the individuals and groups with whom he came into contact."[28]

Zeitlin concludes that "Jesus was neither a Zealot nor a para-Zealot, but rather a charismatic figure, who, despite himself, had an especially strong attraction for such individuals, and who therefore had to come to terms with the Zealot question almost daily."[29]

With respect to the disciples, he believes "that all the textual evidence strongly indicates that Peter, James and John, the sons of Zebedee, and Judas Iscariot were simply unwilling to view Jesus as anything other than what they intensely wished him to be: the victorious Messianic King."[30] Scholars have even suggested that "Judas' real motive was to force Jesus into a confrontation in which he could only prove victorious," Zeitlin suggests.[31]

It has been noted before that the only historical bedrock we have is that Judas was a first-century Jew who followed Jesus. Jesus was a teacher, a miracle worker, and a prophet who felt a special call from God. From this vantage point, he did not likely see himself as *the* Messiah, although he could well have sensed a special call from God. As Marcus Borg has demonstrated, that special call from God was deeply rooted in Jesus' own spiritual awareness. He criticized "the quest for holiness" as pursued by the leaders of God's people and "proposed an alternative path grounded in the nature of God as merciful, gathered a community on that paradigm, and sought to lead his people in the way of peace, a way that flowed intrinsically from the paradigm of inclusive mercy."[32] After his death, the emerging Christian community affirmed his resurrection and with it his special status as Son of God and as God's chosen Messiah.

Jewish scholars are generally in agreement with Richard Rubenstein, although they may not express it as forcefully as he does, who considered "the Judas story as the most damaging single item among Christians' negative association with Jews."[33] Surely, if that is so, it behooves us to continue our work on the figure of Judas.

We do not need to be offended if Judas really did betray Jesus. For we do not invoke any special status to understand what might have happened to him. At the same time, we do not invoke special divine (or demonic) powers to understand what Judas and Jesus did. We play here on the field of history, and only where our sources invite us to transcend that plane do we do so.

Conclusion

Recent studies of the pre-Synoptic layers of the Judas tradition have led to several important conclusions.

First, Judas was neither a symbolic figure nor a product of kerygmatic imagination but a clearly recognizable historical figure, that is, an actual disciple of Jesus. His designated name, Iscariot, comes from a Semitic milieu. Our knowledge that he belongs to the circle of the Twelve also rests on a tradition that comes from the Aramaic-speaking church. Missing from the earliest traditions are any aspects of the paid informant who, in remorse, later commits suicide. We have portrayed, rather, a man who is no worse than his colleagues in the circle of the disciples and who received as much recognition from Jesus as did the rest, and may have been honored by Jesus by being selected for this singular mission.

200 JUDAS

The subsequent understanding of his action as a "betrayal" may come from the Aramaic-speaking church, which later felt compelled to make Judas at least partially responsible for the death of Jesus. More likely it came from the Greek-speaking church, which had lost touch with the two-sided role of the informer in Judaism. It was covered up with a theological rationalization of the death of Jesus in which Judas became villain.

The interpretation of the deed of Judas was soon changed. As the church began to interpret the death of Jesus, increasingly a larger degree of blame was placed on Judas. He initially was remembered only as the first who had parted company with Jesus, even though all the other disciples likewise had occasion to abandon Jesus, leaving him on the cross attended only by a few female followers. However, Judas's initial abandonment eventually was seen as a betrayal and, although Mark 14:21 does not mention him by name, eventually the church used the term "the one who delivered him" to designate his deed, at times avoiding the use of his name.[34] In the subapostolic period, between the years 70 and 120, "the one handing over" came close to being seen as "betrayer," a term that gradually came to designate Judas. The time when that process began is very difficult to ascertain. That indeed is another important area of research.

Notes

1. Maccoby, *Myth*, 17–18.

2. Klausner, *Jesus of Nazareth: His Life, Times, and Teaching*, trans. H. Danby (1929).

3. See Flusser's book, *Jesus*, 114, on Judas. The book was reviewed by Zeitlin, *JQR* 60 (1969/70): 187–196; Oesterreicher, *Brothers in Hope. The Bridge* 5 (1970): 320–333. R. Rendtorff, "NT und die Juden; Flusser and Wilckens," *EvTh* 36 (1976): 191–200; Benoit, *RB* 77 (1970): 445–448; and by Robert Lindsey in a publication reviewing the book.

4. See Vermes's *Jesus the Jew* and, of course, his revision of Schürer. His major contribution has been with the Dead Sea Scrolls and on such matters as Christology.

5. Lindeskog, *Die Jesusfrage*. Their special interest in the passion story is understandable, since the passion story became very much a passion story for the Jews as well, 277, 288.

6. M. Joseph, in his article on Jesus in *JL* 3 (1929): 237–244, concludes that the difficulties in deciding whether Jesus lived "are hardly to be overcome" given the lack of historical evidence outside the Gospels, etc. Still, he suggests that careful critique of the Gospels and a good starting point may make it possible to draw some outlines of Jesus (242). For Judas he has no interest. Quite different is the approach of David Flusser, whose article in the *EnJ* 10 (1971) is a masterful summary of the life and significance of Jesus. However, Judas, treated as a historical figure, is mentioned only in passing.

7. Günter Schlichting, *Ein jüdisches Leben Jesus*. The dating of the *Toledoth Jeshua* varies from the first century (Voltaire); second/third (Gabrieli); fourth/fifth (Schonfeld); fifth/sixth (Krauss); sixth/seventh (Oppenheim and Goldstein); and tenth

(Klausner). William Horbury, who wrote a dissertation on the *Toledoth Jeshua* under the direction of Ernst Bammel ("Critical Examination of the Toledot Yeshu") (Cambridge, 1970), which was apparently never published, dated it early, perhaps even in the first century. Schlichting, 115–121, also dates it as probably early second century.

8. Klausner, *Jesus,* 32. Goldin's translation reads: "The disciples of Balaam the wicked inherit Gehenna and go down to the pit of destruction, as it is written, 'But thou, O God, shalt bring them down into the pit of destruction; bloodthirsty and deceitful men shall not live out half their days'" (Ps 55:23). Judah Goldin, *The Fathers,* 247.

9. Klausner, *Jesus,* 446.

10. Klausner, *Jesus,* 324.

11. Klausner, *Jesus,* 325.

12. Klausner, *Jesus,* 325. Père M. J. Lagrange, *The Gospel of Jesus Christ,* deals with the Jewish treatment of Judas, a "special favourite of anti-Christian critics of the Gospel, especially of Jewish scholars." He agrees with Klausner that Judas was of colder disposition than the enthusiastic Galileans. Gradually Judas, being more perceptive than the others, saw that Jesus was a seducer "and the Law commanded that such a one had to be denounced to the authorities. Judas did his duty. Would such an honest fellow as he was ever have been willing to accept money as the price of his obedience to the laws of his country?" (190).

13. Klausner, *Jesus,* 327.

14. Klausner, *Jesus,* 327.

15. Lapide, "An Judas Iscariot," 18–28.

16. Lapide, *Wer war schuld an Jesu Tod?* 11–42, 114–118.

17. Lapide, "An Judas," 18.

18. Lapide, *Judas, wer bist du?* 25–26; and idem, *Schuld,* 19–20.

19. Lapide, *Schuld,* 23–25.

20. Lapide, *Schuld,* 25.

21. Maccoby, *The Sacred Executioner,* 7–10; and idem, "Who Was Judas Iscariot?" 8–13. The book *Judas Iscariot and the Myth of Jewish Evil* appears to be his most detailed work and is dealt with here.

22. Maccoby, "Who Was Judas?" 8.

23. Maccoby, *Judas Iscariot,* 17.

24. Maccoby, *Judas,* 137.

25. Maccoby, *Judas,* 146.

26. Maccoby, *Judas,* 153. He agrees with Richard Bauckham, *Jude and the Relatives of Jesus in the Early Church.*

27. Irving M. Zeitlin, *Jesus and the Judaism of His Time* (Cambridge: Polity Press, 1988).

28. Zeitlin, *Jesus,* 29.

29. Zeitlin, *Jesus,* 142–143.

30. Zeitlin, *Jesus,* 160–161.

31. Zeitlin, *Jesus,* 161.

32. Borg, *Jesus: Conflict, Holiness and Politics,* 199.

33. Kirsch, *We Christians and Jews,* 60.

34. Vogler, *Judas,* 37; cf. Klauck, *Judas,* 48–76.

CONCLUSION

Our search for the historical Judas began with a particular goal: to listen to the sources and, above all, to look beneath the layer of literary tradition available to us to understand something of who he was. We are as much interested in what the early church made of Judas as we are about what we can learn about the historical Judas.

As we look at what the Gospel writers, historians, artists, and theologians have made of Judas it becomes clear that most efforts have obscured the historical record. Judas was used as a negative moral model even though little was said in the earliest Christian sources about the nature of his deed, his motivation, or even the way his immediate contemporaries felt about him.

It is possible that we rest on solid ground when we accept Judas as a Jew who was a member of Jesus' inner circle. The name Judas Iscariot leads us nowhere in describing the kind of person he was, except that he was a Jew and one of the Twelve, a disciple. Beyond that, we are told that he was even an apostle.

There is no evidence that Judas did anything but function as a valued member of the Jesus community. He plays no discernible role in the community until the last week of Jesus' life, when the sources unanimously report that he played the key role as the one "who handed over" the Son of man.

The most astounding result of our search was the discovery that the deed for which Judas is almost universally blamed—that of "betraying Jesus"—does not rest on linguistic grounds. The Greek verb *paradidōmi*, which virtually always has been translated "betray" in connection with Judas's deed, does not mean "betray" in any classical text we were able to discover; never in Josephus and never in the New Testament. Every authority joined in the consensus on this point. More and more modern translators recognize this.

The early sources do tell us that Judas "handed Jesus over" to the high priest, but that act came as no surprise to Jesus. Indeed, it is never described

by him in any of the sources as a betrayal. When words like treason, in-
trigue, deceit, greed, avarice, disillusionment, villainy, failure, and iniquity
are used to describe the actions or person of Judas, we look in vain for New
Testament texts for support. Above all, the relations between Judas and Jesus
seem to have been warm and friendly. Even the most hostile portrait of
Judas, provided by the writer of the Fourth Gospel, explicitly indicates that
Jesus sent Judas forth on his mission with the words: "Do what you need
to do, quickly" (John 13:27). In that same Gospel, Judas, without any reservations on the part of either of them, apparently had his feet washed by
Jesus and has no role in identifying Jesus to his captors or indeed in anything
important in connection with Jesus' capture. According to John, he stands
there with the party of priests and soldiers and when Jesus identifies himself,
presumably falls to the ground with the rest of them (John 18:6-7).

The different accounts of the death of Judas provided by Matthew and
Luke in a sense cancel each other out, leaving us with the distinct impression that we know nothing about his death. If, as Matthew describes it, he
committed suicide, we should not condemn this act or him or even use it
as a clue to his behavior. The motivations that lead to suicide are notoriously
difficult to interpret, and we are assured by some creditable scholars that
death by one's own hand carried no stigma in first-century Judaism or
Christianity.

The task of "giving over" is seen by the early church as fundamentally
God-centered, initiated and carried out under the direction of God. It is,
we would say today, a theological task. So both the devil (in Luke and John)
and God get involved in this "handing over." Moreover, when God acts
in history, humans are always involved. Because of the lack of theological
sophistication on the part of the early church, but, more important, because
the early church was starting to build walls and boundaries, Judas served
them well and he became the first "insider" to become an "outsider" who
failed and whom the church failed. In such cases we invariably hear more
about the individual's failure than we do of the church's.

In the first instance, the category of failure must be laid at the door of
the earliest community that followed Jesus—there and nowhere else. Judas
did his God-given duty and contributed to the realization of Jesus' mission
by handing him over. The emerging church began to see the need to draw
boundary lines and found Judas a convenient figure—for he was both a
Jew and had been a disciple. Thus, by turning against Judas, the Johannine
community especially could deal with both lapsed Christians and their Jewish antagonists. In doing so, they turned their backs not just on Judas but
also on the way Jesus had taught them to love their enemies. It has taken
many followers of Jesus twenty centuries to recognize this disparity and to
think through its implications.

The style of dealing with the secessionist probably took place in the early years, from 45 C.E. to the 60s C.E. as the community of "Q" began to draw its boundary lines and build its community.[1] By the time the Fourth Gospel was written, Judas was no longer a person, he had become a character in a morality play. There is nothing wrong with playwrights creating characters, but something happens which is not good when a religion based fundamentally on historical events misses a key element in an event and distorts a person into a caricature.

Are we then suggesting a radical revision of our picture of Judas? Certainly, if the evidence provided in this book survives the scrutiny of careful scholarly historical research, such a revision is called for. And even if my reader is unpersuaded by the totality of the evidence, the invitation stands. Consider what enormous harm has been done by the portrayal of Judas as traitor, as an evil character in the divine drama, and ask whether there are not better ways to encourage faithfulness and generosity than to tell harmful tales about others that we cannot prove to be true. Is there anyone in history who has been so hideously slandered as has Judas? We should remember that slander is not just lies told in order to discredit others. It is also "truth" told in order to hurt them. Both are equally condemned by Hebrew and Christian Scriptures.[2] At the very least, those who seek to follow Jesus should examine themselves to see whether it is not possible that Judas was included in Jesus' offer of intercessory prayer from the cross, and whether being loyal to Jesus may not mean that Judas is treated as one of the Twelve disciples who was never rejected by Jesus, even though he has been so totally and fully rejected by the community that names itself after Jesus the Christ.

The answer to the question whether Judas was a disciple or a traitor is not easy. On the one hand, there is no betrayal without friendship or discipleship. At the same time, when discussing historical identity it is important what gets priority of place. If we only follow one lead now, an area in which scholars are virtually unanimous, and refuse to use the word "traitor" in connection with Judas or to use the verb "betray" to describe his action, the future of Judas in history will take care of itself. Then at least we could say that we are taking the sources available to us seriously. It is surely not too much to ask this of translators or of the church which believes that the truth can make us free.

Notes

1. Mack, *The Lost Gospel,* 131–147.

2. While the topic of slander, as proscribed in scripture, seems no longer to be treated in Bible dictionaries, A. E. Garvie wrote a superb article on it for *HDB* 4 (1902): 552–553.

A SUICIDE NOTE FROM JUDAS ISCARIOT,
CA. 30 C.E.

━━━━━━━━━━━━━━━━

A suicide note left behind by Judas Iscariot has recently come to light and been sent on to John Mark in Antioch who is, we are told, writing an account of the days of Jesus. It is being shared with all the followers of the Way, for it throws some light on the role of our much-maligned associate, Judas, in the death of our Lord. It was written in Aramaic and is here translated into Greek for the benefit of those interested.

I, Judas, write with my own hand. My soul is in turmoil. I have seen the guards leading Jesus from the house of Caiaphas toward Pilate's hall of judgment. I am at my wits end and I do not know which way to turn. My heart has turned to water. What made our high priest turn our Lord over to the Romans? Did he forget that to deliver a Jew over to a heathen ruler is a serious transgression of our laws? What is left for me to do?

Jesus cannot possibly escape from the clutches of Pilate—not at feast time! The jaws of Rome do not open to free their victims. If he is not delivered from the fist of Pilate, he will most assuredly be delivered unto death by him.

What did Jesus say to Caiaphas to bring about this drastic change? What questions was he asked? What did he say in his own defense?

For the last few years I have been a disciple of Jesus of Nazareth. They have been years of great joy and much excitement. Exhilarating possibilities of renewal for our people. They have also been frustrating and disappointing. Baffling and painful.

In the last few months especially it has been confusing beyond belief. Jesus seems to have become totally absorbed with his impending death. Why? Why die when things are just beginning to change? We do not know.

It all came to a head during this Passover celebration. As usual we had one of those worshipful and enjoyable dinners with Jesus when we shared deeply with each other and Jesus spoke of the coming kingdom and the meals we would have with him when the kingdom comes. He also returned to a topic that has been much on his mind: his being handed over to the high priests. Each disciple wondered, Am I the one to be chosen? The lot fell to me and Jesus commissioned me to do it. I felt honored but also frightened by the challenge of it. I was confused by what Jesus said about the one who would hand him over. He wanted things to move forward. I did my part.

What is, then, to become of me? What future is there for me? Perhaps during his trial Jesus chose not to confront Caiaphas and will unseat Pilate from his throne. Jesus can be so persuasive. Perhaps he can persuade Pilate voluntarily to give up his throne to Jesus. What a ruler he would be! If not—what then? What if Jesus does not speak out on his own behalf? The priests may have turned against him and testified against him to Pilate. Pilate may well yield to their entreaty and have him killed, since he upsets the people. He lays a charm on them. They follow him, willy-nilly as I, myself, Peter, and many others did. What if Jesus is condemned to die?

I have agonized over whether I should die with him. He often said the disciple is not above his master and that we must suffer with him. If our Lord dies, there is no honor greater than to die with him.

I am terribly frightened, sad, and troubled. I never had all this in mind. Who would ever have thought that the kingdom of God could end this way? If Jesus dies on the cross, surely he cannot be the Messiah.

I am trying to think it all through. I am one of the Twelve whom Jesus chose to represent the new Israel of God. I want to be true to my namesake, Judah. I have had duties to perform. I gave it my best. I discharged those duties as well as I could, always under the mandate of Jesus himself. He never rebuked me. Never called me a "Satan" as he did to Peter. Instead, he embraced me in the garden and called me, "Friend."

For three years I served as treasurer of the wandering group of followers who stayed with him. As treasurer I kept the records and paid the bills. I took in donations from our supporters, among them especially some fine women, and I kept the members informed on the status of our resources. My years with Jesus were the best I have ever had—much better than the time I worked in the treasury of the Temple, the bank of the people.

So much has gone wrong. I was picked to hand Jesus over to the high priest. For weeks Jesus had spoken with certainty about being handed over to evil men to be killed. All of us who traveled with him rejected these predictions and assumed that Jesus once was again speaking in violent metaphors that could not possibly come to pass.

Certainly the high priest is not an evil man! He is divinely ordained to see that law and order are observed in the land. So when the assignment was given to me to hand Jesus over to the high priest, I did it willingly, honored by the trust that Jesus placed in me. I was sure that once the high priest and Jesus would meet, they could agree on the need for the renewal of the people of Israel—and perhaps even on the methods to be used.

At each step Jesus encouraged me to proceed; I did nothing he did not command. If anyone asks, why did I do it? let them be sure that I had learned that the essence of discipleship is to do what Jesus asked of us. What Jesus wanted done, I was prepared to do, even now.

Just now word has come to me that Pilate has condemned Jesus to death. I have come back from the Temple and those misguided priests will not even allow me to cancel the deal! I threw the money at their feet. I told them that Jesus was an innocent man.

Now I will die with him. For the sake of my wife and children, let this act of taking my own life also be seen in the light of my love for my master. If he dies, I want to die with him.

Our great King Saul had an armor bearer who died with his king.[1] God of mercy, if Jesus, your anointed, has chosen to die rather than fight for his kingdom, I am prepared to die with him. I leave my fate to God alone and hand over my life to him, just as I handed God's chosen son over to the high priest, God's highest authority in the land. Adonai, I beg you, please may the children of Israel find peace. Do not desert the Messiah. Do not desert me. Care for my wife and children. Guard them in your tent of peace.

Signed in my own hand,
Judas Iscariot

Note

1. 1 Sam 31:5.—*Ed.*

BIBLIOGRAPHY

Abraham a Sancta (or Santa) Clara (Hans–Ulrich Megerle, 1644–1709). *JUDAS. Ertz-Schelm, Für ehrliche Leuth, oder: Eigentlicher Entwurff, und Lebens-Beschreibung desz Isc(h)ariotischen Böszwicht, Worinnen underschiedliche Discurs, sittliche Lehrs-Puncten, Gedicht, und Geschicht, auch sehr reicher Vorrath Biblischer Concepten.* The title goes on to form something of a preface with the words: *Welche nie allein einen Prediger auff der Cantzel sehr dienlich fallen, der jetzigen verkehrten Welt die Wahrheit under die Nasen zu reiben: sondern es kan sich auch dessen ein Privat und einsamber Leser zur erspriesslicher Zeit Vertreibung, und gewunschten Seelen Hayl gebrauchen,* zusammen getragen Durch Pr. Abraham a Santa Clara, Augustiner-Barfüsser, Kayserlicher Predigten, etc. (Saltzburg: Melchior Haan): 1 (1686): 410 pp.; 2 (1689): 636 pp.; 3 (1692): 556 pp.; 4 (1695): 433 pp. (New edition [not consulted]: *Sämmtliche Werke,* 7 vols., Passau, 1835/36).

Akenson, D. H. *God's Peoples: Covenant and Land in South Africa, Israel and Ulster.* Montreal: McGill-Queens University Press, 1991.

Alvarez, A. *The Savage God: A Study in Suicide.* New York: Norton, 1990.

Anderson, R. S. *The Gospel according to Judas.* Colorado Springs: Helmers & Howard, 1991.

Arbeitman, Y. "The Suffix of Iscariot." *JBL* 99 (1980): 122–124.

Auerbach, E. *Mimesis: The Portrait of Reality in Western Literature.* Garden City, N.Y.: Doubleday, 1957.

Balch, David, et al., eds. *Greeks, Romans, and Christians,* Minneapolis: Fortress Press, 1990.

Barry, R. L. "Suicide in the Bible." *Listening: Journal of Religion and Culture* 26 (1991): 1–6.

Barth, K. "The Election of the Individual: The Determination of the Rejected." In *Church Dogmatics,* II/2: 498–563. Edinburgh: T. & T. Clark, 1957.

Bartnik, C. "Judas l'Iscariote, histoire et théologie." *Collectanea Theologica* 58 (1988): 57–69.

Bauckham, R. *Jude and the Relatives of Jesus in the Early Church.* Edinburgh: T. & T. Clark, 1990.

Baum, P. F. "Judas's Red Hair." *JEGP* 21 (1922): 520–529.

———. "Judas's Sunday Rest." *MLR* 18 (1923): 168–182.

———. "The Mediaeval Legend of Judas Iscariot." *PMLA* 31 (1916): 481–632.

Baumbach, G. "Judas–Jünger und Verräter Jesu." *Zeichen der Zeit* 17 (1963): 91–98.

Baumgarten, J. "Hanging and Treason in Qumran and Roman Law." *Eretz-Israel* 16 (1982): 7–16.

Baxadall, M. *Giotto and the Orators: Humanist Observers of Painting in Italy and the Discovery of Pictorial Composition.* Oxford: Clarendon Press, 1971.

Beare, F. W. *The Gospel according to St. Matthew.* San Francisco: Harper, 1981.

Becker, I. C. "Satan und Judas: Der lukanische Bericht." *Entschluss* 44 (1989): 20–22.

Belcher, F. W. "A Comment on Mark 14:45." *ET* 64 (1952/53): 240.

Benoit, P. "The Death of Judas." In *Jesus and the Gospel,* 1:189–207. London: Dartman, 1973.

Benz, E. *Die Monologie des Judas Ischarioth.* Munich, 1951.

Bettelheim, B. *Freud's Vienna and Other Essays.* New York: Vintage, 1991.

Betz, O. "The Dichotomized Servant and the End of Judas Iscariot. (Light on the Dark Passages: Matt 25,51 and parallel; Acts 1,18)." *RevQ* 5 (1964): 43–58.

Beyer, K. *Die aramaische Texte vom Toten Meer. . . .* Göttingen: Vandenhoeck & Ruprecht, 1984.

Beyschlag, K. "Franz von Assisi und Judas Iskariot." *ThLZ* 85 (1960): 849–852.

Billerbeck, Paul, and Herman Strack. *Kommentar zum Neuen Testament aus Talmud und Midrasch.* Munich: C. H. Beck, 6 vols. 1926–61.

Billings, J. S. "Judas Iscariot in the Fourth Gospel." *ET* 51 (1939/40): 156–158.

Bishop, Eric F. "'He that eateth bread with me. . . .'" *ET* 70 (1959/60): 331–333.

———. "With Jesus on the Road from Galilee to Calvary. . . ." *CBQ* 11 (1949): 440.

Bjerg, S. "Judas als Stellvertreter des Satans." *EvTh* 52 (1992): 42–55.

Black, C. C. *The Disciples according to Mark: Markan Redaction in Current Debate.* JSNTSup 27. Sheffield: Academic Press, 1989.

Blass, F., and A. Debrunner. *A Greek Grammar of the New Testament.* Translated and edited by Robert W. Funk. Cambridge at the University Press, 1961.

Blinzler, J. "Judas Iskarioth." *LThK* 2 (1960), 5:1152–1154.

———. *The Trial of Jesus.* Translated by Isabel and Florence McHugh. Westminster, Md.: Newman, 1959.

Blöcker, G. "Der notwendige Mensch: Die literarischen Deutungen der Judasfigur." *Neue Deutsche Hefte* 1 (1954/55): 64–69.

Boman, T. "Hebraic and Greek Thought-Forms in the New Testament." In *Current Issues in NT Interpretation,* edited by W. Klassen and G. F. Snyder, 1–19. New York: Harper, 1962.

Bonhoeffer, D. "Predigt am Sonntag Judika über Judas." In *Gesammelte Schriften,* edited by E. Bethge, 4:406–413. Munich: Chr. Kaiser, 1961.

Boobyer, G. H. "ΑΠÉΧΕΙ in Mark xiv.41." *NTS* 2 (1955/56): 44–48.

Borg, M. *Conflict, Holiness and Politics in the Teachings of Jesus.* STBibEChrist 5. Lewiston, N.Y.: Edwin Mellen Press, 1984.

Borges, Jorge Luis. *Jesus: A New Vision.* San Francisco: Harper, 1987.

———. *Labyrinths.* New York: New Directions, 1964.

Brelich, M. *The Work of Betrayal.* Translated by R. Rosenthal. Marlboro, Vt.: Marlboro Press, 1988; Italian ed., 1975.

Broderick, R. *Rock Opera: The Creation of Jesus Christ Superstar.* New York: Hawthorn Books, 1973.

Bronikowski, R. J. "Judas Iscariot: The Apostle Who Couldn't Love." *Cross and Crown* 27 (1975): 269–279.

Brown, R. *The Gospel according to John.* 2 vols. Garden City, N.Y.: Doubleday, 1966, 1970.

———. *The Death of the Messiah.* 2 vols. Garden City, N.Y.: Doubleday, 1994.

———. *The Epistles of John.* AB. Garden City, N.Y.: Doubleday, 1982.

———. *The Community of the Beloved Disciple.* New York: Paulist, 1979.

Brownson, J. "Neutralising the Intimate Enemy: The Portrayal of Judas in the Fourth Gospel." *SBL Seminar Papers* 1992: 49–60.

Bruner, F. D. *Matthew: A Commentary.* Dallas, Tex.: Word, 1990.

Büchele, A. *Der Tod Jesu im Lukasevangelium.* FTS 26. Frankfurt, 1978.

Buchheit, G. *Judas Iskarioth: Legende, Geschichte, Deutung.* Gütersloh: Rufer Verlag, 1954.

Büchner, A. *Judas Ischarioth in der deutschen Dichtung: Ein Versuch.* Freiburg, 1920.

———. "Das Judasproblem." *Zeitschrift für den deutschen Unterricht* 27 (1913): 693–698.

Büchsel, F. "παραδίδωμι." *KTWBNT,* 2 (1935): 171–174. Stuttgart: Kohlhammer.

Bühlmann, W. *God's Chosen Peoples.* Translated by R. R. Barr. Maryknoll, N.Y.: Orbis, 1982.

Bulgakov, S. "Judas Ischarioth, der Verräter-Apostel." *Orient und Occident,* Heft 11, 8–24. Leipzig, 1932.

Bultmann, R. *Johannesevangelium.* Göttingen: Vandenhoeck & Ruprecht, 1959.

Büttner, M. *Judas Ischarioth: Ein psychologisches Problem.* Minden, 1902.

Caird, G. *Principalities and Powers: A Study in Pauline Theology.* Oxford: Clarendon Press, 1956.

Carey, S. P. *Jesus and Judas.* London, 1931.

Catchpole, D. "The Answer of Jesus to Caiaphas (Matt 26:64)." *NTS* 17 (1970/71): 213–226.

Cebulj, C. "Die Nachtseite Gottes: Zum Judasbild im Johannesevangelium." *Entschluss* 44 (1989): 16.

Chance, S. *Stronger than Death.* New York: Norton, 1992.

Charlesworth, J. *Jesus within Judaism.* New York: Doubleday, 1988.

Cheyne, T. K. "Judas Iscariot." *EB* 2:2623–2628.

Chilton, Bruce. *The Temple of Jesus.* University Park: Pennsylvania State University Press, 1992.

Christian, P. *Jesus und seine geringsten Brüder: Matt 25:31-46 redaktionsgeschichtlich untersucht.* Leipzig: St. Benno Verlag, 1975.

Chwolson, D. *Beiträge zur Entwicklungsgeschichte des Judentums.* Leipzig, 1910.

———. *Das letzte Passamahl Christi und der Tag seines Todes.* 1892.

———. *Über die Frage ob Jesus gelebt hat.* Leipzig, 1910.

Clements, R. E. "The Form and Character of Prophetic Woe Oracles." *Semitics* 8 (1982): 17–29.

Clemons, J. T. *What Does the Bible Say about Suicide?* Minneapolis: Fortress, 1990.

Cohen, Y. *Nuclear Ambiguity: The Vanunu Affair.* London: Sinclair-Stevenson, 1992.

Cohn, H. *The Trial and Death of Jesus.* New York: Harper, 1967.

Collins, R. F. "Woe in the NT." *ABD,* 6 (1992): 946–947.

Conzelmann, H. *The Theology of St. Luke.* Translated by G. Buswell. New York: Harper, 1961.

Conzelmann, H. "Historie und Theologie in den synoptischen Passionsberichten." In *Zur Bedeutung des Todes Jesu: Exegetische Beiträge,* H. Conzelmann, ed. Gütersloh: Mohn, 1968.

————. *The Theology of St. Luke.* Translated by G. Buswell. New York: Harper, 1961.

Corry, J. *The Manchester Affair.* New York: Putnam, 1967.

Cox, P. *Biography in Late Antiquity: A Quest for a Holy Man.* Berkeley and Los Angeles: University of California Press, 1983.

Crossan, John Dominic. *The Historical Jesus.* San Francisco: Harper, 1991.

————. *Who Killed Jesus? Exposing the Roots of Anti-Semitism in the Gospel Story of the Death of Jesus.* San Francisco: HarperCollins, 1995.

Cullmann, O. "Der zwölfte Apostel." In *Vorträge und Aufsätze 1925–1962,* edited by K. Fröhlich, 214–222. Tübingen: Mohr–Zürich Zwingli, 1966 = "Le douzième apôtre." *RHPR* 42 (1962): 133–40.

————. *Jesus and the Revolutionaries.* New York: Scribner's, 1970.

————. *The State in the New Testament.* New York: Scribner's, 1956.

Czarnecki, J. "The Significance of Judas in Giotto's Arena Chapel Frescoes." In *The Early Renaissance,* edited by A. Bernardo, 35–47. 1978.

Dalman, Gustaf. *Jesus-Jeshua.* Translated by Paul Levertoff. London: SPCK, 1929.

————. *Sacred Sites and Ways.* Translated by Paul Levertoff. London: SPCK, 1935.

————. *The Words of Jesus.* Translated by D. M. Kay. Edinburgh: T. and T. Clark, 1902.

Daub, C. *Judas Ischariot oder das Böse in Verhältnis zum Guten.* Vol. 1–II/1.2. Heidelberg: Mohr und Winter, 1816–1818.

Daube, D. *Appeasement or Resistance? And Other Essays.* . . . Berkeley and Los Angeles: University of California Press, 1987.

————. "Black Hole." *Rechtshistorisches Journal* 2. Frankfurt: Löwenklau Gesellschaft, 1983.

————. *Civil Disobedience in Antiquity.* Edinburgh: University Press, 1972.

————. *Collaboration with Tyranny in Rabbinic Law.* London: Oxford University Press, 1965.

————. "Death as Release in the Bible." *NT* 5 (1962): 82–104.

————. "'For They Know Not What They Do: Luke 23:34.'" *Studia Patristica* 4, pt. 2, edited by F. L. Cross, 58–70. Berlin, 1961.

————. *Sin, Ignorance and Forgiveness in the Bible.* London: Liberal Jewish Synagogue, 1960.

————. "The Linguistics of Suicide." *Philosophy and Public Affairs* 2 (1972): 387–437.

Dauer, A. *Die Passionsgeschichte im Johannesevangelium: Eine Traditionsgeschichtliche und theologische Untersuchung zu Johannes 18:1—19:30.* SANT 30. Munich: Kösel, 1972.

Derrett, J. D. M. "The Footwashing in John 13 and the Alienation of Judas Iscariot." *Revue Internationale des Droits de L'Antiquité.* 3rd series, 24 (1977): 3–19.

————. "Haggadah and the Account of the Passion," *DRev* 29 (1979): 308–315.

————. "The Iscariot, Mᵉsira, and the Redemption." *JSNT* 8 (1980): 2–23.

————. "Miscellanea: A Pauline Pun and Judas's Punishment." *ZNW* 72 (1981): 131–133.

Desautels, L. "La mort de Judas." *Science et Esprit* 38 (1986): 221–239.

Dewey, K. E. "Peter's Curse and Cursed Peter (Mark 14:53-54, 66-72)." In *The Passion in Mark: Studies on Mark 14–16,* edited by Werner H. Kelber, 96–114. Philadelphia: Fortress, 1976.

Dibelius, M. "Die alttestamentlichen Motive in der Leidensgeschichte des Petrus-

und des Johannesevangeliums" (1918). In *Botschaft und Geschichte*. Tübingen: J. C. B. Mohr, 1953.

————. "Judas und der Judaskuss." *Botschaft und Geschichte. Gesammelte Aufsätze I: Zur Evangelienforschung*, 272–277. Tübingen: J. C. B. Mohr, 1953.

Dieckmann, B. *Judas als Sündenbock: Eine Verhängnisvolle Geschichte von Angst und Vergeltung*. Munich: Kösel, 1991.

Dihle, A. "The Gospels and Greek Biography." In *The Gospel and the Gospels*, edited by P. Stuhlmacher, 361–386. Grand Rapids: Eerdmans, 1991.

————. "The Gospels and Greek Biography." In *The Gospel and the Gospels*, edited by P. Stuhlmacher, 361–386. Grand Rapids: Eerdmans, 1991.

————. *Studien zur griechischen Biographie*. Göttingen: Vandenhoeck & Ruprecht, 1970.

Dodd, C. H. *The Apostolic Preaching and Its Developments*. New York: Harper, 1936.

Dorn, K. "Judas Iskariot, einer der Zwölf: Der Judas der Evangelien unter der Perspektive der Rede von den zwölf Zeugen der Auferstehung in 1 Kor 15, 3b–5." In *Judas Iskariot: Menschliches oder heilsgeschichtliches Drama?* edited by H. Wagner, 39–89. Frankfurt: Knecht, 1985.

Dörrie, H. "Xanthippe." Pauly-Wissowa, *Realenzyklopädie*. 2 Reihe, 18 (1967): 1335–1342.

Droge, A. J. "Suicide." *ABD*, 6 (1992): 225–231.

Droge, A. J., and J. D. Tabor. *A Noble Death: Suicide and Martyrdom among Christians and Jews in Antiquity*. San Francisco: Harper, 1992.

Dupont, J. "La destinée de Judas prophétisée par David (Act 1, 16–20)." *CBQ* 23 (1961): 41–51; also idem, "Etudes sur les Actes des Apôtres," 309–320. LeDiv 45. Paris, 1967.

Edelstein, L., and I. G. Kidd. *Posidonius: The Fragments*. Cambridge: Cambridge University Press, 1972.

Ehrman, A. "Judas Iscariot and Abba Saqqara." *JBL* 97 (1978): 572–573.

Eltester, W. "'Freund, wozu du gekommen bist' (Matt XXVI.50)." *Neotestamentica et Patristica* (FS O. Cullmann) (NT,Sup 6), 70–91. Leiden, Brill 1962.

Enslin, M. S. "How the Story Grew: Judas in Fact and Fiction." In *Festschrift in Honor of F. W. Gingrich*, edited by E. H. Barth and R. Cocroft. Leiden: Brill, 1972.

Evans, C. F. *St. Luke*. TPI Commentary. London: SCM, 1990.

Fangmeier, J., and H. Stoevesandt, eds. *Karl Barth Letters (1961–68)*. Translated by G. Bromiley. Grand Rapids: Eerdmans, 1981.

Farrer, A. *A Study in Mark*. Westminster, Md.: Dacre, 1951.

Fascher, E. "Judas Iskarioth." *RGG*³, 3:965–966.

Feldmeier, R. *Die Krisis des Gottessohnes: Die Gethsemaneerzählung als Schlüssel der Markuspassion*. WUNT 2/21. Tübingen: J. C. B. Mohr, 1987.

Feneberg, S.J., P. W. "Im Zweifel für den Angeklagten: Ein neues Judasbild." *Entschluss* 44 (1989): 5.

————. "Von uns verdammt und ausgestossen." *Entschluss* 44 (1989): 2.

Fensham, F. C. "Judas's Hand in the Bowl and Qumran." *RevQ* 5 (1965): 259–261.

Fiorenza, E. S. *The Book of Revelation: Justice and Judgment*. Philadelphia: Fortress, 1985.

Fitzmyer, J. *The Gospel according to Luke*. AB. Garden City, N.Y.: Doubleday, vol. 1, 1981; vol. 2, 1985.

Flusser, D. *Jesus*. Translated by R. Walls. New York: Herder, 1969.
———. "No Temple in the City." In *Judaism and the Origins of Christianity*, 454–465. Jerusalem: Magnes, 1988.
———. "'Sie wissen nicht, was sie tun': Geschichte eines Herrnwortes." In *Kontinuität und Einheit* für Franz Mussner, edited by Paul-Gerhard Müller and Werner Stenger, 393–410. Freiburg: Herder, 1981.
———. "Some of the Precepts of the Torah from Qumran (4QMMT) and the Benediction against the Heretics." *Tarbiz* 6 (1992): 333–374, esp. 340–344 (in Hebrew).
Ford, D. *Barth and God's Story*. Studien zur interkulturellen Geschichte des Christentums, 27. Frankfurt: Lang, 1981.
Ford, J. *My Enemy Is My Guest: Jesus and Violence in Luke*. Maryknoll, N.Y.: Orbis, 1984.
Förkman, G. *The Limits of the Religious Community*. Lund: Gleerup, 1972.
Forsyth, N. *The Old Enemy: Satan and the Combat Myth*. Princeton, N.J.: Princeton University Press, 1987.
Frenzel, E. *Stoffe der Weltliteratur*, 368–371. Stuttgart: Alfred Kröner, 1976.
Freyne, Sean. *Galilee from Alexander the Great to Hadrian*. Notre Dame, Ind.: University of Notre Dame Press, 1980.
Friedrich, J. *Gott im Bruder? Eine methodischkritische Untersuchung von Redaktion, Überlieferung und Traditionen in Matt. 25:31-46*. Stuttgart: Calwer, 1977.
Gager, J. G. "The Gospels and Jesus: Some Doubts about Method." *JR* 54 (1954): 244–272.
Gardner, H. *The Business of Criticism*. London: Oxford University Press, 1959.
Garrett, S. *The Demise of the Devil: Magic and the Demonic in Luke's Writings*. Philadelphia: Fortress, 1989.
Gärtner, B. *Iscariot*. English translation by V. I. Gruhn (FB.B 29); introduction by J. Reumann, v–xvii. Philadelphia: Fortress, 1971.
———. "Judas Iskarioth." *SEÅ* 21 (1956): 50–81.
Gerhardsson, B. "Jesus, ausgeliefert und verlassen—nach dem Passionsbericht des Matthäusevangeliums." In *Redaktion und Theologie des Passionsberichtes nach den Synoptikern*, edited by M. Limbeck, 262–291. Darmstadt: Wissenschaftliche Buchgesellschaft, 1981.
Gillooly, E. *New York Times Book Review*, August 27, 1989.
Ginzberg, L. *The Legends of the Jews*. 7 vols. Philadelphia: Jewish Publication Society, 1966.
Girard, R. *Must There Be Scapegoats?* Translated by M. L. Assad. San Francisco: Harper, 1987.
———. *Things Hidden since the Foundation of the World*. London: Athlone, 1978.
———. *Violence and the Sacred*. Baltimore: Johns Hopkins University Press, 1977.
Glasson, T. E. "Davidic Links with the Betrayal of Jesus." *ET* 85 (1973/74): 118f.
Glazer, M. and P. Glazer. *The Whistleblowers*. New York: Basic Books, 1989.
Gloeckner, R. *Die Verkündigung des Heils beim Evangelisten Lukas*. Mainz, n.d.
Goetz, O. "Hie henckt Judas." In *Form und Inhalt* (FS O. Schmitt), 105–37. Stuttgart, 1950.
Goldin, J. *The Fathers according to Rabbi Nathan*. New Haven: Yale University Press, 1955.
Goldschmidt, H. L. "Das Judasbild im Neuen Testament aus jüdischer Sicht." In

Heilvoller Verrat? Judas im Neuen Testament, edited by H. L. Goldschmidt and M. Limbeck. Stuttgart: 1976.

————. "Judas Iscariot, 2. Eine jüdische Stellungnahme." *TRE,* 17:305–307.

Gollwitzer, H. "Gute Botschaft für Judas Ischarioth." *Krummes Holz-aufrechter Gang: Zur Frage nach dem Sinn des Lebens,* 2nd ed. Munich: Chr. Kaiser, 1970:271—296.

Gordon, A. B. "The Fate of Judas according to Acts 1:18." *EvQ* 43 (1971): 97–100.

Grant, Michael. *Jesus. An Historian's Review of the Gospels.* New York: Charles Scribner's Sons, 1977.

Grayston, Kenneth. *Dying We Live: A New Inquiry into the Death of Christ in the New Testament,* 395–399. New York: Oxford University Press, 1990.

Guardini, R. *The Lord.* Chicago: Regnery, 1954.

Gunther, H. *The Footprints of Jesus' Twelve in Early Christian Traditions.* New York: Peter Lang, 1985.

Guttmann, J. Art. "Judas." *EJ* 9:526–528.

Haenchen, E. "Historie und Geschichte in den johanneischen Passionsberichten." In *Zur Bedeutung des Todes Jesu,* ed. F. Viering, 55–78. Gütersloh: 1967.

————. *John.* Translated by R. Funk. 2 vols. Philadelphia: Fortress, 1984.

Halas, R. B. *Judas Iscariot: A Scriptural and Theological Study of His Person, His Deeds and His Eternal Lot.* SST 96. Washington, D.C.: Catholic University Press, 1946.

Hamerton-Kelly, R. G. *The Gospel and the Sacred: Poetics of Violence in Mark.* Minneapolis: Fortress, 1994.

Hammer, S. *By Her Own Hand: Memoirs of a Suicide's Daughter.* New York: Soho, 1991.

Hand, W. D. "A Dictionary of Words and Idioms Associated with Judas Iscariot. A Compilation Based Mainly on Material Found in the Germanic Languages" (*Modern Philology* 24/3), 289–356. Berkeley and Los Angeles: University of California Press, 1942.

Harper, L. A. "Judas Our Brother." *SLJT* 29 (1986): 96–106.

Harris, J. R. "Did Judas Really Commit Suicide?" *AJT* 4 (1900): 490–513.

————. "St. Luke's Version of the Death of Judas." *AJT* 18 (1914): 127–31.

————. "The Suggested Primacy of Judas Iscariot." *Exp* 8/14 (1917): 1–16.

Hart, J. W. T. *Judas Ischarioth: Eine Selbstbiographie.* Deutsch von H. Ballhorn. Leipzig, 1893.

Hartman, David. *A Living Covenant: The Innovative Spirit in Traditional Judaism.* New York: Free Press, 1985.

Harvey, A. E. *Jesus and the Constraints of History.* Philadelphia: Westminster, 1982.

————. *Jesus on Trial: A Study in the Fourth Gospel.* Atlanta: John Knox, 1977.

Haugg, D. *Judas Iskarioth in den neutestamentlichen Berichten.* Freiburg, 1930.

Hein, K. "Judas Iscariot: Key to the Last-Supper Narratives?" *NTS* 17 (1970/71): 227–232.

Heller, B. "Über Judas Ischariotes in der jüdischen Legende." *MGWJ* 76 (1932): 33–42.

————. "Über das Alter der jüdischen Judas-Sage und des Toldot Jeschu." *MGWJ* 77 (1933): 198–210.

Hengel, M. *The Zealots.* Translated by David Smith. Edinburgh: T. & T. Clark, 1989.

Hengstenberg, E. W. *Commentary on the Gospel of St. John.* Edinburgh: T. & T. Clark, 1865.

Herber, J. "La mort de Judas." *RHR* 129 (1945): 47–56.

Herford, R. Travers. *Pirke Aboth: The Ethics of the Talmud: Sayings of the Fathers.* New York: Schocken Books, 1971.

Herr, M. D. "The Conception of History among the Sages" (in Hebrew). *Proceedings of the Sixth World Congress of Jewish Studies,* vol. 3. Jerusalem, 1977.

Heyraud, J. "Judas et la nouvelle Alliance dans la cène selon Saint Jean." *BVC* 44 (1962): 39–48.

Hill, G. F. *The Medallic Portraits of Christ. The False Shekels. The Thirty Pieces of Silver.* London: Oxford University Press, 1920.

———. "The Thirty Pieces of Silver." *Archaeologia* 59 (1905): 235–254.

Hillers, D. "*Hoy* and *Hoy*—Oracles: A Neglected Syntactic Aspect." In *The Word of the Lord Shall Go Forth* (FS D. N. Freedman), edited by C. L. Meyers and M. O'Connor, 185–188. Winona Lake, Ind.: Eisenbrauns, 1983.

Hillyer, N. "Woe" in the *NIDNTT.* Grand Rapids: Zondervan, 1971 (German): 1978 (English), 3.

Hodges, A. G. *Jesus: An Interview across Time: A Psychiatrist Looks at His Humanity.* New York: Bantam, 1988.

Hofbauer, J. "Judas, der Verräter." *ThPQ* 110 (1962): 36–42.

Höistad, R. *Cynic Hero and Cynic King.* Uppsala: Carl Bloms, 1948.

Horbury, W. "Extirpation and Excommunication." *Vetus Testamentum* 35 (1985): 13–38.

Horsley, G. H. R. *New Documents Illustrating Early Christianity* A Review of the Greek Inscriptions and Papyri published in 1979. Macquarie University: Ancient History Documentation Research Centre, 1987.

van der Horst, P. W. "A Note on the Judas Curse in Early Christian Inscriptions." In P. W. van der Horst, *Hellenism-Judaism-Christianity,* 146–150. Kampen, Holland: Kok Pharos, 1994.

Hughes, K. T. "Framing Judas." *Semeia* 54 (1991): 223–38.

Imbach, J. "'Judas hat tausend Gesichter': Zum Judasbild in der Gegenwartsliteratur." In *Judas Iskariot : Menschliches oder heilsgeschichtliches Drama?* edited by H. Wagner, 91–142. Frankfurt, Joseph Knecht, 1985.

Ingholt, H. "The Surname of Judas Iscariot." In *Studia orientalia Joanni Pedersen dicata,* 152–162. Copenhagen, 1953.

Irmscher, J. "Σὺ λέγεις (Mk. 15,2—Mt. 27,11—Lk 23,3)." *Studii Clasice.* Romania, 2 (1960): 151–158.

Janzen, W. *Mourning Cry and Woe Oracle.* Berlin: de Gruyter, 1972.

Jastrow, M. *A Dictionary of the Targumim, the Talmud.* 2 vols. New York: Pardes, 1950.

Jeffrey, D. L., ed. *A Dictionary of Biblical Tradition in English Literature.* Grand Rapids: Eerdmans, 1992.

Jens, W. *Der Fall Iudas.* 2nd ed. Stuttgart and Berlin, 1975.

Jeremias, J. *Jerusalem zur Zeit Jesu.* Göttingen: Vandenhoeck & Ruprecht, 1958.

Johnson, L. T. "Luke-Acts, Book of." *ABD,* 4 (1992): 403–420.

Jones, G. H. "The Concept of Holy War." In *The World of Ancient Israel,* edited by R. E. Clements, 291–321. Cambridge, 1989.

Jones, J. H. *Bad Blood: The Tuskegee Syphilis Experiment.* New York: Free Press, 1981.

Jursch, H. "Das Bild des Judas Ischarioth im Wandel der Zeiten." In *Akten des VII.*

Internationalen Kongresses für Christliche Archäologie, 565–573. Trier, 1965 (SAC 27); Rome, 1969.

———. "Judas Ischarioth in der Kunst." In *WZ der Friedrich Schiller Universität,* 101–105. Jena, 1952.

———. "Die Rolle des Judas Ischarioth in der Bildtradition der Fusswaschung Jesu." In *Inter Confessiones: Beiträge zur Förderung des interkonfessionellen und interreligiösen Gesprächs,* 25–33. Friedrich Heiler zum Gedächtnis. Edited by A. M. Heiler. Marburg: N. G. Elwert, 1972.

———. "Traditionsort und Aussagekraft moderner Judasbilder." In *Wort und Welt, Festgabe E. Hertzsch,* edited by M. Weise et al., 151–164. Berlin: Evangelischer Verlagsanstalt, 1968.

Kallas, J. *Jesus and the Power of Satan.* Philadelphia: Westminster, 1968.

Kampling, R. *Das Blut Christi und die Juden. Mt 27, 25 bei den lateinischensprachigen christlichen Autoren bis zu Leo dem Grossen.* (NTAbh N.S. 16) Münster: Aschendorff, 1984.

Kann, R. A. *A Study in Austrian Intellectual History: From Late Baroque to Romanticism.* New York: Praeger, n.d. (ca. 1965).

Karris, R. "Luke 23:47 and the Lukan view of Jesus' Death." *JBL* 105 (1986): 65–74.

———. "Missionary Communities: A New Paradigm for the Study of Luke-Acts." *CBQ* 41 (1979): 80–97.

Kaufman, P. S. *The Beloved Disciple: Witness against Anti-Semitism.* Collegeville, Minn.: Liturgical Press, 1991.

Kee, H. *Community of the New Age.* Macon, Ga.: Mercer University Press, 1988.

Kemner, H. *Judas Ischariot: Zwischen Nachfolge und Verrat.* Stuttgart: Neuhausen, 1988.

Kent, J. H. *Corinth,* vol. 8, pt. 3. Princeton, N.J.: American School of Classical Studies, 1966.

Kermode, F. *The Genesis of Secrecy: On Interpretation of Narrative.* Cambridge, Mass.: Harvard University Press, 1979.

Kirsch, P. *We Christians and Jews.* Philadelphia: Fortress, 1975.

Klassen, W. "'A Child of Peace' (Luke 10:6) in First Century Context." *NTS* 27 (1981): 488–506.

———. "Judas Iscariot." *ABD,* 3 (1992): 1091–1096.

———. "Kiss (NT)." *ABD,* 4 (1992): 89–92. Also "The Sacred Kiss in the New Testament: An Example of Social Boundary Lines." *NTS* 39 (1993): 122–135.

Klauck, H.-J. "Judas der 'Verräter'? Eine exegetische und wirkungsgeschichtliche Studie." *ANRW* II.26.1 (1992): 717–740.

———. *Judas, Ein Jünger des Herrn.* Freiburg: Herder, 1987.

Klausner, J. *Jesus von Nazareth.* Hebrew (Jerusalem, 1907); German (Berlin: Jüdischer Verlag, 1934); English, *Jesus of Nazareth: His Life, Times, and Teaching.* Translated by H. Danby. London: George Allen & Unwin, 1929.

Klein, G. *Die zwölf Apostel.* FRLANT 77. Göttingen: Vandenhoeck & Ruprecht, 1961.

Klein, H. "Die lukanisch-johanneische Passionstradition." *ZNW* 67 (1976): 155–86.

Klopstock, F. G. *Ausgewählte Werke.* Edited by K. A. Schleiden. Munich: Carl Hansen, 1962.

Knox, A. B. "The Death of Judas." *JThS* 25 (1924): 289–295.

Koester, H. *Ancient Christian Gospels: Their History and Development.* Philadelphia: Trinity, 1990.

———. "Written Gospels or Oral Tradition?" *JBL* 113 (1994): 293–297.

Komroff, M. *Jesus through the Centuries.* New York: William Sloane Associates, 1953.

Kooy, V. H. "Hospitality." *IDB* 2 (1962): 654. "Heel, Lifted," *IDB* 2 (1962): 577.

Kornetter, J. "Das Judasproblem in der neuesten Literatur." *Das Neue Reich* 8 (Innsbruck, 1926): 553f.

Krauss, S. *Das Leben Jesu nach jüdischen Quellen.* Berlin, 1902.

Krieger, N. "Der Knecht des Hohenpriesters." *NT* 2 (1957): 73–74.

Kugel, J. L. *In Potiphar's House: The Interpretive Life of Biblical Texts.* San Francisco: Harper, 1990.

Künzel, G. *Studien zum Gemeindeverständnis des Matthäusevangeliums.* Stuttgart: Calwer, 1978.

Laeuchli, S. "Origen's Interpretation of Judas Iscariot." *ChH* 22 (1953): 259–268.

Lagrange, Père M. J. *The Gospel of Jesus Christ.* Parts 1 and 2. Theological Publications in India. St. Peter's Seminary, Bangalore, India, 1938.

Lake, K. "The Death of Judas." In *The Beginnings of Christianity,* 5:22–30. London, 1933.

Lampe, G. W. H., ed. *A Patristic Greek Lexicon.* London: Oxford University Press, 1961.

Lapide, P. E. "An Judas Iskariot: Ein Brief." In *Judas, wer bist du?* edited by Raul Niemann Gütersloh: Gütersloher Verlagshaus Gerd Mohn, 1991.

———. "Verräter oder verraten? Judas in evangelischer und jüdischer Sicht." *LM* 16 (1977): 75–79.

———. *Wer war Schuld an Jesu Tod?* Gütersloh: Mohn, 1987: 2nd ed., 1989.

Lapin, Hayim. "Rabbi," *ABD* 5 (1992): 600–602.

Lardner, James. "The Whistle-blower" *New Yorker,* July 7, 1993: 52–70, and July 12, 1993: 39–59.

Laros, M. "Judas Iskariot." *Hochl* 8/1 (1910/11): 657–667.

Lattke, M. "Salz der Freundschaft in Mk 9:50c." *ZNW* 75 (1984): 44–59.

Leclerq, H. Art. "Judas Iscariote." *DACL* VIII/1: 255–279.

Lehmann, P. "Judas Ischarioth in der lateinischen Legenden-überlieferung des Mittelalters." *StMed* NS 2 (1929): 289–346.

Levine, Amy-Jill. *Social and Ethnic Dimensions of Matthean Salvation History.* Lewiston, N.Y.: Edwin Mellen Press, 1988.

Levy, J. *Neuhebräisches und Chaldäisches Wörterbuch über Talmud und Midrasch.* 3 vols. Leipzig: Brockhaus, 1883.

Lightfoot, R. H. *History and Interpretation in the Gospels.* London: Hodder and Stoughton, 1935.

———. *St. John's Gospel.* Edited by C. F. Evans. Oxford: Clarendon, 1956.

Limbeck, M. "Das Judasbild im Neuen Testament aus christlicher Sicht." In *Heilvoller Verrat? Judas im Neuen Testament,* edited by H. L. Goldschmidt and M. Limbeck, 37–101. Stuttgart: Katholisches Bibelwerk, 1976.

Limbeck, M. ed. Art. "παραδίδωμι." *EWNT* 2:491–493.

———. *Redaktion und Theologie des Passionsberichtes nach den Synoptikern.* Wege der Forschung 481; Darmstadt: Wissenschaftliche Buchgesellschaft, 1981.

Lindeskog, G. *Die Jesusfrage im neutestamentlichen Judentum: Ein Beitrag zur Leben-Jesu-Forschung.* Uppsala: Lundequistska, 1938.

Lindsey, R. *A Hebrew Translation of the Gospel of Mark.* Jerusalem: Dugith, 1969.

————. *A Review of David Flusser's Jesus.* Jerusalem: Dugith, Baptist House, 1973.

Linnemann, E. *Studien zur Passionsgeschichte.* FRLANT 102. Göttingen, 1970.

Lohmeyer, E., and W. Schmauch. *Das Evangelium des Matthäus.* Göttingen: Vandenhoeck & Ruprecht, 1958.

Louw, J. P., and E. A. Nida. *Greek-English Lexicon of the New Testament Based on Semantic Domains.* New York: United Bible Societies, 1989.

Lüthi, K. "Judas Iscariot." *TRE,* 17:296–304.

————. *Judas Iskarioth in der Geschichte der Auslegung von der Reformation bis zur Gegenwart.* Zurich, Zwingli Verlag 1955.

————. "Das Problem des Judas Iskariot—neu untersucht." *EvTh* 16 (1956): 98–114.

Maccoby, H. *Judas Iscariot and the Myth of Jewish Evil.* New York: Free Press, 1991; Oxford: Maxwell-MacMillan, 1992.

————. *The Sacred Executioner.* London: Thames & Hudson, 1982.

————. "Who Was Judas Iscariot?" *Jewish Quarterly* (Summer 1991): 8–13.

Mack, B. *The Lost Gospel: The Book of Q and Christian Origins.* San Francisco: Harper, 1993.

Maguire, U. "The Last Supper: A Study in Group Dynamics." *New Blackfriars* (September 1968): 640–645.

Malbon, E. S., and A. Berlin, eds. *Characterization in Biblical Literature.* Semeia 63. Atlanta: Society of Biblical Literature, 1993.

Malcolm, Janet. "Annals of Biography: The Silent Woman" *New Yorker,* August 23 and 30, 1993: 84–159.

Manchester, W. *The Death of a President.* New York: Harper, 1967.

Manning, R. J. S. "Kierkegaard and Post-Modernity: Judas as Kierkegaard's Only Disciple." *Philosophy Today* 37 (1993): 133–152.

Manns, F. "Un midrash chrétienne: Le roit de la mort de Judas (Matt 27:3-10 et Acts 1:16-20)." *Revue des Sciences Religieuses* 54 (1980): 197–203.

Marin, L. "Semiotik des Verräters." In *Semiotik der Passionsgeschichte. Die Zeichensprache der Ortsangaben und Personennamen,* 82–168, 177–187. *Semiotique de la Passion: Topiques et figures.* Translated by S. Virgils. Paris, 1971. BEvTh 70. Munich, 1976.

Maynard, A. H. "The Role of Peter in the Fourth Gospel." *NTS* 30 (1984): 531–548.

McClain, R. O. "Judas Iscariot." Diss. S. Baptist Seminary, 1951.

McLean, Bradley. "A Christian Epitaph: The Curse of Judas Iscariot," OCP 58 (1992): 241–244.

McGlasson, Paul. *Jesus and Judas: Biblical Exegesis in Barth.* Atlanta: Scholars Press, 1991.

Medisch, R. "Der historische Judas—und was aus ihm gemacht wurde." *Theologie der Gegenwart* 31 (1988): 50–54.

Meinertz, M. "Zur Frage nach der Anwesenheit des Verräters Judas bei der Einsetzung der Eucharistie." *BZ* 10 (1912): 372–390.

Mellinkoff, R. "Judas's Red Hair and the Jews." *Journal of Jewish Art* 9 (1982): 31–46.

Menninger, K. *The Vital Balance*. New York: Viking, 1963.

Meye, Robert. *Jesus and the Twelve*. Grand Rapids: Eerdmans, 1968.

Milikowsky, Joseph. "Seder Olam." Jerusalem, 1981. Unpublished.

Momigliano, A. *The Development of Greek Biography*. Cambridge, Mass.: Harvard University Press, 1971.

Montefiore, C. G., and H. Loewe. *A Rabbinic Anthology*. New York: Meridian, 1960.

Moo, D. J. *The OT in the Gospel Passion Narratives*. Sheffield: Almond Press, 1983.

Morel, R. *Das Judasevangelium*. Heidelberg: Kemper, 1949.

Morin, J. A. "Les deux derniers des Douze: Simon le Zélote et Judas Iskáriôth." *RB* 80 (1973): 332–358.

Morison, F. *Who Moved the Stone?* London: Faber, 1930.

Moulton, J. H., and G. Milligan. *The Vocabulary of the New Testament Illustrated from the Papyri*. . . . London: Hodder & Stoughton, 1914–1929.

Müller, K. "ΑΠΕΧΕΙ (Mk 14, 41)—absurda lectio?" *ZNW* 77 (1986): 83–100.

Munro, J. I. "The Death of Judas (Matt xxvii.3–8; Acts i.18–19)." *ET* 24 (1912/13): 235–236.

Myllykoski, M. *Die letzten Tage Jesu: Markus, Johannes, Ihre Traditionen und die historische Frage*. 2 vols. Helsinki: Suomalainen Tiedeakatemia, 1994.

Nepper-Christensen, P. *Das Matthäusevangelium: Ein judenchristliches Evangelium?* Aarhus: Universitetsforlaget, 1958.

Nestle, E. "The Name of Judas Iscariot in the Fourth Gospel." *ET* 9 (1897/98): 140, 240.

Nickelsburg, G. W. E., and J. J. Collins, eds. *Ideal Figures in Ancient Judaism: Profiles and Paradigms*. Atlanta: Scholars Press, 1980.

Niemann, R., ed. *Judas, wer bist du?* Gütersloh: Gütersloher Verlagshaus Gerd Mohn, 1991.

Nigg, W. "Judas Iscarioth." In *Grosse Unheilige*, 58–83. Olten Freiburg, 1981.

Oesterreicher, John M., ed. *Brothers in Hope. The Bridge: A Yearbook of Judaeo-Christian Studies*. 5 (1970): 320–333. New York: Pantheon Books.

Pagels, E. *The Origin of Satan*. New York: Random House, 1995.

———. "The Social History of Satan, Part 2: Satan in the New Testament Gospels." *JAAR* 62 (1994): 17–58.

———. "The Social History of Satan, the 'Intimate Enemy': A Preliminary Sketch." *HTR* 84 (1991): 105–128.

Parker, J. *The Inner Life of Christ, as Revealed in the Gospel of Matthew*. 3 vols. 9th ed. London: Hazell, Watson and Viney, 1885.

Paschen, W. *Rein und Unrein: Untersuchung zur biblischen Wortgeschichte*. SANT 24. Munich: Kösel, 1970.

Peck, S. *People of the Lie*. New York: Simon and Schuster, 1983.

Pedersen, J. *Der Eid bei den Semiten*. Strassburg: Trübner, 1914.

Perera, S. B. *The Scapegoat Complex: Toward a Mythology of Shadow and Guilt*. Toronto: Inner City Books, 1986.

Perkins, P. *Peter: Apostle for the Whole Church*. Columbia: University of South Carolina Press, 1994.

Perrin, N. "The Use of *(para) didonai* . . . Passion of Jesus . . ." In *Der Ruf Jesu und die Antwort der Gemeinde* (FS J. Jeremias), edited by E. Lohse, 204–212. Göttingen: Vandenhoeck & Ruprecht, 1970.

Pesch, R. *Das Markusevangelium*. Freiburg: Herder. Vol. 2, 1980.

Phan, P., ed. *Christianity and the Wider Ecumenism*. New York: Paragon House, 1990.

Phillips, D. R. "We Don't Own the Likeness." *CToday* (April 4, 1980): 3031.

Plath, M. "Warum hat die urchristliche Gemeinde auf die Überlieferung der Judaserzählung Wert gelegt?" *ZNW* 17 (1916): 178–188.

Plummer, A. "Judas Iscariot." *HDB* (1905), 2:796–799.

Popkes, W. *Christus Traditus: Eine Untersuchung zum Begriff der Hingabe im NT.* ATANT no. 49. Zurich: Zwingli Verlag, 1967.

Preisigke, F. *Wörterbuch der griechischen Papyrusurkunden*. Berlin, 1927.

Preisker, H. "Der Verrat des Judas und das Abendmahl." *ZNW* 41 (1942): 151–155.

Puchner, W. *Studien zum Kulturkontext der liturgischen Szene. Lazarus und Judas als religiöse Volksfiguren in Bild und Brauch, Lied und Legende Südosteuropas. Österreichische Akademie der Wissenschaften*. Philosophisch-Historische Klasse. Denkschriften, 216. Vienna: Verlag der Österreichische Akademie der Wissenschaften, 1991.

Quast, K. *Peter and the Beloved Disciple*. Sheffield: Academic Press, 1989.

Räisänen, H. *The Messianic Secret in Mark*. Edinburgh: T. & T. Clark, 1990.

Rand, E. K. "Medieval Lives of Judas Iscariot." *Anniversary Papers by Colleagues and Pupils of George Lyman Kittredge*, 305–316. Boston, 1913.

Reban, J. *Inquest on Jesus Christ*. Translated by Willi Frischauer. London: Frewin, 1967.

Rehkopf, F. *Die lukanische Sonderquelle: Ihr Umfang und Sprachgebrauch*. WUNT 5. Tübingen: J. C. B. Mohr, 1959.

———. "Matt 26:50: Ἑταῖρε, ἐφ᾿ ὃ πάρει." *ZNW* 52 (1961): 109–115.

Reider, N. "Medieval Oedipal Legends about Judas." *Psychoanalytic Quarterly* 29 (1960): 515–527.

Reik, T. "Das Evangelium des Judas Iskariot/Die psychoanalytische Deutung des Judas-problems." In *Der eigene und der fremde Gott: Zur Psychoanalyse der religiösen Entwicklung*, 1923; 75–129. Literatur der Psychoanalyse. Frankfurt am Main, A. Mitscherlich. 1972.

Reim, G. "John 8:44—Gotteskinder/Teufelskinder. Wie antijudaistisch is 'Die wohl antijudaistische Äusserung des NT'?" *NTS* 30 (1984): 619–624.

———. *Studien zum alttestamentlichen Hintergrund des Johannesevangeliums*. SNTSMS 22. Cambridge: Cambridge University Press, 1974.

Renan, E. *Life of Jesus*. London: Walter Scott, 1897.

Rendtorff, Rolf. "Die neutestamentliche Wissenschaft und die Juden. Zur Diskussion zwischen David Flusser und Ulrich Wilckens." *EvTh* 36 (1976): 191–200.

Rese, M. *Alttestamentliche Motive in der Christologie des Lukas*. StNT 1. Gütersloh: J. C. B. Mohr, 1969.

Richter, G. *Die Fusswaschung im Johannesevangelium: Geschichte ihrer Deutung*. Regensburg: Pustet, 1967.

———. "Die Fusswaschung, John 13:1-20." *Studien zum Johannesevangelium*, edited by Josef Hainz, 13, 1977.

———. "Die Gefangennahme Jesu nach dem Johannesevangelium (18:1-12)," 74–87. *Studien zum Johannesevangelium*, 1969.

Rieu, E. V. *The Four Gospels: A New Translation*. Baltimore: Penguin, 1953.

Robertson, A. T. "The Primacy of Judas Iscariot." *Exp* 8/13 (1917): 278–286.

Robertson, J. M. *Jesus and Judas: A Textual and Historical Investigation*. London, 1927.

Roller, O. *Münzen, Geld und Vermögensverhältnisse in den Evangelien.* Karlsruhe, 1929.

Roloff, J. "Anfänge der soteriologischen Deutung des Todes Jesu (Mark 10:45 und Luke 22:27)." *NTS* 19 (1972/73): 38–64.

Roquefort, D. "Judas: Une figure de la perversion." *ETR* 58 (1983): 501–513.

Rostovzeff, M. "Οὓς δεξιόν ἀποτεμνεῖν." *ZNW* 33 (1934): 196–199.

Ruppert, L. *Der leidende Gerechte.* FB 5. Würzburg, 1972.

Russell, J. B. *The Devil: Perceptions of Evil from Antiquity to Primitive Christianity.* Ithaca: Cornell University Press, 1977.

Sabbe, M. "The Anointing of Jesus in John 12:1–8 and Its Synoptic Parallels." In *The Four Gospels,* 2051–2082. (FS Neirynck). Louvain: Louvain University Press, 1992.

―――. "The Arrest of Jesus in Jn 18:1-11. . . ." BETL 44 Gembloux: Duculot (1977): 203–234.

―――. "The Footwashing in Jn 13 and Its Relation to the Synoptic Gospels." *ETL* 57 (1982): 279–308.

Sahlin, H. "Der Tod des Judas Iskariot nach Ag 1,15ff." *ASTI* 12 (1983): 148–152.

Sanders, E. P. *The Historical Figure of Jesus.* London: Penguin, 1993.

―――. *Jesus and Judaism.* London: SCM, 1985.

Sanders, J. N. "'Those Whom Jesus Loved' (John xi.5)." *NTS* 1 (1954–55): 29–41.

Sayers, D. *The Man Born to Be King.* London: Victor Gollancz, 1942.

Scharlemann, R. P. "Why Christianity Needs Other Religions." In *Christianity and the Wider Ecumenism,* edited by Peter Phan, 35–46. New York: Paragon House, 1990.

Schechter, S. *Aspects of Rabbinic Theology.* New York: Schocken Books, 1961.

Schendler, D. "Judas, Oedipus and Various Saints." *Psychoanalysis* 2–3, (1954): 41–46.

Schenke, L. *Studien zur Passionsgeschichte des Markus: Tradition und Redaktion in Markus 14:1-42.* Würzburg: Echter Verlag, Katholisches Bibelwerk, 1971.

Schille, G. *Die urchristliche Kollegialmission.* Zurich: Zwingli, 1967.

Schillebeeckx, E. *Jesus.* New York: Seabury, 1979.

Schläger, G. "Die Ungeschichtlichkeit des Verräters Judas." *ZNW* 15 (1914): 50–59.

Schlatter, A. *Die beiden Schwerter.* Gütersloh: Bertelsmann, 1916.

―――. *Der Evangelist Matthäus.* Stuttgart: Calwer, 1957.

Schleiermacher, F. *The Life of Jesus.* Philadelphia: Fortress, 1975.

Schlichting, G. *Ein jüdisches Leben Jesus: Die verschollene Toldot-Jeschu-Fassung Tam u-mu'ad.* WUNT 24 Tübingen: Mohr, 1982.

Schmidt, K. Art. "Judas Ischarioth." *RE³* 9:586–589.

Schneemelcher, W., ed., and Edgar Hennecke, *Neutestamentliche Apokryphen.* 3d ed. Tübingen: J. C. B. Mohr, 1959.

Schneider, G. *Die Passion Jesu nach den drei älteren Evangelien.* Biblische Handbibliothek 11: Munich: Kösel, 1973.

Schneiders, S. "The Footwashing (John 13:1-20): An Experiment in Hermeneutics." *CBQ* 43 (1981): 76–92.

Schonfeld, H. *The Passover Plot.* New Light on the History of Jesus. New York: Bantam Books, 1965.

Schulthess, F. "Zur Sprache der Evangelien. D. Judas 'Iskariot.'" *ZNW* 21 (1922): 250–258.

Schürer, E. *The History of the Jewish People in the Age of Jesus Christ.* 3 vols. Revised and edited by Geza Vermes, Fergus Millar, and Martin Goodman. Edinburgh: T. and T. Clark, 1979–1987.

Schütz, F. *Der leidende Christus: Die angefochtene Gemeinde und das Christuskerygma der lukanischen Schriften*. BWANT 89. Stuttgart: Kohlhammer, 1969.

Schwager, R. *Brauchen wir einen Sündenbock?* Munich: Kösel, 1978.

————. *Must There Be Scapegoats?* Translated by M. L. Assad. San Francisco: Harper, 1987.

Schwarz, G. *Jesus und Judas: Aramaistische Untersuchungen zur Jesus-Judas-Überlieferung der Evangelien und der Apostelgeschichte*. BWANT 123. Stuttgart: Kohlhammer, 1988.

Schwarz, W. "Die Doppelbedeutung des Judastodes." *Biblical Liturgy* 57 (1984).

Schwier, H. *Tempel und Tempelzerstörung: Untersuchungen zu den theologischen und ideologischen Faktoren im ersten jüdischen-römischen Krieg (66–74 n Chr.)*. NTOA 11. Göttingen: Vandenhoeck & Ruprecht, Universitätsverlag Freiburg, 1989.

Seeley, D. *The Noble Death: Graeco-Roman Martyrology and Paul's Concept of Salvation*. JSNTSup 18. Sheffield: JSOT, 1990.

Segal, Alan. "Matthew's Jewish Voice." In *Social History of the Matthean Community: Cross Disciplinary Approaches,* edited by D. Balch, 3–37. Minneapolis: Fortress, 1992.

Seltmann, M. *Judas Ischariot, Sein Schicksal im Jenseits*. Bietigheim, 1949.

Senior, D. "A Case Study in Matthean Creativity (Matthew 27:3-10)." *BR* 19 (1974): 23–36.

————. "The Fate of the Betrayer: A Redactional Study of Matthew XXVII, 3-10." *ETL* 48 (1972): 372–426; also idem, *Passion Narrative,* 1:343–397. Louvain: Louvain University Press, 1975.

Smith, D. M. *Johannine Christianity. Essays on Its Settings, Sources and Theology*. Columbia: University of South Carolina Press, 1984.

————. "Johannine Christianity: Some Reflections on Its character and Delineation." *NTS* 21 (1974–75): 222–248.

————. "John and the Synoptics and the Question of Gospel Genre." In *Studia Neotestamentica,* edited by M. Sabbe, 1183–1197. Louvain: Louvain University Press, 1991.

Smith, M. *Tannaitic Parallels to the Gospels*. (Philadelphia: SBL) 1958.

Snyder, G. F. "John 13:16 and the Anti-Petrinism of the Johannine Tradition." *BR* 16 (1971): 5–15.

Sonderegger, K. *That Jesus Christ Was Born a Jew: Karl Barth's "Doctrine of Israel."* University Park: Pennsylvania State University Press, 1992.

Spicq, C. *Notes de Lexicographie Néo-Testamentaire,* 504–515. Friburg: Editions Universitaires [OBEO 22/3], 3 (1982): ET: J. D. Ernest, *Theological Lexicon of the New Testament*. Peabody, Mass.: Hendrickson, 3 (1994): 13–23.

Spong, John S. "Did Christians Invent Judas?" *The Fourth R* (March–April 1994): 3–11, 16.

Springer, C. P. E. *The Gospel as Epic in Late Antiquity: The Paschale Carmen of Sedulius*. Leiden: Brill, 1988.

Sproston, W. "Satan in the Fourth Gospel." In *Studia Biblica,* II, edited by E. A. Livingstone, 1978: 307–311.

Stählin, G. "φιλέω." *KTWBNT* 9 (1973): 113–146.

Stauffer, E. *Jerusalem und Rom im Zeitalter Jesu Christi*. Bern: Francks, 1957.

Stein-Schneider, H. L. "A la recherche du Judas historique: Une enque exégétique la luminaire des textes de l'ancien testament et des logia." *ETR* 60 (1985): 403–423.

Storch, R. "Was soll diese Verschwendung? Bemerkungen zur Auslegungsgeschichte von Mk 14:4f." *Jeremias Festschrift*, 1970: 247–258.

Strauss, D. F. *The Life of Jesus Critically Examined*. Translated by George Eliot. Philadelphia: Fortress, 1972.

Stuart, D. R. *Epochs of Greek and Roman Biography*. Berkeley, 1928.

Suggit, J. N. "Poetry's Next-Door Neighbour." *JThSA* 25 (1978): 3–17.

Suhl, A. *Die Funktion der alttestamentlichen Zitate und Anspielungen im Markusevangelium*. Gütersloh: Gerd Mohn, 1965.

———. "Die Funktion des Schwertstreichs bei der Gefangennahme Jesus: Beobachtungen zur Komposition und Theologie der synoptischen Evangelien." *The Four Gospels: Festschrift Neirinck*, 295–223. Louvain: Louvain University Press. I 1992.

Swartley, Willard. *Mark: The Way for All Nations*. Scottdale, Pa.: Herald Press, 1979.

Tabachovitz, D. "Der Tod des Judas Iskariot." *Eranos* 67 (1969): 43–47.

Tacitus. *The Annals of Imperial Rome*. Translated by C. H. Moore. LCL. 1937.

———. *The Annals of Imperial Rome*. Translated by Michael Grant. London, 1956.

Talbert, C. H. "Biography, Ancient." *ABD*, 1 (1992): 745–749.

Tarachow, S. "Judas, der geliebte Henker," Y. Spiegel, ed., 1992, 1:745–749. *Psychoanalytische Interpretationen biblischer Texte*, Munich, 1972: 243–256 = "Judas, the Beloved Executioner." *Psychoanalytic Quarterly* 29 (1960): 528–554 abbreviated.

Taylor, A. "The Burning of Judas." *Washington University Studies* 11 (1923): 159–186.

———. "The Gallows of Judas Iscariot." *Washington University Studies* 9 (1922): 135–156.

———. "Judas Iscariot in Charms and Incantations." *Washington University Studies* 8 (1920): 3–17.

———. "'O Du armer Judas.'" *JEGP* 19 (1920): 318–339.

Taylor, V. *Behind the Third Gospel*. London: Oxford University Press, 1926.

Taylor, Vincent. *Jesus and His Sacrifice*. London: Macmillan, 1959.

———. *The Passion Narrative of St. Luke*. Cambridge: Cambridge University Press, 1972.

Teichert, W. *Jeder ist Judas. Der unvermeidliche Verrat*. Stuttgart: Kreuz, 1990.

Temple, Sydney. "The Two Traditions of the Last Supper, Betrayal and Arrest." *NTS* 7 (1960–61): 77–85.

Thümmel, H. G. "Judas Ischariot im Urteil der altkirchlichen Schriftsteller des Westens und in der frühchristlichen Kunst." Diss., Greifswald, 1959.

Tolbert, M. A. *Sowing the Gospel: Mark's World in Literary-Historical Perspective*. Minneapolis: Fortress, 1989.

Torrey, C. C. "The Name 'Iscariot.'" *HTR* 36 (1943): 51–62.

Trüdinger, L. P. "Davidic Links with the Betrayal of Jesus: Some Further Observations." *ET* 86 (1975): 278–279.

Upton, J. A. "The Potter's Field and the Death of Judas (Matt 27:3-10; Acts 1:15-20)." *Concordia Journal* 8 (1982): 213–219.

van Hooff, A. J. L. *From Autothanasia to Suicide: Self-killing in Classical Antiquity*. London: Routledge, 1990.

van Unnik, W. C. "The Death of Judas in Saint Matthew's Gospel." In *Gospel Studies in Honor of Sherman Elbridge Johnson (ATRS* 3). Milwaukee, 1974.

Vermes, G. *Jesus and the World of Judaism.* London: SCM, 1983.

————. *Jesus the Jew.* London: Libral Jewish Synagogue, 1973.

Vielhauer, Philipp. "Gottesreich und Menschensohn in der Verkündigung Jesu," *Festschrift für Günther Dehn.* edited by W. Schneemelcher. Neukirchen Kreis Moers: Verlag der Buchhandlung des Erziehungsvereins, 1957: 51–79.

Viviano, B. "The High Priest's Servant's Ear: Mark 14:47." *RB* 96 (1989): 71–80.

————. *Study as Worship: Aboth and the New Testament.* Leiden: Brill, 1978.

Vogler, W. *Judas Iskarioth: Untersuchungen zu Tradition und Redaktion von Texten des Neuen Testaments und außer kanonischer Schriften.* ThA 42. Berlin: Evangelischer Verlag, 1983; 2nd ed., 1985.

von Dobschütz, E. "Legend, Legendary." *The New Schaff-Herzog Religious Encyclopedia,* 6:441–442. Grand Rapids: Baker, 1956.

Vorster, W. "Gospel, Genre." *ABD,* 3 (1992): 1077–1079.

Wagner, H. "Judas: Das Geheimnis der Sünde, menschliche Freiheit und Gottes Heilsplan." In *Judas Iskariot: Menschliches oder heilsgeschichtliches Drama?* edited by H. Wagner, 11–38. Frankfurt: Josef Knecht 1985.

Weeden, T. *Mark: Traditions in Conflict.* Philadelphia: Fortress, 1971.

Wehr, G. "Judas Iskariot, unser schattenhaftes Ich. Analytische Psychologie im Dienste der Bibelauslegung." *DtPfrBl* 74 (1974): 146–147.

Weiger, J. *Judas Iskarioth: Eine Betrachtung.* Munich, 1951.

Weiss, Johannes. *Die Schriften des Neuen Testaments.* Göttingen: Vandenhoeck & Ruprecht, 1917³.

Westcott, B. F. *The Gospel according to St. John.* Grand Rapids: Eerdmans, 1951.

Whelan, C. F. "Suicide in the Ancient World: A Re-examination of Matt 27:3-10." *LavTP* 49 (1993): 505–522.

Wieser, S. *Judas. Der Kreuzweg des Verräters in sechs Stationen.* Neutestamentliche Predigten 8. Paderborn, 1922.

Wilcox, M. "The Judas-Tradition in Acts i.15-26." *NTS* 19 (1972/73): 438–452.

Williams, D. J. "Judas Iscariot." In *Dictionary of Jesus and the Gospels,* edited by J. B. Green and S. McKnight, 46–48. Downers Grove, Ill.: Intervarsity Press, 1992.

Williams, D. S. "Rub Poor Lil' Judas's Head." *Christian Century,* October 24, 1990.

Wilson, W. *The Execution of Jesus.* New York: Scribner's, 1970.

Windisch, Hans. *Der messianische Krieg und das Urchristentum.* Tübingen: J. C. B. Mohr, 1909.

Wolff, H. W. *Jesaja 53 im Urchristentum.* Berlin: Evangelische Verlagsanstalt, 1952³.

Wrede, A. "Judas." *HWDA* 4:800–808.

Wrede, W. "Judas Ischarioth in der urchristlichen Überlieferung," 127–146. *Vorträge und Studien.* Tübingen, 1907.

Zehrer, F. "Zum Judasproblem." *ThPQ* 121 (1973): 259–264.

Zeitlin, Irving. *Jesus and the Judaism of His Time.* Cambridge: Polity Press, 1988.

SCRIPTURE INDEX

OLD TESTAMENT

Genesis
16:5—63
18:4—150
19:1-3—149
29:25—48
37:2,4—66
37:11—66
37:26-27—66
44:18—161
49:8-12—66
50:21—66

Exodus
4:13—134
21:32—98
25:3-5—157
29:20—130

Leviticus
8:23—130
14—183
14:14—130
16—183
16:8.10.26—17
17:4-9—93
20:3,4,5—93
27:1-8—98

Numbers
5:6—74
15:26—125
31:5—48, 74
31:16—48, 74

Deuteronomy
11:18—158
13:1-18—55
13:2-12—197
15:17—129
21:23—163

Joshua
9:22—48
15:25—32, 40

Judges
1:25—59
4:7,14—53
19:15-21—149

1 Samuel
9:15—129
19:17—48
28:12—48
31:5—207

2 Samuel
7:27—129
12:17—101
17—170
17:23—170
19:27—48
20:1-22—64
20:21-22—63
24:1-2—140

1 Kings
13—183
20:2,13—135
22:8,17—135

2 Kings
21:16—163
22:45—135

1 Chronicles
12:17—48
12:18—48
21:1—140

INDEX OF OTHER
ANCIENT WRITINGS

MODERN AUTHOR INDEX

TOPICAL INDEX